Y0-BLF-340

Second Edition

A Guide to Educational Research

DAVID R. COOK
Northeastern University

N. KENNETH LaFLEUR
University of Virginia

Allyn and Bacon, Inc.
BOSTON·LONDON·SYDNEY·TORONTO

Copyright © 1975 by Allyn and Bacon, Inc.

Copyright © 1965 by Allyn and Bacon, Inc.
470 Atlantic Avenue, Boston, Massachusetts 02210

All rights reserved. Printed in the United States of America. No part of the material protected by this copyright notice may be reproduced or utilized in any form or by any means, electronic or mechanical, including photocopying, recording, or by any informational storage and retrieval system, without written permission from the copyright owner.

Library of Congress Cataloging in Publication Data

Cook, David R
    A guide to educational research.

    Includes bibliographies and index.
    1. Educational research. I. LaFleur, N. Kenneth, 1942-   joint author. II. Title.
LB1028.C59   1975   370'.78   74-19393

ISBN 0-205-04747-5

Fourth printing... August, 1979

To Carol Ann Cook, a little older and much wiser than the time of the first edition.

To Michelle and James LaFleur, who were not present for the arrival of the first edition.

A Guide to
Educational Research

Contents

Preface   ix

I   A Framework for Understanding Educational Research   1

II   The Research Study   11

III   Historical Research   29

  Study 1   Social Centers, Politics, and Social Efficiency in the Progressive Era / Edward W. Stevens, Jr.   34

IV   Descriptive Research   51

  Study 2   Coeducation and Adolescent Values / J. C. Jones, J. Shallcrass, and C. C. Dennis   62

  Study 3   The Teacher Subculture and Curriculum Change / Donald J. Willower   77

  Study 4   Prediction of Successive Terms Performance in College from Tests and Grades / Arvo E. Juola   90

  Study 5   School Board Changes and Superintendent Turnover / John C. Walden   100

V   Experimental Research   109

  Study 6   Effects on Classmates of a Deviant Student's Power and Response to a Teacher-Exerted Control Technique / William J. Gnagey   119

Contents

Study 7 The Relationship Between Sequences of Instruction and Mental Abilities of Retarded Children / G. Phillip Cartwright   134

Study 8 Dissonance, Self-Perception, and Honesty in Children / Mark R. Lepper   143

Study 9 The Application of Operant Conditioning Techniques in a Secondary School Classroom / L. W. McAllister, J. G. Stachowiak, D. M. Baer, and L. Conderman   162

Study 10 Teachers' Belief Systems and Preschool Atmospheres / O. J. Harvey, B. J. White, M. S. Prather, R. D. Alter, and J. K. Hoffmeister   177

Index   195

Preface

As was stated in the preface to the first edition, this book is intended primarily for the beginning graduate student in a required course in research methods. However, it might also be helpful to instructors and other school personnel who are interested in research and want to refresh their understanding of it. In another sense, it is also written for the instructor of a research methods course. The content has been planned to make the teaching of a research course easier and more interesting. It is our hope that the instructor will find this book helpful in providing relief from spending too much time lecturing on elementary concepts and understandings and enabling classroom time to be spent on more complex technical matters that are not dealt with in this book.

It should be clear that this book does not pretend to be a comprehensive textbook in research methods. It must be supplemented, but the manner in which it is supplemented can be very flexible. It can be used as a supplementary text with a basic standard textbook or it can serve as the basic required text and be supplemented through the instructor's lectures and outside reading assignments.

A revision ought to improve a book without altering the basic value and appeal of the original edition. That was our aim in this second edition. The essential value and appeal of the original edition was undoubtedly in the simplicity and straightforwardness of the basic material and in the use of published studies with written analyses as a vehicle for learning about research. Hopefully that remains unchanged in this new edition.

The effort to improve the first edition took the following

Preface

directions: *First,* the original chapters 5 and 6 (dealing with the research problem, proposal, and report) have been combined into one chapter (now Chapter 2). *Second,* the first chapter has been extensively rewritten to provide a more coherent and focused framework for the book. The role of theory in research has been stressed more in the rewriting and several new sources of ideas have been drawn upon. The content of this first chapter, however, parallels the original. *Third,* nine new studies have been used in the book, replacing all but one of the original studies. The new edition has ten illustrative studies rather than nine as in the first edition. *Fourth,* the analyses of the studies in this edition place greater stress on the theory and assumptions upon which each study was based. The studies continue to serve as vehicles for explaining statistical and methodological approaches to research. Other material in the last three chapters has been revised where necessary to improve clarity and in some cases correct errors of omission or commission.

Since the major attractive feature of the book has probably always been the published research studies and the accompanying analyses, the use of nine new studies, several of them with potentially high interest value for students in education, will probably constitute the major change and improvement from the first edition. We hope that regular users of the book will welcome new studies and new ideas about them.

As always, we wanted to produce a book that students would find helpful and readable in this sometimes confusing and frustrating field of research. The success of the book from our point of view depends on whether students find that it helps them learn what they need to know about research and stimulates them to continue as active consumers of research, and perhaps even producers of research.

Our thanks again to the authors and publishers who gave their permission to publish in reprint form the studies that make the existence of this book possible.

David R. Cook
N. Kenneth LaFleur

I

A framework for understanding educational research

Our purpose here is to provide a framework in which the concepts, the processes, and the research presented in the remaining chapters will be more easily understood, although no single construct can completely accomplish this purpose. Our discussion will be organized around three main topics: (1) a philosophical framework, (2) theory as a framework for understanding educational research, and (3) basic and applied research in education. Finally, we shall discuss the methodology of the remaining chapters in the book and of the analysis of research that will follow in those chapters.

THE PHILOSOPHICAL FRAMEWORK

We speak seriously today of the "knowledge industry" as one of the "growth industries" of the future. Much, though not all, of the knowledge industry is institutionalized within the formal structures of education. The very assumption that there is such an entity as a knowledge industry requires the existence of research activity. And research is fundamentally a process whereby knowledge is generated. Knowledge, in turn, is supposed to enable us better to control our lives and our environment and to

1

help accomplish the objectives we set for ourselves as human beings.

In the context of education, research knowledge should enable the improvement of those processes whereby human beings come to learn about themselves and their surroundings, one process of which is research itself. There is, then, a sense in which research is simply one of the normal, fundamental activities of human beings. The main differences between that normal human activity and the kind of activity we will discuss in this book are the rigor and discipline with which formal research is carried on and the making of that process a highly self-conscious activity.

Self-awareness or self-consciousness is possible only for human beings. There would be no knowledge in the sense in which we use this term without self-awareness. Self-awareness enables us to step back from our activity in our minds and become aware of what we are doing and thinking. It will help if we recognize this human activity as we undertake our study of the research process. We shall return to this point later in the chapter. In the meantime, we shall look at two major processes man has invented for generating knowledge: empiricism and rationalism.

Empiricism

Empiricism, with its philosophical roots in the work of Bacon, Locke, and Hume, stresses the development of knowledge as an external process. The empiricist looks outside himself to observable phenomena as the source of knowledge. Facts discovered through experience or objective observation of the senses become the basis for knowledge. This approach was the basis for the scientific revolution of the last 300 years, enabling the development of modern technology and all the gifts and problems that have accompanied that development. There is little doubt as to the power of the empirical mindset.

The empirical approach to knowledge has proved to be most powerful in the physical sciences. Attempts to adapt this approach to the psychological and social sciences has done much to establish scientific rigor and respectability for these fields. However, empiricism as an exclusive approach to the study of human behavior is becoming more and more of a dead end so far as advancing knowledge of human activity is concerned. Too little important human behavior can be understood through strict empirical observation.

Rationalism

Descartes, Spinoza, and Leibniz are some of the forebears of rationalism as an approach to generating knowledge. Rationalism proceeds from an internal frame of reference, with knowledge being generated first in the form of clear and distinct ideas. In this process, what can be intuited with the mind is what becomes fundamental to the shaping of reality.

Historically, both these philosophical strands merged in debate during the Renaissance and helped give birth to the Age of Reason or what we can generally call the rational mindset of contemporary man. Both empiricism and rationalism are essentially anthropocentric activities, i.e., man is the actor in his universe rather than one who is acted upon. This emerging attitude gave man the possibility of taking control of his environment and shaping it more to his own ends.

The enormous expansion of self-awareness that was brought about by the scientific revolution has provided us with new possibilities for understanding ourselves and in turn is beginning to influence our concepts of research.

DEDUCTIVE AND INDUCTIVE REASONING

We are now clear that the processes of empirical thinking and rational thinking are not mutually exclusive but are inter-related, complementary, and inseparable.

You have probably encountered before the terms *deductive reasoning* and *inductive reasoning* as names for these thought processes. Deductive reasoning, representing the earlier development in the history of man's attempts to reason, begins with a generalization and moves from there to inferences about particular instances. In its raw form, a generalization is first a product of the imagination such that inferences to specific events are therefore given shape by what was first a creation of the mind.

Inductive reasoning proceeds in the opposite direction, beginning with the specific instance and generalizing to whole classes of specific observations. The raw beginning of induction is the fact of the basic observation, external to the self, that is first made; this essentially is repeated for a sample of the universe one is observing. From this raw fact the imagination is informed to give shape to the whole.

CHAPTER 1

These two modes of thought—the empirical-inductive method and the theoretical-deductive method—must merge in a self-awareness mode for the production of any really useful knowledge. Yet each of these approaches has its own problems and pitfalls, and the necessity for a critical self-awareness about each is of great importance to both the production and the consumption of research. For what we have on the one hand are techniques or processes for uncovering facts and on the other hand we have the creative and imaginative processes for making sense out of those facts. Because technique is an essentially external, observable, and more or less tangible activity, the tendency is to be much more aware of that activity than we are about the more internal creative process. But to the extent that this is true, we sometimes fall into the trap of assuming that the results from our techniques are the reality that we are seeking to understand. What an expanded self-awareness reveals is that reality is finally the creation of our minds which emerges in whatever shape our values dictate, regardless of the facts. And this makes it imperative that we take a further look at the role of theory in research.

THEORY AS A FRAMEWORK FOR UNDERSTANDING RESEARCH

To avoid confusion in the discussion that follows, you should understand that the terms *theory, model,* and *ideology* will be used on an essentially interchangeable basis to refer to what Bruner describes as "a way of using the mind, the imagination—of standing off from the activities of observation and inference and creating a shape of nature."[1]

The twentieth-century Spanish existentialist philosopher, Ortega y Gasset, speaks of the process this way[2]:

> Science is the interpretation of facts. By themselves, facts do not give us reality; on the contrary, they hide it, which is to say that they present us with the problem of reality. If there were no facts, there would be no problem, there would be no enigma, there would be nothing hidden which it is necessary to de-hide, to dis-cover.

Science has never been without theory, at least in the sense in which Ortega speaks of it. It is the failure to make theory explicit,

---

1. Jerome Bruner, "Culture, Politics, and Pedagogy," *Saturday Review,* May 18, 1968.
2. José Ortega y Gasset, *Man and Crisis,* New York: W. W. Norton, 1958, p. 13.

A FRAMEWORK FOR UNDERSTANDING EDUCATIONAL RESEARCH

i.e., self-conscious, that leads to problems in understanding the results of our observations. For our theories not only inform our understanding of facts but *they also suggest what facts we should observe.*

What is clearer to us today than it was to the early philosophers and scientists of the modern age is the existential fact that man must interpret reality. Reality is not revealed in unvarying form. If, therefore, we are to be disciplined, objective, and rigorous in our efforts to expand our knowledge, we must be able to describe the model which we are using to guide our investigations and the interpretation we make of our observations. The process of research assumes that the model is always open to change when evidence from observations suggests other possible interpretations than the one the model provides for. But unless we are clear about the model in the first instance, we may not be clear about what ideas need to be altered.

Another problem with the models has to do with their comprehensiveness. The narrower and more restrictive the model, the smaller will be the scope of our investigations and the more limited will be the understanding we can reach of complex problems. By restricting the scope of the observations, the raw accuracy of the observations made increases. As the complexity and breadth of your observations increases, precision is lost. A simple illustration may help:

> Two people are watching a football game. One is concerned with the activity of the left side linebacker on defense. The other is concerned about the overall pattern and activity of the total play of both teams. The first will be making very precise observations of all the moves of the left side linebacker and will be able to describe them in detail and report on the results of that activity with a high degree of accuracy. He will not, however, be able to make too many accurate generalizations about the overall process of the play of all twenty-two men on the field. The second observer will have a much clearer perception of the interaction of the play of all twenty-two men on the field and will be able to make a good many accurate generalizations about the process of the entire game. But, when questioned about the activities of the left side linebacker and the effect of his performance, he is likely to respond with a good deal of vagueness.

Whose model for observing the game is best? The obvious answer is that it depends on what is important. The rookie substitute for the left side linebacker will probably find it more important to make accurate generalizations about the play of his alter ego. The coach would find that model too narrow and restrictive for his purposes. He needs a model that will enable him to generalize about the total process of the entire game as it progresses.

In education we are dealing with rather complex human behavior. Yet research can reflect different purposes and therefore differing levels of comprehensiveness in the models used to guide the research process. One way to distinguish purposes calling for different degrees of comprehensiveness is to differentiate between basic and applied research.

BASIC AND APPLIED RESEARCH IN EDUCATION

The differentiation between basic and applied research can be made largely on the basis of the role of theory in each of them. Although any research undertaking begins with one or more assumptions (the givens of our theory), there is a difference between research for the purpose of testing out the validity of assumptions and research for the purpose of enabling better immediate decision-making or planning. The former defines *basic research* and the latter *applied research.* Benedict[3] has clarified this distinction as being one between "conclusion-oriented research" and "decision-oriented research." The latter is considered more relevant for the purpose of educational evaluation than is basic or conclusion-oriented research.

It may make more sense to see these two types of research as being on either end of a continuum, not dichotomies. Either type of research can be helpful in making decisions, but basic research does not have decision-making as its fundamental purpose. Either type can contribute to the advancement of knowledge, but applied research does not have the advancement of knowledge as its fundamental purpose. And when the purpose for which research is to be undertaken is clear, it would be a mistake to follow an approach that emphasizes a different purpose.

This is not to say, however, that the essential research approach discussed in this book, which is a methodology for gathering observable or empirical data, is not equally applicable to both ends of the continuum. It is more likely that you would be

---

3. Larry G. Benedict, "Traditional Research Versus Evaluation," University of Massachusetts, Amherst, 1971, mimeo. See also Lee Cronbach, *Research for Tomorrow's Schools,* Toronto: Macmillan, 1969.

applying your research skills in the future to decision-making research than to conclusion-oriented research.

In addition to the necessity for maintaining the tension between empirical-inductive and theoretical-deductive processes, it is also important to support both basic and applied research efforts if education is to continue to advance in effectiveness. Long-term, sustained, basic research helps to buttress the evaluative, decision-making research. It does this partly through its contributions to improved research methodology and partly through establishing a body of knowledge about educational processes that can be expected to produce certain results under certain conditions.

A LOOK AHEAD

The chapters that follow are designed to implement the framework for understanding research that was developed in this chapter.

Chapter 2 is designed to assist you in a limited way with your task as a producer of research should that be a necessary part of the learning process in which you are engaged. It contains a number of suggestions, ideas, and concepts that should be helpful in undertaking a research project as part of a research course.

Chapters 3, 4, and 5 are designed primarily to improve your competency as a consumer of research, but they also contain information that will be useful if you must produce some research. These chapters deal with three arbitrarily organized types of research: historical, descriptive, and experimental. Each chapter begins with a brief review of the major methodological problems and approaches inherent in the type of research under discussion. Whereas this opening chapter has stressed theory, the beginning of each of these chapters on types of research will stress technique. You will therefore find some information that will be useful to you if you are doing research as well as learning how to read and understand the research of others.

The published research studies that make up the bulk of these three chapters illustrate the concepts discussed both in this chapter and in the remaining chapters. The analysis that follows each study is designed to increase your awareness of the process in which the researcher was engaged when he produced the research.

The approach we shall be taking in our analyses of the studies in this book can be described under three broad categories:

CHAPTER 1

1. *The methodology.* Our concern here will be to make explicit the methodology that the researcher followed in designing his investigation. When special concepts, particularly statistical concepts, are utilized, we shall provide some explanations of those concepts in the context of the analysis. The very methods by which observations are made or controls imposed on the situation being investigated can lead to distortion or bias in the data that were collected. So we shall try to point out any possible sources of such bias or distortion that might not have been corrected.

2. *The theory or assumptions.* First, we will make the assumptions of the study explicit if the researcher has not already done so. We will then comment on the comprehensiveness of the theory or the extent to which it may unduly focus our perceptions to the exclusion of other important processes related to the ones under investigation. And it is important to relate the theory to the methodology used to test the theory. Sometimes the methods used to investigate a problem can do violence to the assumptions on which the investigation was based.

3. *The purpose and significance.* Comments on the significance of any research are obviously a matter of the opinion and values of the commentator. Nevertheless, this is a legitimate aspect of any critical reading of research. We should ask what the purpose of any research study is and to whom and for what the results might be important or significant. Some technically good research is lacking in any real significance, and some flawed research can be highly significant for a variety of reasons. We need to address this issue.

The primary purposes of the studies presented here are to illustrate various types of research and to provide a useful vehicle for learning about various concepts and techniques of research. Each study in this book, therefore, had to meet that criterion of usefulness to be included. Since many published studies could meet that criterion, we made an effort to find studies that would also be interesting to read and fairly recent.

Any research study is open to criticism or at least question on some ground. The studies reprinted in this book range in quality. But quality is related to the standards one has for making a qualitative judgment. It is probably well for both the student and the instructor to be aware that the purpose of the analyses is not to render a judgment of the quality of the research but to point out the salient features of methodology, theory, and purpose from which the student can learn something important about reading and doing research. Naturally, judgment will often be implied in some of our comments, but the absence of explicit judgment is intentional.

At the same time, we believe that it is important for students to make qualitative judgments about these or any other research studies. The analyses following each study included here will suggest some of the critical standards that you as a consumer of research can use.

SUMMARY AND CONCLUSION

The focus of this book, as developed in the analyses of the research that follows, is on theory as the basis for understanding educational research. The importance of sound methodology in research design and data collection is undeniable. However, unexamined assumptions often lead both the producer and the consumer of research to unwarranted conclusions. We have stressed, therefore, the importance of research as self-conscious inquiry. And that self-consciousness must be applied equally to the rigor of one's methods of inquiry and to the assumptions or theory with which one begins any investigation. Whether a consumer or a producer of educational research, such a critical self-consciousness is the most useful and productive human stance you can take toward the process of research.

II

The research study

The typical beginning course in research has at least two major purposes: to equip the student with some elementary skills for carrying out a research study and to help the student become a better and more critical consumer of research. This book emphasizes the latter on the grounds that consumers of research in education will always outnumber the producers of research, especially in beginning courses required for a degree. However, many of you will have to conduct some research project so that you can experience firsthand the requirements and difficulties that researchers regularly encounter.

We shall deal with three major topics in this chapter: (1) finding and stating a research problem, (2) preparing a research proposal, and (3) writing the research report. This arrangement will leave two important gaps unfilled in the process at this point. First, the matter of the design of your research, including how you plan to analyze your data, is not included here. Secondly, the techniques or methods you will use to collect your data, i.e., make your observations, are also not included. These gaps will be dealt with in the remainder of the book. Techniques of data collection and statistical analysis are not treated in this book except through the illustrative material. The published studies include a number of examples of data collection techniques, and the statistical analyses made in these studies are discussed in the context of the study. Our aim is to help you develop understanding of these matters, not expertise. You will need to consult other references for further detail on design and data collection techniques.

CHAPTER 2

FINDING A PROBLEM

Many potential research studies flounder because the researcher has failed to give a clear statement of the problem. Unless the researcher can clearly delineate his problem, he will not be able to design a proper study to investigate the problem. Without some idea as to what educational problem is to be studied, there is nowhere to go. For the specialist in research, of course, this is no difficulty since he usually is aware of far more problems needing research than he can devote himself to in a lifetime. But for the beginning student, finding a problem is a problem in itself.

Accordingly, we shall try to suggest some guidelines for locating a problem to work on and then proceed to the matter of stating the problem clearly so that research methods may be designed for gathering data bearing on the problem which has been posed.

Since most people who actually carry out research studies do so of their own free will rather than because of a course requirement, it is natural to expect that the problems they study arise out of their own interest and curiosity about educational problems. It follows that the more aware you are of general educational problems, the more likely you are to find a specific problem that challenges you and is at the same time of manageable proportions.

R. M. W. Travers's *Second Handbook of Research on Teaching* (Chicago, 1973), published under the auspices of the American Educational Research Association (AERA), contains reviews of research and methodological procedures relevant to education. Some of the topics covered in the *Second Handbook* are:

1. Techniques of observing early childhood teaching and outcomes of particular procedures
2. Assessment of teacher competence
3. Social psychology of teaching
4. Research on the urban school
5. Teaching the emotionally disturbed
6. Teaching of affective responses
7. Skill learning
8. Gaming and simulation
9. Research on teaching in higher education

These broad categories suggest where you might begin to look for a problem if one does not spring readily to mind. By consulting

THE RESEARCH STUDY

the *Second Handbook* on these topics, you will find comprehensive reviews of numerous research studies in each of the areas. In addition to the topical areas listed above, the *Second Handbook* contains an entire section devoted to research reviews on the teaching of specific school subjects.

Another excellent source of reviews is the journal published by the AERA, *Review of Educational Research*. The journal is a quarterly publication and contains research reviews focused on particular issues in education.

A third valuable review source is the annual publication, *Review of Research in Education* (Itaska, Ill., 1973), also under the auspices of the AERA. The annual volumes are directed toward disciplined survey of educational issues and contain reviews on various topical areas in education. The objective of the varied reviews is to improve educational research. The annual volumes of the *Review* should provide the researcher with source material references and aid in the conceptualization of the individual research goals.

Additional sources that may be helpful in making your problem identification or completing a review of related research are listed below. Most of these references are available in college and university libraries and many larger municipal libraries.

1. *Dissertation Abstracts:* abstracts of all doctoral dissertations completed in over 200 institutions of higher education
2. *Psychological Abstracts:* summaries of articles and books published in psychology and related areas
3. *Sociology Abstracts:* similar to the *Psychology Abstracts* only in the field of sociology
4. *Education Index:* an index by subject and author of journal articles, yearbooks, and professional meeting proceedings in education
5. *Research in Education:* a publication of the United States Office of Education that contains abstracts of completed and in-progress research in education
6. *Current Index to Journals in Education:* a subject, author, and descriptive title word index of articles in the broad field of education, published by the United States Office of Education

The publications *Research in Education* and *Current Index to Journals in Education* are part of an information retrieval system. The manner of using the system is described in the issues of the two publications. The American Psychological Association and the American Sociological Association also have information retrieval systems that may be of use in problem identification and literature review activities of research. Information about these latter two information retrieval systems can be obtained by contacting the respective professional organizations. After consulting these references, you should be able to formulate some general idea of the kind of problem that interests you.

The next step is to develop a small bibliography of original references for further reading. Each study reviewed will have a full reference given for it, and you can usually find the journal in which it appears on the shelf of your library. There you can read in detail about the method and the findings of the study. In addition to this, you will almost always find a bibliography at the conclusion of each research study that will suggest further reading. This reading should help you refine your thinking to the point where you can put down a specific question or problem that you would like to undertake as your research project.

Unless you have already had a problem germinating in your mind when you enrolled in the research course, you will find that this initial perusal of the research literature, especially the reviews of research, will be the best way to stimulate ideas. Even so, it may be of some help to know what others in similar circumstances have done. Since limitations of time, money, available subjects, and other practical matters restrict somewhat the choice of a problem, the experience of other graduate students in a research methods course might be helpful.

The following is a list of titles of research papers that have been completed by candidates for the master's degree in education in a one-semester course in research methods. It provides a typical cross-section of problems that are within the scope of the graduate student. Most of these students, it might be added, were teachers attending graduate school on a part-time basis.

Effect of Homogeneous and Heterogeneous Grouping on Group Mean Spelling Scores

High School Achievement as a Predictor of Nursing Performance

Relationship of Intelligence to Elementary School Achievement

A Comparison of Intelligence Quotients to the Retention of Shorthand

Effect of Parents' Educational Backgrounds on the Intelligence Quotient of Their Children

Functions of School Counselors in Certain Massachusetts Secondary Schools

An Evaluation by High School Students of the Guidance Counselor's Role

Problems Encountered in the Classroom by Substitute Teachers in Framingham, Massachusetts

The Effect of Suggestions for Improved Performance Given in an Eyes-Closed Induced State of Relaxation

Effect of Home Television Viewing on High School Achievement

Teacher Praise and Criticism: Their Effect on Student Achievement

Driving Habits and Their Relationship to Selected Background Factors and School Achievement

Teaching Arithmetic by Two Approaches

The Relationship of Social Class Status and Intellectual Achievement

The Effects of the Written Word on Learning Beginning Spanish for High School Students

A Comparison of the Effect of Using Written Compositions and Formal Drill in Diagramming Sentences on the Application of Grammatical Principles

The Relationship of Emotional Maladjustment to Reading Disability in Primary Grade Children

The Effect of Entrance Age on Elementary School Achievement

The Effects of Leadership Ratings Upon Leadership Performance

The Influence of Graphic Presentation on Student Understanding of Algebraic Relationships

The Effect of an Enrichment Program on Reading Speed and Comprehension at the High School Level

Relationship of Parental Occupational Level to Eighth Grade Tentative Vocational Choice

ASKING QUESTIONS/STATING PROBLEMS

Asking questions is an art. Unfortunately, students in our schools get little practice in this art, although they get a lot of practice in the drudgery of answering. But without clear questions we have no basis for research. The questions we raise, like the ideas we form about any observations we make, depend a lot upon our operating assumptions or our theory. Indeed, as we pointed out in Chapter 1, our theory will lead us to ask some questions and completely

CHAPTER 2

ignore other questions which may be equally important but are blocked out by the limitations of the theory. Another football anecdote provides a vivid illustration of this point.[1]

> A group of spectators sat watching a football game. They saw two groups of eleven men facing each other, heard a whistle blow, then suddenly action erupted, followed by another blast of the whistle, whereupon everyone stopped. One of the spectators said, "That was a good draw play, we gained eight yards." Someone asked a second spectator, "What did you see?" "Well," he replied, "I saw the acting out in different degrees of the needs for aggression and achievement in the players and the effects of how each views himself in relation to the other 21 men." A third spectator said, "I saw 11 men on either side engage in a pattern of coordinated behavior with very well worked out expectations of action for each position in regard to other positions, until these patterns were disrupted by the other side." A fourth spectator said, "I also saw your role relationship and integration. But additionally, I saw a leadership structure, which included a man in one position calling signals during the play and a captain exercising some limited authority. I saw a social system of 11 men opposing another social system, each of which was composed of many subsystems and structures like leadership, conflict, plus a coach attached to each system." A fifth spectator said, "I saw two kinds of traditions: the ritualistic and emotional meaning of a game of this sort and the heightened excitement and tension of this particular game due to the traditional rivalry between these two teams. Both traditions reflect the competitive and peer values of our young adult culture."

Who were the spectators? The second spectator was probably an individual psychologist, the third a small-group man, the fourth a sociologist, and the fifth a cultural anthropologist. The first, of course, was a football fan.

Relating this illustration to the matter of asking questions, we can see how the individual psychologist, operating out of a model of human behavior that is particularly relevant to his field, would raise quite different questions about the observed activity of the football game than would any of the other spectators in this story.

It should be obvious, pursuing this illustration further, that the kind of data which the psychologist would collect on the basis

---

1. W. Bennis, K. Benne, and R. Chin, "Conceptual Tools for the Change-Agent: Social System and Change Models," in E. M. Lloyd-Jones and N. Rosenau (eds.), *Social and Cultural Foundations of Guidance*, New York: Holt, Rinehart and Winston, 1968, pp. 622–23.

THE RESEARCH STUDY

of his questions would differ from the data collected by the others. One might even suppose, without too much stretching, that the data collected by the psychologist is almost certain to confirm his model of "aggression and achievement" as the basic motivators of human behavior. This anecdote also reminds us that each spectator was dipping into the same ball game for his observations. There is a clear sense in which each spectator's observations were "correct." None, however, had a total picture of what was going on.

As far as research goes, what we are trying to do through our questions is to point toward the kind of observations that will produce data which in turn will enable us to clarify our theory. We want to generate the clearest and best possible information we can, but we must recognize that having done this we are still left with the problem of making sense out of our observations. The questions multiply and in some way they keep coming back to the theory. Part of the discipline of research is to raise the kind of questions that will effectively direct our observations toward the kind of information or data that we need in order to test our theory.

SOURCES OF THEORY

One question that might have occurred to you in the midst of this discussion is: How do I get my theory? Since so much of the focus of this book is on the importance of theory, we shall make a brief but important digression here to discuss the question.

There is no single way to answer the question of where theory comes from. At the most fundamental level, we would need to return to the discussion in Chapter 1 in which theory was described as a product of the imagination or a way of using the mind to make sense out of nature. In this sense, a theory can emerge from whatever you are able to imagine in your mind about some phenomenon. It is rare for such imaginings to emerge from a vacuum of previous thought or observations, although that is possible. More often a theory emerges as an explanation for observed events.

A friend recently pointed out that children seem to be able to organize themselves in a rather orderly fashion for play or other activity when they are left completely free of externally imposed adult constraints. On the other hand, he observed that when a teacher leaves a classroom of students unattended disorder and

17

CHAPTER 2

chaos often follow. He then went on to theorize: If order is imposed from without by external authority, order breaks down when that authority is removed; if there is no externally imposed authority, a group will tend to create its own order to accomplish its purposes. In this case, the theory (whether good or bad) was created out of the imagination in order to explain the observed data. And once the theory has been stated it is then subject to further testing.

Buckminster Fuller has called attention to some historical research using the diaries, letters, and family conversations of scientists who had made great discoveries to determine if there was any commonality as to what had brought about the discovery.[2] The commonality uncovered by this research was intuition. Intuition, or the realization of a relationship operating in the universe, had indicated to these scientists the existence of very extraordinary generalized principles which would hold true in every special case. Such a realization constitutes a theory.

At a very mundane level we can say that theory comes from the accumulated research studies that one might read in preparing to investigate a question or problem of interest. Various disparate findings from different research studies might begin to suggest a theory which could be subjected to further testing.

Formulating Hypotheses

Generally speaking, we can sharpen our understanding of the research data if we frame our research problem in terms of a statement of expected outcomes, or a *hypothesis*. Your theory, of course, suggests to you what outcome to expect from a set of operations. If data collected from your research effort imply different outcomes from what you anticipated, you will have to revise your theory. Should the outcomes correspond to your predictions, your theory may then be strengthened.

But formulating a hypothesis is not a particularly easy thing to do. Furthermore, there are different types of hypotheses which the research discipline calls for us to understand. Let us begin by distinguishing between two kinds of hypotheses: *statistical hypotheses* and *research hypotheses*.

A statistical hypothesis is actually a *null hypothesis,* or in other words, a hypothesis that there is no difference between the

2. B. Fuller, Preface to *A New Learning Environment* by H. Cohen and J. Filipczak, San Francisco: Jossey-Bass, 1971, p. xii.

18

groups being studied. Most of the time null hypotheses are used in studies when previous theory and research do not suggest which group being studied will be different or in what direction it will differ. You will encounter some examples of null hypotheses in the studies following this chapter. Any statistical test of a hypothesis is essentially a test of the null hypothesis, since the statistical test only tells us the probability that a difference occurred by chance.

A research hypothesis is the statement of expected outcomes that is based on theory or previous research. Such a hypothesis is formulated as a guide to developing a research design. Our theory may suggest that in a certain specified situation a particular outcome would be expected; our hypothesis states this outcome and suggests the kind of experiment that might be designed to test the hypothesis.

You will find some good examples of research hypotheses in Gnagey's study of deviant students (see Study 6). For example, after citing a related finding from a study by Lippitt, Gnagey states, "We believed that if a high-powered deviant submitted to the teacher's control effort, his overt acceptance of the teacher's dominance would spread to the others in the class for whom the deviant was an identifying figure." Though not formally stated, this is clearly a statement of expected outcomes, and it formed the basis for one aspect of his study. Notice, however, that the actual statistical test of this hypothesis (see p. 125) was really a test of whether the groups differed from each other significantly, a test of the null hypothesis. The research hypothesis was explanatory and provided for a test of Lippitt's theory in another context.

Not all hypotheses provide an equally good basis for developing research studies. Travers has suggested some criteria for judging whether a hypothesis is a suitable one on which to base an experiment. He suggests the following desirable characteristics of a hypothesis[3]:

1. It should be rooted in a framework of theory or previous research.
2. It should be testable. One reason why a hypothesis may be untestable is the possibility that one or more variables cannot be measured. Other general sources of untestable hypotheses are areas where little or no organized knowledge exists on which to formulate clear and testable hypotheses.

3. R. M. W. Travers, *An Introduction to Educational Research,* New York: Macmillan, 1964, pp. 88–94.

CHAPTER 2

3. It should state relationships between variables.
4. It should be limited in scope. It is better to get a small corner of the universe in your hypothesis than to try something of global significance which may ultimately require a lifetime of work.
5. It should be consistent with most known facts.
6. It should be stated as far as possible in simple terms. Simplicity can increase clarity at no loss of significance. One aspect of simplicity is avoiding vague terminology.
7. It should be amenable to testing within a reasonable length of time. If you have one semester in which to complete a research paper, your experiment should not require a lapse of time greater than that allowed to complete the project.

Most good questions and hypotheses can be alternate forms of one another. However, not all problems can properly be stated in the form of a hypothesis. In a survey where you are merely seeking to describe an existing situation, there would be no statement of expected outcomes as in a research hypothesis nor any statistical test of differences between groups. You would simply formulate a question such as: What are the most frequent problems encountered by substitute teachers in community X?

Questions and hypotheses regarding problems in education are formulated for the purpose of enabling us to generate some clear and objective data against which we test our theory. These data, however, never answer our questions, prove our hypotheses, or solve our problems. They only provide a better basis for reshaping our theory, out of which we can then make the decisions and take the action to improve education.

THE RESEARCH PROPOSAL

These suggestions for preparing a research proposal are frankly geared to the needs of the beginning student of research and should not be confused with the requirements of a proposal for a major research project such as a doctoral dissertation or a funded research study. Nevertheless, the suggestions are in keeping with high standards of research.

It would be difficult to overemphasize the importance of the research proposal as a basis for carrying out research. For a student in a beginning course in educational research, without a carefully worked-out proposal, there is no assurance that he will know what he is doing. By the same token, the more thought and effort the student puts into his proposal, the more likely he will be to successfully execute the research itself. The proposal is somewhat like a roadmap that is studied carefully in advance of the trip so that you will know "how to get there from here."

What should a good research proposal contain? There is no absolute answer to this question, and any answer must depend to some extent on the setting in which the research is to be carried out. Since we are concerned with the kind of proposal a beginning student should submit before undertaking a research project for the research methods course, such a proposal should probably have five or six main parts.

Tentative Title

Your proposal should have a tentative title that is stated in fairly precise terms. "Television and Achievement" is too vague and general. "The Effect of Home Television Viewing on High School Achievement" is much better and suggests rather clearly what is to be studied. Remember, the title at this point is tentative, and you may want to alter it when the research is completed.

Statement of the Problem

You should now give the clearest statement of your actual problem that you can. The problem statement should be directly tied to the theory from which it is derived. Since this is just a proposal, you may not have your problem completely refined in the form of a precise question or hypothesis, but it is at least necessary to make it clear to the instructor what issue it is that you want to investigate. Along with a statement about the problem, some statement of the purpose of the study or what you hope to accomplish should be made. The object of this part of your proposal is to clarify the corner of the universe that you want to isolate and study. If your proposal is fuzzy on this, you may simply not know what you wish to study. Then you will be lost as soon as you try to consider design and data collection. If this is so, you had better wrestle with your problem some more until it is made clearer.

Research Design

Describe briefly the research procedures or methods to be used in attacking the different elements in the problem. This is your research design. Here you explain how you intend to investigate your problem. You explain the techniques you plan to use, the samples, the controls, the statistical techniques, and so on. The guiding criterion here is that your methods fit the requirements of both your problem and your practical situation. You must have time, subjects, and equipment to meet the demands of your methods.

This part of the proposal often poses a difficulty for the student. Admittedly, you are trying to design a research project before you have read enough or heard enough lectures to enable you to have any idea how to solve a problem that interests you. The only solution to this difficulty is trial-and-error. Plan your study as best you can with your limited knowledge now and refine it in the light of your instructor's criticisms, your reading, and your thinking about it. You will learn much faster this way than if you sit hopelessly and say that you cannot do it.

Data to Be Collected

List the specific data, facts, or items of information to be gathered. This may overlap with the description of methods above. However, it is included as a safeguard to force you to clarify just what data are to be collected. Are they test scores? Observations of a particular kind? Answers to questionnaires? A count of the number of times first graders pick fights during the course of a week's observation? Be specific!

Sources of Data

You should explain how and where each item or set of data is to be obtained. If you are a student, your access to certain data may be very limited. It is important, then, that you determine in advance where and how you will be able to collect the data that your problem and methods require. If you simply cannot get the tests you were counting on using or the subjects or whatever else you need in connection with data collection, you will have to make compromises or find another problem.

Relevant Research and Theory

We began this section by saying the proposal should have five or six main parts. Under ordinary circumstances a section on relevant research and theory would be highly important, and it would most logically follow the statement of the problem. Since, as you will see below, your research paper must contain a section reviewing the related literature on your problem, if you can cover this thoroughly in your proposal, this section will more or less be written. However, the circumstances of the student are seldom ordinary. If it is possible in the time available to the student for completing the project, then this topic should appear in the proposal. It will appear in the final report in any case.

ORGANIZING AND WRITING A RESEARCH PAPER

When your data have been collected and analyzed and you are ready to write the report of your research, how do you organize your material? There is no hard and fast rule, but the five divisions we suggest are generally accepted as important and necessary. These divisions, however, are most relevant to the type of paper you will submit for your research methods course. Published research, as you will see from the examples in the following chapters, does not necessarily follow the order of these divisions, nor are all of these divisions included in every published paper. Space limitation is the main reason for this. Even so, most published research will contain all the following five categories, however briefly presented:

1. Introduction and Statement of the Problem
2. Review of Related Research
3. Research Methods
4. Analysis and Results
5. Summary and Conclusions

In addition to these five divisions, we will also discuss the bibliography and appendix, if any, and make some general suggestions for preparing the report.

Introduction and Statement of the Problem

Long-winded, tangential introductions are not appropriate to research papers, but some kind of leading in to the problem is usually good style. Two or three paragraphs usually suffice to set the stage for your problem or to put it in some perspective. The problem itself should be clearly and concisely stated, either in question form or as a hypothesis. Most good introductory sections will contain a statement about the purpose of the study, the importance of it, or the need for it. In other words, try to support the idea that your study is worth doing, for reasons other than that it is required for a grade in a course.

Review of Related Research

Reviewing the related research is usually not as difficult as locating the research was in the first place. There is no substitute for persistent searching in the periodical room of the library. We have already suggested some sources which will help you in compiling a bibliography. You must locate, read, and take notes on a good sampling (usually a minimum of ten references) of the research that has been carried out and published in the area of your problem. The library references given in this chapter will help you compile and prepare this section of your report.

The essentials to note (preferably on 3 x 5 index cards) from each study are:

1. A statement of the author's problem
2. The scope of the study, including a description of the subjects, their number, and similar information
3. The author's procedures or methods
4. The major findings and conclusions

In addition, a routine but very important procedure in your library research is to note fully, in the exact bibliographic style specified by your instructor, the author, title, journal, issue, and page numbers for each reference. This will save you much time and trouble later when you come to footnoting and preparing a bibliography.

When the articles have been read and notes made, you come to the task of incorporating the information into an organized and meaningful narrative. There are undoubtedly numerous ways you can organize your review of these studies, but three standard ways can be mentioned as prominent examples: (1) by chronological order, usually from the most recent to the earliest studies, (2) by the closeness of their relation to your study, and (3) by categories or related groups.

The first method is self-explanatory and refers to the date of publication of the study. The second method assumes that the studies you reviewed ranged along a continuum from very closely related to your study to indirectly related to your study. Usually you cite the studies which are most closely related first. It may be that you will have more than one study with the same degree of relatedness, and in that case you can order these chronologically within the category of relatedness.

If your study is in any way complex, there may be several aspects to the related research you review. For example, your problem may involve the use of a particular test or other method, and you may wish to review studies utilizing the same method or test, even though it was applied to a different problem. In this situation you may find it better to group your related studies into meaningful categories and review a series of studies in each category.

Whatever method of organization you use, you should still give a summary or overview of the studies at the end of this section. You should be brief and draw together the common thread or threads that can be found in all the studies. In this way, you try to make sense out of the differing studies so that later you can relate your own findings more clearly to the findings which you have gathered together in your review.

Research Methods

You should answer the question: What did you do and who did you do it to or on? You describe your research design in this section in such a way that another researcher could replicate it if he decided to check on your results with another sample. You can almost think of this chapter in terms of writing a recipe for a cake you just invented. You want it to be clear enough so that someone else can bake the cake the same way you did.

Some of the information you must supply includes: a description of your population of subjects; the sample you chose and how you sampled; tests, questionnaires, scales, and so on which you used and how they were constructed, if original; how the data were analyzed, including the statistical methods used and level of confidence accepted; and the nature of the experimental controls or procedures, if any. The description of research methods should be clear, concise, and to the point. Don't waste words.

Analysis and Results

Analysis and results present your findings in a clear, objective fashion. This may well be the most difficult section to write unless your findings are confined to a single experimental observation. Descriptive survey studies, for example, may require many tables and a fairly lengthy discussion to cover all the important findings, whereas the test of a clear-cut hypothesis may involve only an explanation of the basis for accepting or rejecting the hypothesis.

Your basic quantitative results should always be summarized in one or more tables. Often, the inclusion of one or more graphic figures will further clarify the meaning of your data. This means that you must begin by constructing clear and meaningful tables and figures before you undertake any descriptive writing. Thus, your narrative will be anchored around your tables and figures which will normally contain more total information than you actually discuss.

These tables and figures should be clear enough so that a reader can examine them and draw some of his own conclusions. However, your job is to facilitate this process by pointing out in your narrative the significant aspects of your findings that appear in the table. To repeat everything in words that is obvious from looking at a table is a waste of time. Touch on the highlights, pointing up those bits of information that are most striking, or significant, or interesting and perhaps tying together separate pieces of information from several tables so that the meaning of your results is made more clear.

You should stick to straight expository writing rather than flowery prose. Also, avoid drawing conclusions as you go; rather just present the facts as you found them. The creative task of this section lies in the way you present your data so as to call attention to those aspects which are significant and important in relation to the original problem you posed.

Summary and Conclusions

In the final section you should recapitulate briefly your problem statement and the methods by which you attempted to study the problem, i.e., summarize sections one and three. Then proceed to state your conclusions based on the findings just reported in section four. Your conclusions should relate to the relevant literature reviewed in the second section.

The difference between a *finding* and a *conclusion* is more or less the difference between the data and the theory. What you want to do in your final chapter is to suggest something about the way your theory has been altered or strengthened as a result of the information generated from the research data. It should be obvious to you that your conclusions or statements about your theory must be directly related to the information which you have reported earlier. Many beginning students of research make the mistake of drawing broad and far-reaching conclusions that go way beyond the data which they report. This is a serious flaw in reporting research. You should be able to substantiate the conclusions which you reach from the data which you report.

Because of the inexactness of most data in educational research, conclusions must be stated with appropriate caution. Qualifying words like "tend to," "generally," "usually," and "on the whole" call attention to the fact that we are dealing in probability, not mechanical cause-and-effect. The entire section should be written in the past tense.

The summary and the statement of conclusions is the heart of this final section, but it is important to add to this some discussion of your conclusions, the implications for educational practice of the results of your study, and suggestions for further research. In addition, this would be a good place to discuss particular weaknesses of your study if these weaknesses may have had an important effect on the interpretation of your results. Suggestions for additional research may include a suggestion to repeat the study with certain improvements designed to sharpen the clarity of the results. In any case, there is room for some creative and insightful discussion in this section, as long as you make it clear when you are basing statements on your data and when you are speculating.

Bibliography and Appendix

Whether you have used footnoted references or references to a numbered bibliography in your text, you must include a complete bibliography of all sources consulted in connection with the research and the report of the research. For this you should follow carefully the style prescribed by your instructor.

If you have a special test, questionnaire, rating form, basic table(s) of raw data, or any other material which will not fit naturally into the context of one of the sections but which contains important information to the reader, it should be included in an appendix.

These two sections will complete the required content of your paper. Remember that, while a bibliography is definitely necessary, an appendix is included only if there is something to go in it.

CHAPTER 2

General Suggestions for Preparing the Report

1. Do not make the report longer than necessary. Always be concise and succinct in writing up research. Quality counts more than quantity of pages.

2. You should write in your best expository style. Grammar, punctuation, and diction are important and should be correct. Have someone edit your paper if you are weak in writing. Your verb tense should remain fairly consistent throughout your paper. In general, most research is written in the past tense, since any report on research must necessarily follow the data collection process and describe what *was* observed. At times this may seem awkward, but usually it makes good sense.

3. Mechanical style, i.e., the style in which the report is typed—the appearance of the title page, table of contents, chapter headings, format for tables and figures, manner of footnoting, form of bibliographical references, and so on—is important. Your instructor will probably specify the style manual he wants you to follow, and he will expect you to adhere to it carefully. This may seem picayune, but it is part of the discipline of doing the project correctly.

4. You may find these few criteria useful for judging your own paper before you turn it in:

Is the presentation such that what you did and what you observed stand out clearly?
Do you show an awareness of the weaknesses, underlying assumptions, and so forth, in your study?
Are your conclusions valid and in keeping with your findings?
Were the data handled and presented accurately and effectively?
Was the research designed adequately within the practical limitations you faced?

In general, your paper will probably be judged in a research methods course according to these criteria and others which your instructor may specify.

III

Historical research

The historian of education in some ways is the forgotten man of educational research. Textbooks in research methods pay brief homage to him and his methods and then pass on to the concerns of the present. No one is to blame for this since the conduct of historical research is inherently difficult and time consuming. It is a field that is more attractive to the scholar than to the activist bent on searching out truth in the present.

    A student can learn the rudiments of designing and conducting an experiment with relatively little difficulty, but the problem of locating historical source material, subjecting it to careful, objective criticism, and then relating and interpreting the facts that are discovered is a process that takes considerable study and practice. It would be a rare student who could hope to conduct a legitimate piece of historical research in education as part of a research methods course. This is not said to discourage the attempt, but to promote a realistic understanding of the difficulties involved in doing such research. As we shall see, it involves more than reading books in the library.

THE NATURE AND PURPOSE OF HISTORICAL RESEARCH IN EDUCATION

A knowledge of history is often glibly defended as enabling us to avoid making the same mistakes in the future, or in some cases even to predict the future. There is a grain of truth in this, but it makes more sense to think of an understanding of history as providing us with a perspective on the future.

Any problem will be easier to deal with if we can get some perspective on it, can step back and view it in its context of past and present events. It was often pointed out in a connotation clearly favorable that John F. Kennedy was a student of history. His knowledge of history did not necessarily make it easier for him to arrive at decisions as president, but this knowledge gave him a perspective on the events that he was a part of, and this perspective often enabled him to see consequences and alternatives that might not have been so clear to a man without his historical acumen.

In the same way, a historical perspective can serve the educator involved in educational policy-making, and it can serve any member of the profession in dealing with educational problems. But historical research for the purpose of gaining perspective on present problems is not the only purpose which such research can serve. Historical research can also be carried out for its own sake, that is, an interest in the truth about the past.

A historian may be interested in reconstructing as accurately as possible the events of the past regarding some specific situation or institution. Such reconstructions may have a worthy value locally even though they do not contribute much to larger and more general problems of education. The history of an institution (for example, *The History of Northeastern University*) is an example of research undertaken for limited or local purposes.

What kind of problems in education can be studied by historical methods? Since historical method represents essentially a means of investigating events, personalities, institutions, and similar phenomena in the past, almost any educational problem may be investigated this way. What is of historical significance or, to put it another way, worth remembering, is whatever has had a significant effect on present circumstances. What constitutes significance here is a matter of judgment.

Education, being so much a part of the fabric of our culture and our society, is preeminently a product of historical forces. The history of social change, the movement of men and events in any time and any place, is in some part the history of education and educational institutions in a society. Thus, whatever significant struggles are going on within education at any particular time, historical method may be applied to a study of them.

Some of the most important current struggles involve such issues and problems as the role of teachers' unions and teacher strikes in education, decentralization and community control of school policy in large urban areas, the role of students in educational policy- and decision-making, the development of more effective ways of educating minority groups who have been "educationally deprived" for so long, and the effect of racially segregated schools on learning. Among these problems and issues may be found almost the full range of possible research topics one might undertake to investigate by any method. We merely suggest here that historical method may be brought to bear on any of these areas.

Perhaps an example of how historical research can contribute to education will make the discussion clearer. The guidance movement in public education is one of the newest and most rapidly growing fields of education. Although it has a history in American education that can be traced back to formal beginnings around the turn of the century, it is just at present suffering from growing pains. Part of these growth pains are manifested in a search for clearer objectives and sounder philosophy of operation in the practice of guidance.

An important contribution to this search was made by Perry J. Rockwell in a study entitled "Social Concepts in the Published Writings of Some Pioneers in Guidance, 1900–1916," an unpublished doctoral dissertation at the University of Wisconsin, and in a briefer article published with John W. M. Rothney.[1] This study explored the social ideas of these pioneers of guidance as revealed in their own published material. The study showed the kind of ideas that motivated and guided the guidance services that these pioneers sought to develop. Through an examination of these ideas, Dr. Rockwell has provided an interesting perspective for examining some of the competing ideas that are causing a struggle in the present-day guidance movement.

For example, Rockwell points out, "All of the guidance activities organized by these early workers were designed to make the individual fit closer to a mold that would include all the values which these workers thought would result in successful living."[2] He goes on to cite present-day echoes of this same idea in a slightly different context, suggesting that the issue has still not been resolved. He then poses the question of what kind of society guidance workers are dedicated to moving toward today. Such a study provides a much needed perspective for the guidance profession in resolving its philosophical dilemma.

---

1. Perry J. Rockwell and John W. M. Rothney, "Some Social Ideas of Pioneers in the Guidance Movement," *Personnel and Guidance Journal*, 40, No. 4 (1961), 349–54.
2. ibid., 354.

CHAPTER 3

METHODS OF HISTORICAL RESEARCH

Modern historical research leans heavily on scientific method. The historian strives to insure as far as possible that the images from the past which he uncovers and organizes are as free from bias and distortion as possible. Of course, many historical documents are in themselves biased reports, but these can still be examined objectively in the light of other available evidence.

The historian cannot be a witness to the facts he seeks the way other researchers can. He must rely on the silent witnesses of documents and other remains or relics. Consequently, the collecting of source materials is a fundamental stage in historical research.

Source materials are classified roughly into two categories: primary and secondary. Primary sources are those closest to the events being studied and secondary sources are those one or more times removed. How a source is classified depends somewhat on the problem being studied. In Rockwell's study cited above, the writings of the guidance pioneers were primary sources for their social ideas. However, a historian interested in specific guidance programs of the time might find these writings to be no more than secondary sources.

When source materials have been collected they must be subjected to criticism to establish their authenticity. Two lines of evidence must be pursued. First, is the document or relic what it appears to be? Is this book purportedly written by this guidance pioneer actually what it claims to be? This is called external criticism.

The second line of criticism is designed to establish the meaning and trustworthiness of the data contained in the document itself. What did the guidance pioneers mean by what they wrote in their books and articles? Are the things they said credible? This is internal criticism.

The aimless collection of records and relics, however, does not contribute any more to our understanding of events than the unrelated collection of any other kind of data. Consequently, the historian, like any other researcher, must develop a model of what he is looking for. The historical significance of any set of historical data stems from the context in which it is presented.

Sometimes the historian's model leads him to look for particular developments or trends in the material he is studying. Other times, he may simply be searching for all possible material relating to a particular event or issue and will apply some after-the-fact organizational structure to these data.

The importance of the model in historical research cannot be overestimated. Because of the nature of historical data, particularly when original sources in the form of persons are no longer available, the only questions one may address to one's data must be addressed and answered in the historian's own imagination. If the historian's presuppositions about the events he is investigating are too restrictive, he may never see what is there to be seen.

Recent developments in the history of science provide a good illustration of this phenomenon. Thomas S. Kuhn writes:[3]

> Gradually, and often without entirely realizing they are doing so, historians of science have begun to ask new sorts of questions and to trace different, and often less than cumulative, developmental lines for the sciences. Rather than seeking the permanent contributions of an older science to our present vantage, they attempt to display the historical integrity of that science in its own time. They ask, for example, not about the relation of Galileo's views to those of modern science, but rather about the relationship between his views and those of his group, i.e., his teachers, contemporaries, and immediate successors in the sciences. Furthermore, they insist upon studying the opinions of that group and other similar ones from the viewpoint—usually very different from that of modern science—that gives those opinions the maximum internal coherence and the closest possible fit to nature.... By implication, at least, these historical studies suggest the possibility of a new image of science.

Kuhn suggests that simply to look at the same historical data from a different point of view and to ask different questions of the data is to open the possibility of emerging with new images of what was taking place historically. We may, in fact, be long overdue for historical studies of educational research itself, studies which would investigate the effects of research on educational practice, the development of scientific models in education, trends in the development of research methodology, and so on.

Meanwhile, we shall turn to an example of historical research in education to illustrate some of the points we have made about both purpose and methodology.

3. Thomas S. Kuhn, *The Structure of Scientific Revolutions,* Chicago: The University of Chicago Press, 1962, p. 3.

STUDY 1

INTRODUCTION TO STUDY 1

This study represents an investigation of a series of events that take on historical significance because they were forerunners of similar events that are presently operative nationwide and with considerable visibility. Furthermore, these events are part of a development that has significant social implications far beyond the realm of education alone. These are issues of community identity in relationship to neighborhood schools, public support of private services, use of public facilities, and focus of curriculum in education.

Study 1

Social Centers, Politics, and Social Efficiency in the Progressive Era

EDWARD W. STEVENS, JR.

It is in the social centers of Rochester that I should look for an answer to the question, whether in a great democratic community you were realizing the purposes of society.[1]

In 1911 the state of Wisconsin wrote into law a provision for the establishment of social centers. The law, the first of its kind in the United States, authorized school directors to establish "evening schools, vacation schools, reading rooms, library stations, debating clubs, gymnasiums, public playgrounds, public baths, and similar activities." It further provided that "nonpartisan, nonsectarian, and nonexclusive associations of citizens shall have use of schoolhouses free of charge."[2] According to Charles Zueblin, seventy-one cities in twenty-one states had established social centers by 1913, and by 1914 seventeen states had provided "wider-use" legislation—five in the East, five in the mid-West, four in the far-West, and three in the South.[3] The social center movement had captured the imaginations of educational decision-makers and legislators alike. Although leaders of the movement invariably adjusted the features of their programs in light of regional differences, the movement itself was not "regional" in nature. Moreover, it administered to both urban and rural constituencies.

Reprinted with permission of author and publisher from *History of Education Quarterly*, **12**, No. 1 (Spring 1972), 16–33.

Local leaders, of course, made social center programs operative, but support was plentiful at the national level. In fact, the prestige of the movement might be gauged by the support and recognition awarded it by nationally known figures and organizaitons. Presidents Theodore Roosevelt, Taft, and Wilson all recognized it as a significant contribution to the development of American democracy. The Rochester experiment (1907–1911) attracted the attention of the National Municipal League, the Playground Association of America, the National Education Association, and the Russell Sage Foundation. University extension divisions soon recognized the social center idea as a means of the implementation of their own services. Numerous bulletins from the U.S. Bureau of Education kept the idea alive in officialdom, and the organization of a National Conference on Civic and Social Center Development gave the movement a forum of its own making. Finally, a number of publications, among them Edward J. Ward's *The Social Center* (1913), Clarence A. Perry's *How To Start a Social Center* (1914), Henry E. Jackson's *A Community Center, What It Is and How To Organize It* (1918), and Ida C. Clarke's *The Little Democracy* (1918), familiarized educators and municipal reformers with the basic philosophy of the movement and "how-to-do-it" suggestions.[4]

The rapid increase in numbers of social centers operating in the United States was matched only by the proliferation of the types of activities offered. Surveys by Clarence A. Perry and Eleanor Glueck show a variety of athletics to have been the most popular type of activity carried on in public schools used as social centers. Clubs, social occasions, games and entertainment (concerts, etc.) also were popular, while lectures and civic occasions (mass meetings and public discussions) were moderately successful. In addition to these core activities, social centers served as local art galleries, branch public libraries, movie theaters, polling places, places for party caucuses and political rallies, and Americanization centers.[5]

As might be expected in an era of efficiency, leaders of the movement, particularly Edward J. Ward, its most ardent spokesman, soon began speaking in the rhetoric of social engineering. What the movement needed, said Ward, were specialists and managers. Because the superintendent of schools must direct his energies to the "regular work of the school," a "social engineer" should be employed to coordinate social center work. He should be "technically qualified to advise upon methods found successful in community organization elsewhere, and should cooperate efficiently with the school principals in the service of the various neighborhoods."[6] According to Ward the social engineer with a staff (which might include a property specialist, a specialist in schoolhouse architecture, and paid secretarial service) could then administer more efficiently to the citizens in whose behalf the social centers were organized.[7]

Late nineteenth-century attempts at moral uplift and municipal reform had made use of the social center idea, although in a limited way by the

STUDY 1

standards of the Rochester experiment.[8] Yet these earlier attempts to extend the social function of the public school, while anticipatory, cannot properly be considered a part of the social center movement. What distinguished the movement as it developed after 1907 was its commitment to the ideal of social efficiency espoused by Progressive leadership. The concept of social efficiency as it emerged in the Progressive Era was used to denote a method whereby maximum predictability and probability might be achieved in any socially oriented process. In the early twentieth century, advocates of social efficiency usually adopted what they called scientific methods for achieving these ends. Some, however, continued to rely upon moral suasion. Collectively, social efficiency was a method for achieving stability *in* and control *of* the environment. In general, then, the term denoted a method for effecting social control.[9]

Progressive leaders, and most likely their followers, were generally committed to an attack on what they perceived as the evils of an urban-industrial society. Their methods were those defined by "science" and a new organizational ethic of social efficiency, sometimes accompanied by an older rhetoric of rural fundamentalism and a competitive ethos. The model for developing the socially efficient organization was that offered by corporate enterprise. In the arena of municipal reform, political capitalism achieved some of its greatest successes as municipal reformers came to see efficient government as businesslike government led by a professional-business elite. Among social missionaries, agrarian reformers, conservationists, labor union leaders, proponents of Americanization programs, and civil service reformers, an appeal to moral individualism and self-restraint had its place, but the method and the model that finally emerged triumphant were those of corporate enterprise. In reform organizations personal concern gave way to efficiency and individual responsibility gave way to organizational responsibility.

Educators were not far behind in their quest for the socially efficient society. The ideal society of Irving King, an articulate spokesman for social efficiency in rural life, was one in which conflicting interests had been resolved and a cultural homogeneity achieved. While idealizing the rural community King attempted to make the school an agency for adjustment by yoking together a rather traditional moral education with a new concern for vocational education. Social efficiency, as it was applied to the school, said King, merely concerned itself with the "best means scientifically determined to accomplish the generally recognized function of the school to train the child and to cultivate in him the right and useful habits needful for adult life."[10] Social efficiency, according to King, essentially concerned itself with the development of community, the central theme of which was cooperative capitalism.

David Snedden, an urban-oriented spokesman for social efficiency, did not, like King, look to the past for an ideal by which to guide his attempts to define the socially efficient society. Rather, he looked forward to the day "when educational aims and processes could be systematically improved and advanced by methods that can properly be called scientific."[11] Snedden hoped to hasten that day by publishing his *Sociological Determination of Objectives in Education* (1921) and by bringing a science of education to bear upon the problems of social efficiency in modern society. Snedden perceived modern civilized life to be "like modern industry" or a "modern army organization," the most significant aspect of which was its highly differentiated and specialized nature. The modern industrial and military model, then, was for Snedden the model to which men must conform. Whenever the individual was involved in group action, as he inevitably was in such a model, it was necessary, according to Snedden, that "individuality of action ... be greatly subordinated to the requirements of subjection to orders and enforced limitations, uniformity of stimuli, and conformity in behavior."[12] The school, the master agency for adjustment, was to carefully cultivate behavior patterns that would result in "efficient personal growth, individual efficiency, and ultimate social usefulness."[13]

It was part of the social center idea that citizens, particularly adults, should make worthy use of their leisure time. To advocates of social efficiency the very concept of leisure was problematic and a source of difficulty. If leisure time were to be interpreted generally as free time, then the former would be an obstacle to the building of a socially efficient society. If leisure, however, could be interpreted as only freedom *from* (from an occupation or from compulsion, for example), then the problem was solvable. As long as freedom *to* was limited by specific and prearranged alternatives for action, then leisure would pose no threat to order and stability. The argument was put succinctly by H. R. Knight of the Russell Sage Foundation when he explained the way in which a task-oriented schoolhouse eliminated the threat of free time:

> Young people go wrong during their leisure hours. While at work or study their thoughts and actions are controlled by their tasks. When free to do what they will they may or may not make the right use of their time.[14]

The problem was no less real for the adult. Herbert S. Weet, Superintendent of the Rochester Public Schools, noted the following in an article entitled "Citizenship and the Evening Use of School Buildings" (1911):

> The leisure life problem is yet to be solved. A comparatively weak man may be a good citizen while he is at his work, but it takes a strong man to use his leisure hours with advantage to himself and with profit to the community.[15]

The impact of this "tremendous force for righteousness" captured the imagination of Clarence A. Perry, the movement's most thorough researcher. Citing the 847,935 attendances at social centers for the year 1914, Perry urged his readers to think of these as "so many evenings spent in wholesome activity within an improving environment by persons many of whom would otherwise have spent that time in less beneficial and positively harmful pastimes."[16]

The relationship between the proper use of leisure and the making of a moral citizen was made visible in the many recreational activities designed for moral uplift and the teaching of "proper" values. Citing the Rochester experience as a case in point, Harriet L. Childs noted that "clean, decent amusements are almost impossible to a girl outside of the social centers." She continued:

> Here under supervision girls and boys can dance, can play, wholehearted, happy, safe, in the assurance of no expense for liquor that the boy cannot afford, and no evil result for the girl.[17]

In an article entitled "How a Community May Find Out and Plan for Its Recreation Needs," Rowland Haynes explained that recreation should build character, particularly the habits of "quickness of thought, fair play and teamwork."[18]

Temperance sentiment was strong in the arguments of social center advocates, a fact not surprising in view of the nationwide strength of prohibitionist sentiment. In a speech opening the first social center in Rochester the President of the Board of Education implored his listeners that "If the instinct of fellowship is not satisfied in wholesome and uplifting ways, if people of all classes are compelled to find companionship when and where they can, if those who would profit by it [saloon keepers and dancehall owners] are permitted to make their appeal in evil ways, and with mercenary prompting, then we have the harvest of crime, insanity, and moral disintegration and shipwreck which is so terrible a characteristic of existing society."[19] While the Board President addressed himself to "all classes," he singled out those leisure time abodes most frequented by the immigrant and the poor as the evils to be attacked by the building of social centers. Uplift, it would appear, was for one socioeconomic class but not another.

A number of social center advocates saw the center as a means to the restoration of family unity. Advocates concerned with urban centers spoke of the moral evils of the city and the deleterious effects of industrialism on family life. Those more concerned with the establishment of rural centers stressed the out-migration from the country to the city and the isolation of rural people as a result of increasing specialization of farming as problems that the social center could solve. In both cases (rural and urban) facilities for family recreation were to be provided.[20] The restoration of family life, like so many other functions of the social center, was linked to the proper use of leisure time. "The schoolhouse social center," said H. R. Knight, "brings the whole family together for its recreation, for intelligent use of its leisure time."[21]

Attitudes toward family unity were easily transferred to the community in general. For most purposes the word community was synonymous with neighborhood, and the concept of neighborhood, in many respects, was that of the family enlarged. American democracy was "the organization of society on the basis of friendship," and "the aim of the Community Center Movement," said Clarence A. Perry, "is to organize America into a society with the schoolhouse as the society's home and clubhouse in each local unit."[22] The neighborhood school was to be the agency "through which the economic, social, intellectual, political, and religious conditions in the neighborhood are to be transformed according to the spirit of order, progress, and national well-being."[23] A number of leaders stressed that social centers should counteract ethnic and class divisions that might be present in the neighborhood. Edward J. Ward's fear of the political left was evident when he spoke of that "sense of solidarity and power of collective action upon which all those who do not accept the doctrine of 'class struggle' base their hope of human progress."[24]

Democracy meant efficiency, and discord was to be avoided if centers were to operate in a democratic way. Of the Rochester social centers specifically, Ward noted that the social instinct "should not be left to satisfy itself *at haphazard*...."[25] Clarence A. Perry was specific about the model to be followed. Commenting upon the "machinery" needed for the neighborhood to become "an intelligent, co-ordinated, wise-acting civic unit," he made the following analogy:

> An efficient manufacturing corporation maintains a research staff to carry on and systematize experimentation with new processes. It provides machinery to keep its board of directors fully informed of the concern's affairs. It believes that an intelligent mind on the board is worth more than a dummy. It forms shop committees and establishes channels through which complaints can flow without hindrance. It consciously takes the necessary steps to keep up the morale of its organization. A municipality which provided a staff to organize its communities and establish community centers would be imitating an up-to-date business corporation.[26]

It is one of the ironies of the social center movement that, as it attempted to initiate reform along the lines of social efficiency and the corporate model, it clung to a concept of community that was rural in origin, and whose genesis, according to Ward, was the New England town meeting. Ward, the organizer and administrator of the Rochester social centers, saw in them "the restoration to its true place in social life of that most American of all institutions, the Public School Center, in order that through this extended use of the school building, might be developed, in the midst of our complex life, the community interest, the neighborly spirit, the democracy that we knew before we came to the city." The same rural sentiment was behind the

STUDY 1

School Extension Committee's decision to open the centers to discussion on all subjects, such freedom being essential, they said, "to the development of an institution which shall serve the people in the city as the Little Red School House served the folks back home."[27] Ward's "Dedication" to his short history of the social centers in Rochester exceeded most in its nostalgia:

> To Governor Hughes, and the rest of us, who recognize the spirit of the Social Centers and Civic Clubs because we remember how, back home, the folks used to get together in the school house, evenings, for spell downs, singing schools and festivals, where there wasn't any difference between the postmaster's wife and the hired girl, because the women took their hats off; and how the men folks got together there, evenings, and decided things, by free, honest discussion. . . .[28]

In the political ethos of the social center movement, social efficiency, a rural ideal of community, and liberal politics met to form the Progressive outlook. One of the most visible means by which social centers tapped the spirit of Progressive efficiency was to make the school the polling place for local, state, and national elections. "The voting machine or ballot box should be kept in the schoolhouse as the symbol of efficiency in self-government," said Edward J. Ward. Such a practice, moreover, would "make a monumental declaration of the community of civic interest that transcends all our disunities."[29] Using the schoolhouse as a polling place was only one of several policies, said supporters, which would bring "order, efficiency, economy of effort, and strength of a united citizenship out of . . . inter-individual chaos."[30] Fighting corruption and the political machines that spawned them was another, as was making the social center a political forum to air issues and to promote "intelligent" voting. A faith in human reason, free speech, and the tendency of informed men to moderation made social center leaders optimistic in their efforts. Men who were reasonable, they said, would vote "for measures and men rather than for parties and machines."[31] Free speech would give truth a chance and would, furthermore, operate as a safety-valve for those whose grievances might otherwise erupt in violence.[32] Arthur E. Bostwick, speaking on behalf of social centers, offered evidence from his own experience as a librarian in St. Louis regarding the tendency of men to moderation given the proper conditions:

> In one of our branches there meets a club of men who would be termed anarchists by some people. The branch librarian assures me that the brand of anarchism that they profess has grown perceptibly milder since they have met in the library. It is getting to be literary, academic, philosophic. Nourished in a saloon, with a little injudicious repression, it might perhaps have borne fruit of bombs and dynamite.[33]

EDWARD W. STEVENS, JR.

In an address delivered before the first National Conference on Civic and Social Centers in 1911 Woodrow Wilson capsulized, better than most, the liberal-Progressive politics that lay behind the social center movement. After exhorting his listeners to remember that the schoolhouse is the civic center of the community, Wilson went on to explain the "process of modern politics" and its relation to liberty. Modern politics, he noted, must "exclude deadly rivalries, make men understand other men's interests, bring all men into common council, and so discover what is the common interest." The way to reconciling the opposing concepts of private interests and community interest was through an agreed-upon definition of liberty, said Wilson. Liberty, he continued, was a matter of "adjustment": "the individual is free in proportion to his perfect accommodation to the whole . . . men are free in society in proportion as their interests are accommodated to one another. . . ." With adjustment of interests comes control in the form of "sovereignty" of the people. Liberty could not work, he said, without enlightenment, a state to be achieved primarily via a liberal education—the kind of education that "disconnects [a man] from . . . special interests and marries his thought to the common interests of great communities. . . ."[34]

The political spirit of the social center movement was most evident in the civic clubs, usually organized for adults and sometimes for the explicit purpose of Americanizing newly arrived immigrants. The social center, said Mrs. Thomas W. Hayes, a county superintendent of schools, was "the greatest socializing and Americanizing agency in the country today."[35] Through its extensive use of the civic club as an agency of political socialization, the social center movement in Rochester, N.Y., became widely recognized as a model whose successes were to be imitated and whose failures were to be avoided.[36] Among the former, according to its advocates, were the enlightenment of voters on municipal and national issues, its broad-based constituency, its supervision by the school board, and its tendency to curb radicalism. Chief among the latter was its dramatic collapse after four "glorious" years—a collapse explained variously as the result of machine politics, a weak mayor, and the reactionary forces of self-seeking industrialists and conservative clergy. The reasons for the Rochester failure offered above do provide, in part, an explanation of that failure. The fact that the centers were subject, also, to the budgetary discretion of the Common Council helps explain the mechanism through which opposing forces wielded their power. (The appropriations made to maintain civic clubs were denied in 1911, although the appropriations for recreation centers and a lecture course were continued. With this denial the broad-based social center movement became primarily a recreation movement.)[37] Still, these explanations only touch upon the inherent weaknesses of a liberal-Progressive political theory that, in the long run, was unable to cope with the demands of liberty in democracy. A closer look at the Rochester centers should prove instructive.

The breadth of interest in social centers in Rochester was evident from

STUDY 1

the beginning. Eleven organizations* represented by the School Extension Committee received a five thousand dollar appropriation in 1907 for the establishment of the centers. Civic clubs were always part of the centers in Rochester and experienced the same rapid growth (from one club with twelve members in 1907 to sixteen clubs with 1,500 members in 1909) as did the centers generally.[38]

From its inception the movement in Rochester partook of a rural sentiment best expressed by Ward himself when he spoke of "an institution which shall serve the people of the city as the Little Red School House served the folks back home." The feeling that the social centers were community centers—where all could meet on an equal basis—was one compatible with the city neighborhood from the point of view of the center leaders. The restriction by the Board of Education that the civic clubs were "not to be partisan or exclusive either in meetings or discussions" was one designed to combat ethnic prejudice formed as a result of urban living.[39] Professor George M. Forbes of the University of Rochester saw the centers as a way to avoid both the "monarchy" of the public elementary school and the exclusiveness of "every institution within the state." The centers "must be free from the limitations of the public schools," he said; they must appeal to relatively mature minds dealing with actual experiences of community life, and they must be all inclusive, "the one institution within the state that takes in everybody solely by virtue of his living in the community."[40]

Moral uplift, too, was part of the social centers in Rochester, and, according to the Board of Education, was demonstrably successful:

> ... it has already been demonstrated that the groups of boys and young men who have been such a nuisance in various quarters of the city are not inherently vicious, but are driven to loafing and mischief by the lack of any opportunity for wholesome activity.[41]

Civic clubs themselves extended their activities in the direction of uplift when they undertook the supervision of playgrounds to maintain order "without the aid of the police."[42] This, they said, would foster the spirit of self-government, self-control, and good citizenship, all of which, it seemed, were defined as the maintenance of good order by the civic clubs.

In order to properly "exercise the franchise" the Rochester clubs made it a point to discuss issues and hear lecturers on topics of fundamental political and social importance. A sampling of the Men's Civic Club activities at School No. 14, for instance, illustrates the breadth of the program carried on by the club: "Why Vote for Taft," "Why Vote for Debs," "Social Values

---

*Central Trades and Labor Council, Children's Playground League, College Women's Club, Daughters of the American Revolution, Humane Society, Labor Lyceum, Local Council of Women, Officer's Association of Mother's Clubs, Political Equality Club, Social Settlement Association, and Women's Educational and Industrial Union.

of Theater," "Woman Suffrage," "Trade Unions," "The Peaceful Revolution," "The Negro Problem," "Credit Abuses," "Direct Primaries," "Industrial Training," and so forth.[43] Certain of the civic clubs such as the Italian Men's Civic Club were organized, also, for the express purpose of Americanization. A resolution passed at the number fourteen social center by this club told of the possibilities that such clubs offered for the assimilation of the immigrant:

> Resolved, that we ... hereby ... express our gratitude to the city of Rochester, for the Social Centers and the opportunities they offer for educational, civic, social and recreational advantage, and ... pledge ourselves to the loyalty of the American ideal of good citizenship and human brotherhood for which they stand.[44]

As might be expected the airing of critical issues did not go unopposed. School authorities called on to justify the existence of the civic clubs did so on the basis that it would be improper to "withhold from non-exclusive, responsible organizations of citizens the opportunity for free discussion in a public building because of occasional objectionable utterances of individuals occurring in the midst of addresses or discussions and leading to no partisan or exclusive action on the part of the responsible body." The central point here seems to have been that the free discussion of all should not be sacrificed for the objectionable words of a few so long as those words did not result in any action; as long as the civic club forum remained a forum for debate and *not for action*. The Board further defended the clubs as forums for free discussion on the grounds that the most "effective antidote" to "economic and political theories of extremists and dreamers who look for the transformation of society by revolutionary processes" was an "atmosphere of free discussions." "These extreme views thrive and become dangerous," said the Board, only "when cultivated by isolated groups who intensify their one-sided and unbalanced opinions by mutual encouragement." "The average citizen is not made a socialist by these discussions," the Board maintained. "On the contrary, the socialist has in many cases been brought to saner and more healthy views of the conditions of social progress."[45] Professor Forbes of the University of Rochester agreed, saying that in his opinion "the net result of the movement was to modify extreme opinion and bring it into line with rational progress."[46] From 1907 to 1911 the Board took the position, then, that radical and unprogressive views could best be kept in check by exposing them to the rigors of debate. But debate was to be short-lived. The case of Kendrick P. Shedd at number nine social center brought free discussion to an end.

Kendrick P. Shedd, Professor of Government at the University of Rochester, director of the number nine social center from 1909 to 1911, and director of the Rochester Socialist Sunday Schools and Young People's

Socialist League, had been a popular speaker at various social, civic, and labor functions held in the City of Rochester. The year 1911, the same year that Mayor Edgerton expelled the Labor Lyceum controlled by socialists from the city hall, was a critical one for Shedd also. Shedd had been very much in the news for criticizing, among other things, the "2 X 4 patriotism that was taught in our public schools and churches."[47] On February 4, 1911, Shedd, sponsored by the Women's Civic Club at No. 9, with the unanimous approval of those at number nine social center, and with the permission of Superintendent Weet, spoke at the center. The following day Mayor Edgerton announced that Professor Shedd would not be allowed "to speak in the public schoolbuildings of Rochester again." Soon after, the Board of Education explained that while they approved of the use of public schools for recreational activities, they disapproved of their use "at public expense for the adult civic clubs."[48] Funds were thereby discontinued for civic club activities.

Shedd's speech that caused such repercussions among authorities was, concluded Superintendent Weet, "essentially a plea for socialism." There was no manuscript for the speech, but Shedd allegedly made unpatriotic references to the American flag and "indulged in radical and sensational statements in the course of the address...." The Council of Civic Clubs quickly insisted that in saying what he did, Shedd "was voicing his personal views and opinions and did not in any respect represent us."[49]

Shedd himself called the whole affair a "tempest in a teapot," and insisted that the *Herald's* reporting of his address was so incomplete and the phrases so taken out of context as "to be misleading and entirely to misrepresent me." Said Shedd, "I did not insult the American flag, and this charge is so silly as to be unworthy of discussion." In his own defense he noted that the subject of his speech was "Privilege's Fear of Democracy" and that "the allusion to the flag came in collaterally, and merely by way of illustration." He was explaining, he said, that the red flag did not denote "murder and assassination," but, rather, "universal peace and love and fraternity," and that the "flag of our country, or any other country, was geographically limited" while the "red flag of brotherhood was international...." Still the Board disapproved and resolved to confine activities at the social centers to those which "by common consent" are regarded as of a "wholesome recreational and educational character."[50]

The question, of course, remains why a mildly socialistic speech had such an impact. Some reasons have already been suggested previously. Added to these would be the general climate of antagonism toward socialists that paralleled their steady gain in popularity in Rochester. All of these—machine politics, reactionary opposition from powerful industrial and religious interests, susceptibility to budgetary manipulation, and the climate of antagonism—explain the reaction of Rochester officials in terms of local conditions. The question remains, however, why the centers were so vulnerable.

EDWARD W. STEVENS, JR.

The social center was first, and always, an agency of adjustment—an organizational response to the threat of instability, uncontrolled change, and the loss of traditional values faced by an industrial society. Its aim was collective stability; its method that of the technocrat. By legitimizing prearranged alternatives for the use of leisure time, and thereby eliminating the threat of freedom, moral uplift could be achieved. Social engineering, the "specialized" institution, scientific methodology, and the corporate model all did service to the goal of social efficiency.

Both the social and political rationale for social centers was strongly utilitarian. The liberal-Progressivism (often a conservative liberalism) of the social center in Rochester, while committed to liberty of speech and the supposition that the competition of ideas would arrive at some consensus called truth, suffered that liberty only so long as it resulted in no plan of action nor offered any fundamental challenge to the status quo. Effects were the measure of tolerance, and that espoused by the centers was for established organizations, not for outspoken individuals. Moreover, it was tolerance only for those values within the "community" framework already established and within the bounds that social efficiency could manage.

Advocates of the social centers could, with the aid of the corporate model, accommodate tolerance if its effects could be predicted. As practitioners of "technique" they could predict the activities of organizations, but found unorthodox individuals a problem of a different order. Organizations were safe, individuals were not. Social efficiency and liberal-Progressive politics, then, were in agreement. They agreed, also, that a "community of values" must underlie any social progress. Yet the "source" of this community was a puzzle. If, as Woodrow Wilson had suggested, community arose from a variety of competing interests, how could that community, except through some magical dialectic, ever transcend those interests? Further, if the social center were a political forum—a marketplace for competing ideas (interests), and if the centers themselves were to promote a community based on neighborhood, how were these two functions reconcilable? The marketplace was no place for community, nor was community any place for competing values and interests. The problem was simply magnified by a retreat to the Little Red School House and the idealized rural community it represented.

It was fitting, perhaps, that an experiment in the free discussion of public issues should complete its life cycle in the public school system, for it dramatically pointed up the inability of liberal-Progressivism and social efficiency to contend with the problems of democracy in education. The experiment began as one inspired by the myth of community and governed by the ideals of social efficiency. When faced with the realities of mass urban society, the assumption of community and the ideal of participative democracy proved false. The tolerance of a liberal tradition proved illusory.

ENDNOTES TO STUDY 1

1. Edward J. Ward, *The Social Center* (New York, 1913), p. 191.
2. Clarence A. Perry, "Recent Progress in Wider Use of School Plant," *Report of the U.S. Commissioner of Education* (Washington, D.C., 1915), p. 471.
3. Charles Zueblin, *American Municipal Progress* (New York, 1916), pp. 422–23; Perry, "Recent Progress," p. 471.
4. Edward J. Ward, "The Schoolhouse as the Community Center," *NEA: Journal of Proceedings and Addresses* 50 (1912): 438; idem., "The Schoolhouse as the Polling Place," U.S. Bureau of Education, *Bulletin* no. 13 (Washington, D.C., 1915): p. 9; idem., "The Rochester Social Centers," *Proceedings of the Third Annual Playground Congress* (New York, 1909), pp. 389–96; Woodrow Wilson, "The Social Center, A Means of Common Understanding," *Bulletin of the University of Wisconsin* (Madison, December 1911).
5. Ward, "Schoolhouse as Polling Place," pp. 18–19; idem., *The Social Center;* idem., "A Point of Agreement," *American City* (October 1912), pp. 325–28; Zueblin, p. 259; Clarence A. Perry, "The Extension of Public Education," U.S. Bureau of Education, *Bulletin* no. 28 (Washington, D.C., 1915), pp. 46–47; idem., "School Extension Statistics," U.S. Bureau of Education, *Bulletin* no. 30 (Washington, D.C., 1917), pp. 18–19; Eleanor T. Glueck, "Extended Use of School Building," U.S. Bureau of Education, *Bulletin* no. 5 (Washington, D.C., 1927), pp. 8–9; Robert A. Carlson, "Americanization as an Early Twentieth-Century Adult Education Movement," *History of Education Quarterly* 10 (1970): pp. 451–52; Herbert S. Weet, "Citizenship and the Evening Use of School Building," *The Common Good* 4, no. 5 (1911): 7–9; Arthur E. Bostwick, "The Public Library, The Public School, and the Social Center Movement," *NEA: Journal of Proceedings and Addresses* 50 (1912): 240–46.
6. Ward, *The Social Center,* p. 35.
7. Ibid.; idem., "Schoolhouse as Community Center," p. 447; Erich C. Stern, "The Organization and Administration of Recreation and Social Center Work," *NEA: Journal of Proceedings and Addresses* 50 (1912): 249; Dwight H. Perkins, "The Relation of Schoolhouse Architecture to the Social Center Movement," *NEA: Journal of Proceedings and Addresses* 50 (1912): 234–39.
8. Joel Henry Spring, "Education and the Rise of the Corporate State, the Role of Socialization and the Corporate image in the Development of American Public Education in the Late Nineteenth and Twentieth Centuries" (Ph.D. diss., University of Wisconsin, 1969), p. 15.
9. Edward Stevens, Jr., "The Political Education of Children in the Rochester Public Schools, 1899–1917: An Historical Perspective on Social

Control in Public Education" (Ed.D. diss., University of Rochester, 1970), p. 21.
10. Irving King, *Education for Social Efficiency* (New York, 1913), pp. 17–18.
11. David Snedden, *Sociological Determination of Objectives in Education* (Philadelphia, 1921), p. 278.
12. Ibid., p. 44.
13. Ibid., pp. 26–46.
14. W. S. Bittner, "The Community Schoolhouse: Lecture Notes," *Bulletin of the Extension Division,* Indiana University **1,** no. 4 (Bloomington, 1915), p. 5.
15. Weet, p. 8.
16. Clarence A. Perry, *Contributions to Community Center Progress; A Report on the Community Center Sessions at the NEA Department of Superintendence Meeting* (New York [Russell Sage Foundation Reprint], 1920), p. 11.
17. Harriet L. Childs, "The Rochester Social Centers," *The American City* **5** (1911): 20.
18. Rowland Haynes, "How a Community May Find Out and Plan for Its Recreation Needs," *NEA: Journal of Proceedings and Addresses* **50** (1912): 234.
19. Edward J. Ward, *Rochester Social Centers and Civic Clubs* (Rochester, N.Y., 1909), p. 23.
20. Mrs. Thomas W. Hayes, "Rural School as a Social Center," *NEA: Journal of Proceedings and Addresses* **56** (1918):602–5; L. J. Hanifan, *A Handbook Containing Suggestions and Programs for Community Social Gatherings at Rural Schoolhouses* (Charleston, W. Va., 1915), p. 8.
21. Bittner, p. 6.
22. Perry, *Contributions to Community Center Progress,* p. 11.
23. George W. Guy, "Community Leagues of Virginia and Their Contribution to Rural Education," *NEA: Journal of Proceedings and Addresses* **60** (1922): 1206.
24. Ward, "Schoolhouse as Community Center," p. 442.
25. Ward, *Rochester Centers and Clubs,* p. 24.
26. Perry, *Ten Years,* p. 10.
27. Ward, *Rochester Centers and Clubs,* pp. 12–13.
28. Ibid., "Dedication."
29. Ward, "Schoolhouse as Polling Place," pp. 5, 7.
30. Ward, *The Social Center,* p. 8.
31. Social Centers in the Southwest (San Antonio, Tex., 1912), p. 11.
32. Perry, *Contributions to Community Center Progress,* pp. 10–11.
33. Bostwick, "Public Library," p. 244.
34. Wilson, pp. 6, 11, 9.

STUDY 1

35. Hayes, "Rural School as Social Center," p. 605.
36. Perry, *Ten Years,* pp. 3–4, 8; Ward, *The Social Center,* pp. 53, 197, 199; idem, *Rochester Centers and Clubs;* idem, "The Rochester Movement," *The Independent* 62 (1909): 860–61; Eleanor T. Glueck, *The Community Use of Schools* (Baltimore, 1927), p. 24; Zueblin, p. 257; Ethel Cleland, "Social Centers," *National Municipal Review* 3 (1914): 137–138.
37. City of Rochester, *Common Council Proceedings,* 1911, p. 536.
38. Ward, *Rochester Centers and Clubs,* p. 68.
39. Rochester Board of Education, *Proceedings,* 1908, p. 51.
40. George M. Forbes, "Buttressing the Foundations of Democracy," *The Common Good* 5, no. 4 (1912): 9.
41. Rochester Board of Education, *Proceedings,* 1908, p. 51.
42. ———, *Proceedings,* 1910, p. 2.
43. ———, *Annual Report,* 1907, p. 126.
44. ———, *Annual Report,* 1908–1910, p. 140.
45. ———, *Proceedings,* 1909, pp. 60, 64.
46. Forbes, p. 10.
47. John Dutko, "Socialism in Rochester, 1900–1917" (A.M. thesis, University of Rochester, 1953), pp. 23, 169–74.
48. Rochester Board of Education, *Annual Report,* 1913, pp. 336–37.
49. ———, *Proceedings,* 1911, p. 7.
50. Ibid., p. 8.

ANALYSIS OF STUDY 1

The "historical problem" in this report was to describe some specific historical events that the author views as representative antecedents and correlates to contemporary events in education. Stevens became aware that the Rochester social centers had been organized out of desire to expand the services of education and that the successes and failures of the centers became dependent on organizational and procedural issues within a particular social context.

The explicit model out of which this historian did his research would appear to be relatively simple and straightforward. Current events with regard to educational governance, school curriculums, community schools, and the finance of education are not new to education. As before, the events must be critically examined in the social context in which they occurred. Stevens, therefore, uses sources to examine the social context of the organization and operation of the Rochester social centers.

Stevens presented the purpose of his study in the first paragraph. While the question under investigation is directly stated, the procedure used to examine the issue is not explicitly detailed. As suggested in Chapter 1, research questions and procedures can evolve out of the investigator's theory. Stevens's research procedure and the meaning of his research question are not directly stated but become evident as the study report continues. The Rochester social centers were used as a vehicle to study a larger question, and through the use of this vehicle meanings were placed on the terms of "great democratic community" and "purposes of society."

Having decided that the centers had enough historical significance to investigate further, Stevens's problems as an historian were to identify and to locate the documents and remains that would enable him to develop as full and objective account of what went on as possible. The list of notes at the end of the report provides the evidence of the source materials used. A careful study of these notes reveals that the major sources consulted were National Education Association (NEA) proceedings and addresses of the time and the reports and proceedings of the Rochester Board of Education. The latter could probably be described as a primary source and the former as a secondary source. Thus the report of events is generally scientific and objective insofar as another investigator can check the same source material and confirm or deny the validity of the reporting.

Two possible exceptions to this generalization are the use of a doctoral thesis by the author of the study as documentation for the fifth paragraph of the report and the point that social efficiency denoted a method for effecting social control. Another investigator might view social efficiency differently and, based on this differing view, develop an entirely different model to examine the research question. The use of source material is important in the completion of historical research, and it is dependent on the researcher's theory, the point again being that we search for data from a personal theoretical frame of reference.

IV

Descriptive research

Types of research can be distinguished on the basis of methodological differences, that is, how the researcher collects data. Another way to differentiate types of research is by the purpose for which the research is conducted. But purposes of research can overlap from one type of research to another while methodology will also vary. For example, a researcher might pursue the same purpose in his research through either a descriptive approach or an experimental approach but in each case his methodology would certainly vary.

Taking the methodological distinction first, we can begin by stating that descriptive research entails the collection of data that essentially describe, accurately and objectively, the way things presently are. The descriptive data can range from very simple to very complex, but the element of description is still present. What presently exists with regard to this problem or phenomenon? This is the basic question of descriptive research.

When the researcher wishes to get a picture of present conditions as a normative basis for making judgments or decisions, the approach is generally a descriptive one. Here we have the matter of the purpose for which the research is to be conducted. Many important decisions in education can be better made if descriptive data are available. Decisions about the curriculum of a school can certainly be considered relevant to employment opportunities in the community which the school serves. Accurate survey data as to employment opportunities in the community, the mobility of the school's graduates, and similar information would therefore be necessary in making good decisions about what to include or exclude in the school curriculum.

CHAPTER 4

In addition to setting forth descriptive data about relevant situations, the researcher is often interested in the relationships among events or among phenomena. In other words, the researcher may be interested in observing not only what exists, but how existing situations seem to be altered, if at all, in relation to other existing situations. Obviously, we move very quickly into a much more complex problem when we begin to examine relationships than when we deal with single situations. We also begin to increase the demand for model-building as we explore more complex relationships. In fact, we can make the generalization that the simpler descriptive studies are more likely to be undertaken for the purpose of aiding in specified decision-making, while the more complex studies are generally carried out as an adjunct to model-building.

TYPES OF DESCRIPTIVE RESEARCH

Labels for descriptive research have been extensively proliferated. A perusal of only a few educational research textbooks has turned up over thirty different labels. There is much overlapping, and we shall consider three basic types, from the simple to the complex, in this discussion:

1. Survey research
2. Correlational research
3. Causal-comparative (or *ex post facto*) research

Survey Research

No type of descriptive research is probably more familiar or more widespread in education than survey research. Little in the way of explanation is required to understand this type of research, since a survey is primarily the way in which an educator answers the "What exists?" type of question. Although there is much nonsense that passes for research in this category, the kinds of questions that lead to surveys are often of great importance to educational decision-making or to planning further research of a different type. Usually, survey research serves local purposes such as aiding in management decisions.

Survey studies appear deceptively easy to carry out, and this is one reason why they are done so often. Another reason for their proliferation is the seemingly endless number of things in education that can be surveyed. It should not be surprising that the list of labels that can be applied to survey research is a long one: appraisal surveys, community surveys, documentary frequency studies, follow-up studies, interview surveys, job surveys, market surveys, problem checklist surveys, public opinion surveys, questionnaire surveys, rating studies, school surveys, social surveys, and test surveys.

It is important to note, with more detail, that many survey studies are made for the purpose of aiding in specific kinds of decisions. These studies, therefore, often serve decision-making purposes as opposed to conclusion-oriented purposes. The yearly school census would be an example of this use of the survey. The point here is that these purposes are essentially different from each other, and the difference is largely related to the role of theory in a given research study. Is the study designed to examine a theoretical position or to provide data for decision-making? That question ought to be asked prior to conducting the research. We certainly can raise the question with regard to the published studies we read as well.

Correlational Research

Most correlational studies of the type that would be included under descriptive research have as their purpose prediction. A correlational study, however, is primarily defined by the use of the technique of correlation as the means whereby the variables in the study are observed.[1]

Correlation coefficients express numerically the degree of relationship between two or more variables. We might do a study in which the scores on a test of academic aptitude given in the fall were correlated with grades given in school at the end of the school year. The correlation coefficient will indicate the extent of the relationship between these two variables and also the extent to which grades could be predicted from the test scores. What is being described through this approach is the nature and extent of the relationship(s) involved. The correlation is essentially a probability statement about the relationship.

One danger in interpreting correlations is to assume that because two variables are related in predictable fashion to one another with a high degree of probability, they are also in a causal

---

1. The term variable is discussed in greater detail in Chapter 5. Briefly, a variable is anything that can change—a function, an attribute, a characteristic, and so on.

CHAPTER 4

relationship. This is not necessarily the case. For one thing, there is never more than a probable relationship between variables in any case. For another, it is quite possible for two variables to be related to one another with a high degree of probability but with a third variable accounting for the nature of the relationship.

Turning to some facts about correlation coefficients, the first thing to understand is that the numerical value can vary between −1.00 and +1.00. A value of 1.00, whether positive or negative, represents a perfect relationship between the two variables. In reality, perfect correlations are never found. The extent to which a correlation approaches perfection is indicated by the size of the coefficient—how close to 1.00 it comes—and not by the sign, positive or negative.

A positive coefficient (usually shown without any sign) means that the two variables vary directly, that is, when one increases, the other increases, when one decreases the other decreases. A negative coefficient (always preceded by a minus sign) means that the two variables vary inversely, that is, when one increases, the other decreases and vice versa. The closer a correlation comes to .00, the less relationship there is between the variables. Zero correlation indicates no relationship at all between the variables.

One good way to understand the extent of the relationship represented by the correlation coefficient is to square it. The resulting figure represents a percentage of the shared elements between the two variables. Suppose an aptitude test correlates .50 with grades earned in school work. When we square .50 we get .25. This means that 25 percent of what goes into earning the grades in school is shared with what goes into the score on the aptitude test. By the same token, we must recognize that 75 percent of the elements in each are not common. This procedure demonstrates vividly the fact that even seemingly high correlations leave many things unexplained. If you will perform this manipulation with all predictive correlations you meet in research literature, you will have a ready way to grasp much of what the correlations mean in predictive effectiveness.

A correlation between only two variables is called a *zero order correlation.* However, we may add additional variables to the correlational analysis in an effort to find combinations of variables that increase the accuracy of prediction. These are called *multiple correlations.* The correlation between an aptitude test and grades at the end of the year, made to see how well the test predicts grades, is a zero order correlation. We might want to add to our correlation additional measures such as a reading test, a study habits inventory, or even grades made the previous year to see if the accuracy of the prediction of end of year grades can be increased. The multiple correlation will indicate precisely how much of the variation in end of year grades is accounted for by each of the variables in the multiple correlation.

As we indicated at the beginning of this section, prediction is the main purpose of most correlational studies. For such a purpose to be carried through, it is essential that there be a time lapse between the measure by which we want to predict and the criterion that is to be predicted. In other words, the aptitude test in our example must have been given some time prior to the assignment of year-end grades for there to be a prediction.

There are correlational studies in which the variables are measured essentially concurrently with each other. There are many possible purposes for a researcher to be interested in how those variables relate to each other but prediction would not be one of those purposes. One of the experimental studies presented in this book used correlation as one of the techniques of experimental analysis (see Study 10). That study had descriptive research as one of its purposes.

Factor analysis is a complex correlational technique in which many different variables are all correlated with one another in order to determine the patterning of the interrelationships among many variables. Clusters of interrelated variables can then be studied for their similarities and new insights revealed as to the nature of the relationships involved.

Causal-Comparative Research

Under the general label of causal-comparative we can lump all those descriptive studies that emphasize relationships among variables which cannot be accounted for under the two types of descriptive research already mentioned. The causal-comparative study typically involves the analysis of characteristics associated with two different groups of subjects. Characteristics which are observed to be closely related to one group but not the other are often presumed to have some sort of causal relationship to the factor on which the groups differ.

Familiar examples of this type of research outside the field of education were the studies relating smoking to lung cancer. The incidence of lung cancer was compared for smokers and nonsmokers, and the results indicated a much higher probability of lung cancer developing in smokers than in nonsmokers. This did not by itself prove that smoking *caused* lung cancer. But one could be certain within a particular degree of probability that if he smoked

CHAPTER 4

he would be more likely to develop lung cancer than if he didn't smoke. On the face of it, one might suppose that this knowledge would be sufficient reason to consider giving up smoking in order to lower the probability of getting lung cancer. But the causal-comparative research does not isolate the cause, and there could be an "X factor" related also to smoking that is the actual cause of the cancer. Only experimental research can isolate the causal factor.

Causal-comparative studies in education can enlighten us about how important variables relate to one another in particular circumstances and with particular groups. However, we would usually need to subject these insights to experimental research before we could proceed to act with confidence on the basis of the causal-comparative data. We might demonstrate that there is a significant and positive correlation between the achievement level and the weight of all the students in an elementary school. Does that mean that in order to increase achievement we merely feed the students more? Obviously not, since a third variable, age, can be shown to have a fundamental relationship to weight and to achievement.

PROBLEMS OF DESCRIPTIVE RESEARCH

Before considering the specific matter of data collection, we need to confront the fact that data are gathered in the first place from people, objects, or situations. In some cases the researcher may be interested only in the information he collects from the original sources of that information. If he asks 100 people to complete a questionnaire, he may only be interested in the responses of those 100 people. But in most cases a researcher is really interested in generalizing beyond the original sources. In this case, the 100 people who are asked to respond to a questionnaire merely represent a good many more people whose responses can be assumed to be like the responses of the 100 actually sampled. Nearly all descriptive research, then, must deal first with the problem of sampling.

Sampling

The starting point for careful sampling must be an identification of the population to which the results are to be generalized.

Unfortunately, the unsophisticated researcher often begins by drawing his sample and then later tries to find a population to which he can generalize. If you are going to conduct a study in which you want to be able to generalize the results to all elementary pupils in your school district, then you have a basis for planning your sampling procedures in order to be sure you draw a sample that will represent all the elementary pupils in the district.

The essence of careful sampling is to ensure that the process of sampling does not introduce any bias into the sample. A biased sample is one in which the difference between the sample and the population is systematic. There will always be differences between the sample and the population, but if those differences can be distributed randomly so that they tend to cancel each other out, the sample will not be biased.

As an example, consider the situation of two boys given the opportunity to pick 100 marbles from a bag of 1,000 marbles of varying sizes. If one of the two boys were to select the sample of 100 for each of them, the sample would probably be biased in the direction of all big marbles for one and all small ones for the other, and neither sample would resemble the population of 1,000 marbles. This would obviously be a systematic difference. But now suppose we place the marbles in an opaque bag and have a disinterested adult pick one marble at a time, alternating to whom they are given. We shall find that each boy will tend to get about as many big marbles as small marbles, and the proportion of big to small marbles for each boy will be in approximately the same proportion of big to small marbles for the entire population. This would be *random sampling.* The technical feature that defines a random sample from other kinds of samples is simply that in a random sample each member of the population has an equal chance of being selected every time a member is drawn.

The *population* (or *universe* as it is often called) is usually defined by the researcher. It may be broadly or narrowly defined; but the broader the population represented by the sample, the broader are the generalizations that can be made from the results of the research. However, the broader the population from which the researcher is sampling, the greater will be the sampling error. It is not too difficult to get a really representative sample of all first graders in a particular school system, but it is much more difficult to get a representative sample of all first graders in the United States. Any sample which purports to represent a national population must involve very complex sampling procedures since the many facets of the population must be represented in the sample in the same proportion in which they appear in the population.

While sampling is usually thought of in connection with subjects or groups of subjects, sometimes the universe that is involved can be things. A study involving textbook analysis, for example, must assure that the sampling of textbook content represents the entire contents of all the relevant textbooks involved. Similarly, any study of pupil achievement involves the sampling of both content and skills, as well as pupils.

Actual sampling from a universe is of great importance in descriptive survey studies in education. A researcher wishing to survey the way secondary school principals conduct faculty meetings would certainly want to take pains to question a representative sample of secondary school principals. He may legitimately want to limit his population to a particular state, but on a question of this type the results would be worthless unless they could be shown to represent the practices of a good-sized universe. Questionnaire surveys in education often founder on this point making it impossible to say that the questionnaire responses represent the responses of anyone except the actual persons who answer the questions.

The usefulness of careful sampling procedures worked out in a highly sophisticated and complex fashion can be seen in the accurate reflections of voting and opinion trends for millions of voters obtained by professional pollsters who actually question only a few hundred persons.

Validity of Data Collection Techniques

There are seven widely used techniques of data collection in descriptive research: critical incidents, interviews, observation of behavior, opinionnaires and questionnaires, rating scales, standardized tests, and word counts. An obvious, but often overlooked, requirement for adequte descriptive research is that these techniques must be valid for the purpose of the study, or the data collected by means of their use will be meaningless.

Validity is a technical concept, a full discussion of which we cannot go into here. In relation to standardized tests it has several meanings, all connected to the purpose for which the test is to be used. Since we are concerned here with the general problem of valid techniques of data collection, including many techniques in addition to standardized tests, we shall propose a basic explanation of validity.

We would say that a technique of data collection is *valid* if it is meaningful and doing the job the researcher intends it to do.

But it is not a simple matter to determine whether the technique you are using meets some minimum standard of validity. Indeed, there is no simple answer to what constitutes a minimum standard.

In the case of standardized tests there are well-developed techniques for establishing various kinds of validity, and the researcher who uses such tests can often rely on the data already provided to establish the validity of his instrument. But in the case of a newly developed questionnaire or other measuring device, determining validity is a complex matter.

One reason why questionnaires should be tried out in advance of the main data collection is so that the difficulties and ambiguities in the questions can be weeded out. It is usually a good idea to administer a few questionnaires in person so that the respondent can ask questions and verbalize responses while the researcher observes what difficulties of understanding exist in the questions.

Ingenious devices are often worked out for quantifying a variable so that it can be measured. The measurement itself can be made completely objective, but it is not always possible to determine if what is being measured is what you intend to measure. Sometimes, however, the research study itself will provide some insight into the validity of the technique used. Another good way to make some assessment of the validity of a technique is to read other research studies that used the same or a similar technique.

In any case, since the interpretability of results in descriptive research may rest squarely on the validity of the instruments used to collect the data, it is at least necessary that you become aware of this and take whatever steps you can to assure the meaningfulness of the data-gathering technique.

INTERPRETATIVE THEORIES IN DESCRIPTIVE RESEARCH

The lack of an explicit (and often an implicit one as well) theory for making sense out of descriptive research data is probably the major continuing weakness in this type of research. Descriptive research carries the aura of meaningfulness by virtue simply of the presence of facts and figures. If the "facts" have been carefully collected and analyzed there is further reason for presuming the presence of useful knowledge. But, when all the data are collected, we still must apply our theory before we can make sense out of any data. Too often there is an after-the-fact interpretation made

CHAPTER 4

of these data that may bear little or no relation to the *a priori* assumptions that were only implicit in the collection of data. A researcher may mount what can only be described as a "data collection binge" that is vaguely related to some problem. Selection and development of the data collection techniques probably occurred in the absence of any self-conscious decisions about an interpretative theory. Then, with the data collected, the researcher set about making various interpretations which were again based on purely implicit theories.

On the one hand, masses of unrelated facts and figures do not constitute meaningful research. Yet carefully collected and systematically analyzed data do not become meaningful until they have been grasped in the context of a theory, however rudimentary that theory might be.

> A student surveyed the mass media that were read, watched, or listened to by college freshmen and seniors. In some vague way the student felt that the difference in educational level between the two groups would contribute to differences in the mass media data that were collected. Sure enough, after the questionnaire results were tabulated, differences were found. Twenty-seven percent of the freshmen read *Time* magazine as compared with only 10 percent of the seniors.

Anyone reading this information would have to ask the question: So what? Assuming for the moment that this was a representative sample of college freshman and seniors, we are still lacking a theory with which to make sense out of this datum. The problem, however, is not simply the lack of a theory at the point of having data to interpret. Anyone who cares to can conjure up a number of explanations for this finding, regardless of plausibility. But because there was no explicit theory in the first place that suggested why the data we now have should even have been collected, we are left with an uncertain basis for interpretation.

ANALYSES OF RESEARCH

Before introducing the illustrative descriptive studies, we shall review the three aspects of our analysis mentioned in Chapter 1. They are stated here in the form of the questions to be asked.

1. Was the methodological discipline undertaken with due consideration for the possible sources of bias and distortion in the

resulting data? What sources of distortion were overlooked, and how could the researcher have done a better job of correcting this problem?
2. <u>What is the theory out of which the researcher undertakes the research</u>? <u>What assumptions are made by the researcher</u>? <u>How comprehensive is the theory</u>? <u>How does the theory relate to the methodological discipline?</u>
3. <u>What was the researcher trying to do through his research? What does he seem to want to have happen as a result of this research?</u> Of what significance is the study and to whom?

As we proceed with the analyses of the studies in this book, we shall use these questions as our point of departure. In addition to this, we shall utilize the studies to illustrate various points about statistics and other pertinent technical matters that will help to deepen your understanding of the process of research. From time to time we shall also include some questions for you to ponder.

STUDY 2

INTRODUCTION TO STUDY 2

The following published research study is an example of survey research which has been subjected to an analysis based on certain relationships. Notice that the authors begin by citing a few published survey studies of the effects of coeducation on adolescent values. The authors detail the difficulties in studying these effects in American society. The educational system in New Zealand is briefly described, and a rationale is provided for the use of students in the New Zealand schools to counteract the difficulties in examining the relationship between coeducation and adolescent values. As you read, note how the authors attempt to use the students in New Zealand to proceed with their questions. The procedures employed and the manner of analysis of the data collected should be of particular interest.

Study 2

Coeducation and Adolescent Values

J. C. JONES
J. SHALLCRASS
C. C. DENNIS

Many psychologists have viewed the early and preadolescent period as a definitive point in intellectual development. During this stage, intelligence, as a truly coordinated mental organization involving sensory-motor, cognitive, and conceptual abilities, can be said to appear. (Piaget, 1952; Vinacke, 1951) Ausubel (1962) has noted the transition during early adolescence from "a predominantly concrete to a predominantly abstract mode of understanding and manipulating complex relational propositions [p. 268]." And Braham (1965) has stated that "the prior years may be considered as the period of intellectual birth, with adolescence as the period of true intellectual growth [p. 251]."

However, as Braham has also noted,

> The continued development of intelligence through adolescence requires an intellectually stimulating environment. It also requires inter-

Reprinted with permission of the authors and publisher from *Journal of Educational Psychology*, **63**, No. 4 (1972), 334–41. Copyright 1972 by The American Psychological Association.

est in, and motivation for, intellectual activities on the part of the adolescent. . . . The problem, however, is that when intelligence is just beginning to function as a coordinated structure, and requires the most nurturing circumstances, the adolescent meets a major deterrent to its development, that of the intellectually negating adolescent peergroup structure, or sub-culture [p. 252].

This opinion, that the "adolescent society" in our secondary schools exerts a stultifying effect on intellectual activities, has been supported by the results of Coleman's (1961a) study of the adolescent society in 10 American high schools.

Coleman, pointing out that status in this adolescent society is dependent upon popularity, rather than upon scholastic or intellectual achievement, has suggested that these adolescent values stem, at least in part, from the coeducational organization of our schools, with a consequent emphasis upon "rating and dating." He observes that, although educators and laymen have commonly assumed that it is "better" for boys and girls to be in school together during adolescences, coeducation "may be inimical to *both* academic achievement and social adjustment [p. 51]."

If Coleman is correct, one of our fondest beliefs is in need of reexamination. But an assessment of the effects of coeducation on adolescent values is complicated by two factors: First, there is the difficulty of separating the effects of coeducation from the effects of other aspects of our society. Second, there is the lack of single-sex schools, comparable to our coeducational high schools, whose students could be used in making comparisons. The New Zealand public secondary schools, however, provide an opportunity for evaluating some of the views on the effects of coeducation upon adolescent values. Although the high schools have been traditionally single-sex, in recent years a number of coeducational high schools have been established. Some of these have been patterned on the American comprehensive high school and are regarded in New Zealand by the general public as being innovative, if not radical departures from educational tradition. Other coeducational schools, however, although admitting both sexes, follow the same curricular plan as the single-sex schools and the students, their parents, and the instructional and administrative personnel appear to hold essentially the same values and attitudes. In its broader outlines, the New Zealand educational system is quite similar to that of the United States, as are societal attitudes toward the role and importance of education. For these reasons, this study made use of New Zealand secondary school students to assess the effects of coeducation on student attitudes and behaviors related to academic motivation and achievement.

STUDY 2

METHOD

Subjects
Subjects were 1,255 students in their third and fourth years of secondary school in Wellington, New Zealand, the capital city with a population of approximately 200,000. Of these students, 697 were males, 455 enrolled in an all-boys' school and 242 in a coeducational school. The total of 528 females was divided between 364 in an all-girls' school and 164 in the same coeducational secondary school.

The three schools were similar with respect to curriculum organization, degree of student regimentation, the requirement that all students wear school uniforms, and instructional methods. In Wellington, a small proportion of students elect to attend schools outside their assigned district. However, the large majority attend a particular school because it is in their zone. The girls' school in this study, for example, draws less than 10% of its students from outside its zone.

This pattern of attending the school in one's district is probably accentuated by the fact that instructional programs, whether in single-sex or coeducational schools, are virtually indistinguishable from one another. All programs are traditional university preparatory curricula and all are based on syllabi determined by the demands placed upon the schools by the national public examinations for graduation and university entrance.

While it was not possible to assign students randomly to single-sex or coeducational schools, the above factors, taken in conjunction with the generally egalitarian nature of New Zealand society, suggest that the three groups probably did not differ markedly from one another in background or motivation upon entry into secondary school.

Procedure
Items from the questionnaire used by Coleman (1961a) were selected to assess student attitudes and beliefs in the following areas: scholastic activities and attitudes, and popularity, peer influences on behavior, and self-regard. These items were combined into a single questionnaire and administered on a group basis in each school with the explanation to student subjects that a study was being made to compare the attitudes of New Zealand and American secondary school students. All questionnaires were answered anonymously.

RESULTS

The responses of boys in the all-boys' school were compared with boys in the co-ed school; co-ed girls' responses were compared with those of girls in the all-girls' school. Chi-square analysis of responses indicated significant differences between responses of students in the co-ed school and those in the single-sex schools in each of the following categories.

Scholastic Activities and Attitudes

When asked to indicate the number of hours spent on homework, significant differences were found with co-ed students, both boys and girls, reporting that they spent less time than students in the single-sex schools.

Thirty-eight percent of the co-ed boys reported spending, on the average, from 1½ to more than 3 hours per day on homework. Over 55% of the boys attending the all-boys' school reported averaging this much time. While differences were not as great between the two groups of girls, they were significant. Fifty-five percent of the girls at the all-girls' school spent 1½ to 3 or more hours per day on homework, while 44.6% of the co-ed girls reported spending this much time.

When asked how they would spend a free hour in school if given a free choice, co-ed boys differed significantly ($p < .05$) from boys attending the all-boys' school. More co-ed boys indicated they would spend the time on sports and fewer would spend it in study. The differences between co-ed girls and girls attending the all-girls' school were even greater ($p < .01$) and followed a somewhat different pattern. Nearly 32% of those attending the girls' school would spend the time studying as opposed to 12.2% of the co-ed girls who would spend the time this way. More of the co-ed girls would spend the additional time in a club or activity (18.9% versus 13.6%) and over twice as many (24.4% versus 9.5%) would spend the time at something other than the choices offered.

TABLE 1. Item 7: How much time, on the average, do you spend doing homework outside school?

Response	Co-ed boys N	Co-ed boys %	Boys N	Boys %	Co-ed girls N	Co-ed girls %	Girls N	Girls %
None or almost none	10	4.1	15	3.3	14	8.5	11	3.0
Less than ½ hour a day	11	4.6	10	2.2	9	5.5	19	5.2
About ½ hour per day	31	12.9	16	3.5	15	9.1	21	5.8
About 1 hour per day	53	22.0	75	16.6	22	13.3	58	15.9
About 1½ hours per day	43	17.8	86	19.0	33	20.0	55	15.1
About 2 hours	55	22.8	167	36.9	49	29.7	145	39.8
3 or more hours	38	15.8	84	18.5	23	13.9	55	15.1
	$\chi^2 = 36.43, p < .01$				$\chi^2 = 14.43, p < .05$			

STUDY 2

TABLE 2. Item 8: Suppose you had an extra hour of school, how would you use it?

| | Co-ed boys || Boys || Co-ed girls || Girls ||
Time spent	N	%	N	%	N	%	N	%
Course	37	15.2	65	14.4	36	22.0	81	22.1
Sport	94	38.7	136	30.2	37	22.6	84	22.9
Club activity	30	12.3	61	13.5	31	18.9	50	13.6
Study	39	16.0	121	26.8	20	12.2	117	31.9
Something else	43	17.7	68	15.1	40	24.4	35	9.5
	$\chi^2 = 12.34, p < .05.$				$\chi^2 = 36.81, p < .01.$			

There were no significant differences between the two groups of boys in the percentages who reported they had been truant during the past year. There were, however, significant differences ($p < .01$) between the co-ed girls and girls attending the all-girls' school. The same percentage of co-ed girls as co-ed boys (63.0%) reported that they had been truant, while less than 40% of the girls attending the all-girls' school indicated they had been absent without authorization during the past year. In their overall appraisal of their years in high school, boys at the all-boys' school gave more ($p < .05$) favorable ratings. Differences were even greater between co-ed girls and girls attending the girls' school ($p < .01$). Again, a greater percentage of girls' school students said their school year had been interesting and hard work, and fewer of them rated their school years as dull or unhappy. However, unlike the co-ed boys, significantly more co-ed girls described their time in school as "full of fun and excitement" ($p < .01$).

TABLE 3. Item 9: In the last year have you been truant from school?

| | Co-ed boys || Boys || Co-ed girls || Girls ||
Response	N	%	N	%	N	%	N	%
Yes	155	63.0	263	57.7	102	63.0	146	39.9
No	89	37.0	193	42.3	60	37.0	220	60.1
	$\chi^2 = 2.26, ns.$				$\chi^2 = 24.0, p < .01.$			

TABLE 4. Item 11. The years at high school have been:

Response	Co-ed boys N	Co-ed boys %	Boys N	Boys %	Co-ed girls N	Co-ed girls %	Girls N	Girls %
Fun and exciting	24	9.9	50	11.1	29	17.7	25	6.8
Interesting and hard work	73	30.2	164	36.4	46	28.0	172	47.0
Fairly pleasant	104	43.0	179	39.8	68	41.5	141	38.5
Fairly dull	39	16.1	48	10.7	14	8.5	16	4.4
Unhappy	2	0.8	9	2.0	7	4.3	12	3.3
	$\chi^2 = 12.43, p < .05$				$\chi^2 = 42.06, p < .01$			

Prestige and Popularity

Students at both co-ed and single-sex schools rated being a leader in activities and being in the leading crowd as most important in achieving prestige and coming from the right family and having a nice car as being relatively unimportant. However, co-ed students, both boys and girls, ranked membership in the leading crowd significantly higher and scholarship significantly lower than did boys and girls at single-sex schools. Boys attending the

TABLE 5. Item 1. What does it take to get to be important and looked up to by the other students at school?

Response	Mean rank Co-ed boys	Mean rank Boys	Mean rank Co-ed girls	Mean rank Girls
Coming from right family	4.34	4.92*	4.61	4.45*
Leader in activities	2.16	2.29	1.78	1.64
Having a nice car	4.17	4.83**	4.90	5.56**
A good scholar	3.62	3.01*	3.56	2.68**
Being a sports star	3.09	2.60**	3.54	3.45
Being in leading crowd	2.27	2.95*	2.54	3.15**

*$p < .05$.
**$p < .01$.

STUDY 2

TABLE 6. Item 6. If you could be remembered here at school for one of the three things listed below, which one would you want it to be?

	Co-ed boys N	Co-ed boys %	Boys N	Boys %	Co-ed girls N	Co-ed girls %	Girls N	Girls %
Brilliant student	92	39.0	202	45.7	44	25.9	146	41.0
Leader in activities	77	33.3	144	32.7	63	39.9	141	39.6
Most popular	64	27.7	96	31.6	54	34.2	69	19.4
	$\chi^2 = 3.49$, ns.				$\chi^2 = 16.83, p < .01$.			

TABLE 7. Item 10. If you want to be part of the leading crowd around here, you have to sometimes go against your principles.

Response	Co-ed boys N	Co-ed boys %	Boys N	Boys %	Co-ed girls N	Co-ed girls %	Girls N	Girls %
Agree	151	64.0	296	66.0	79	49.0	181	51.0
Disagree	85	36.0	152	34.0	82	51.0	175	49.0
	$\chi^2 = .31$, ns.				$\chi^2 = .14$, ns.			

TABLE 8. Item 12. Which of the following would be hardest for you to take?

Response	Co-ed boys N	Co-ed boys %	Boys N	Boys %	Co-ed girls N	Co-ed girls %	Girls N	Girls %
Parent's disapproval	93	39.0	191	43.5	55	35.3	153	43.3
Teachers' disapproval	6	2.5	5	1.5	7	4.5	5	1.4
Breaking with a friend	138	58.5	240	55.0	94	60.3	195	55.2
	$\chi^2 = 2.85$, ns.				$\chi^2 = 6.53, p < .05$.			

all-boys' school ranked sports as a means of achieving prestige significantly higher than did co-ed boys.

When asked how they would best like to be remembered at their school, as brilliant students, leaders in activities, or as the most popular, co-ed boys distributed their choices rather uniformly across the three categories while a majority of the boys at the all-boys' school chose being remembered as a brilliant student or a leader in activities. There were, however, no significant differences between the two groups of boys. The girls, on the other hand, did differ significantly ($p < .01$) with 41% of the girls at the all-girls' school preferring to be remembered as a brilliant student as compared with 26.9% of the co-ed girls making this choice, and 34.2% of the co-ed girls wished to be remembered as "most popular" while 19.4% of the students at the all-girls' school wished to be remembered for this reason.

Peer Influences

A majority of the total group agreed that membership in the leading crowd sometimes required that one compromise his principles, and there were no significant differences between students, boys or girls, attending the single-sex schools and those attending co-ed schools.

The disapproval of a friend had more impact than the disapproval of parents or teachers for all groups. But, while there was no difference between co-ed boys and boys attending the all-boys' school, significantly more ($p < .05$) co-ed girls rated the loss of friendship as more difficult to take than parental disapproval.

Although "having a good time" ranked high among the things that were important to all four groups, it was ranked significantly higher by co-ed girls than by girls at the all-girls' school ($p < .01$). Groups and activities outside the school were more important to boys and girls attending the single-sex

TABLE 9. Item 4. Rank the following in terms of their importance to you.

Criteria	Co-ed boys	Boys	Co-ed girls	Girls
Outside groups and activities	2.62	2.53*	2.76	2.50**
Activities associated with school	3.35	3.14**	3.32	3.27
Having a good time	1.68	1.92	1.90	2.30**
A good reputation	2.18	2.40*	2.03	1.91*

*$p < .05$.
**$p < .01$.

STUDY 2

TABLE 10. Item 3. Among the things you strive for, just how important is each?

Response	Co-ed boys	Boys	Co-ed girls	Girls
Pleasing my parents	2.35	2.25	2.40	2.19*
Learning as much as possible	1.90	1.82	2.06	1.85*
Living up to my religious ideals	3.67	3.66	3.54	3.62
Being accepted and liked by the students	2.06	2.25*	1.97	2.33**

*$p < .05$.
**$p < .01$.

schools than they were to co-ed boys and girls. Maintaining a good reputation was valued more highly by co-ed boys than by boys at the all-boys' school.

When asked to indicate the relative importance of the things they strove for in school, more students ranked "learning as much as possible" in first place than any of the alternatives. However, significantly more ($p < .05$) girls from the all-girls' school ranked this as a first choice than did co-ed girls. They also ranked "pleasing my parents" higher ($p < .05$) and "being accepted and liked by other students" lower ($p < .01$). The two groups of boys differed only on this last category, co-ed boys ranking acceptance by other students higher ($p < .05$) than did boys from the all-boys' school.

TABLE 11. Item 2. Which category comes closest to your feeling about yourself?

Response	Co-ed boys N	Co-ed boys %	Boys N	Boys %	Co-ed girls N	Co-ed girls %	Girls N	Girls %
Don't like the way I am; would change completely	9	3.0	14	3.0	3	2.0	10	3.0
Many things I'd like to change; but not completely	130	54.0	237	52.0	104	64.0	245	67.0
Like to stay much the same; little I would change	103	43.0	204	45.0	55	34.0	108	30.0
	$\chi^2 = .46$, ns.				$\chi^2 = 1.19$, ns.			

Self-Regard

Adolescence has usually been considered as a period when young people are frequently less than satisfied with themselves and the results seem to bear this out. Less than half of the boys and even fewer of the girls indicated that there was very little about themselves they would like to change. And in this respect, there were no significant differences between students attending co-ed or single-sex schools.

A less direct question asked students to choose the category they felt best described a person who was alone. While no differences were found between the two groups of boys, 62% of the co-ed girls indicated that they thought such a person was bored, unhappy, lonely, or afraid. A greater percentage of girls attending the all-girls' school described such a person as better off, relaxed, thinking, reading, or happy.

DISCUSSION

Various explanations for these results are possible. Students electing to attend co-educational schools, as opposed to single-sex schools, could conceivably differ in ways that are reflected in academic achievement and attitudes. This possibility, however, for reasons mentioned in the discussion of the selection of subjects, seems rather remote. It is also possible that significant differences exist between teachers in single-sex schools and those in coeducational schools and that, even with the restrictions imposed by a remarkably uniform curriculum and visiting inspectors from the national office, they are able to make these differences felt. Since there is no central assignment of secondary teachers, this possibility cannot be ruled out. But the uniformity of curricula,

TABLE 12. Item 5. A person who is alone is:

Response	Co-ed boys N	Co-ed boys %	Boys N	Boys %	Co-ed girls N	Co-ed girls %	Girls N	Girls %
Bored or unhappy	50	22.0	100	24.0	15	10.0	44	12.9
Lonely	79	35.0	135	32.0	68	45.3	123	36.2
Afraid	17	7.5	35	8.3	10	6.7	20	5.9
Better off	21	9.2	34	8.0	10	6.7	8	2.4
Relaxed, thinking, or reading	55	24.0	100	24.0	43	28.7	122	35.9
Happy	6	2.6	20	4.7	4	2.7	23	6.8
	$\chi^2 = 3.04$, ns.				$\chi^2 = 13.15, p < .05$.			

salaries, facilities, and administrative philosophy would suggest that this is probably an unlikely source of differences. A simpler, more direct explanation is that the adolescent social structure promoted by a coeducational system exerts a strong influence on adolescent values and on the attitudes these adolescents hold toward scholastic activities, themselves, and their peers and parents.

That the adolescent society strongly influences its members, whether they attend coeducational or single-sex schools, seems clear enough. For a majority of the adolescents in this study, the disapproval of their friends is more serious than parental disapproval, and a majority also indicated that maintaining status sometimes required that they go against their principles.

There do, however, seem to be critical differences in the degree of pressure and in the end results of these social pressures for students in the two types of schools. Coleman (1961a) has suggested that, for the American adolescent attending secondary school, the school, especially for the small-town student, is the focal point of the adolescent society. He achieves status and prestige here or he fails to achieve it at all. The data from this study suggest that this is more likely to be true for those attending coeducational schools, even when these are urban schools. Out-of-school groups and activities were less important to them than to students attending single-sex schools. The pervasiveness of the adolescent society for students in coeducational schools may account for the fact that, despite the social pressures shaping their behavior, they seemed relatively unaware of these effects. Girls attending the all-girls' school, for example, were less frequently truant than were boys in either type of school. Co-ed girls were not only more frequently truant but were truant at the same rate as the boys in their schools. Yet they indicated no more frequently than the girls in the single-sex school that social pressures sometimes required violating personal principles.

It also appears that the rewards and sanctions of the adolescent social system weigh more heavily on the girls than on the boys. Truancy rates for boys in the co-ed school do not come down, they remain at the same level as for boys in the single-sex school; rates for the girls go up in the coeducational school. And, in general, differences on most items were larger between the two groups of girls than between the two groups of boys. When asked how they would best like to be remembered at their schools, more boys in both groups rated being remembered as a brilliant student above being remembered for their popularity or their leadership in activities. This was also true of girls at the all-girls' school. However, co-ed girls placed both popularity and leadership in school activities above being remembered as a brilliant student. And this orientation toward popularity and status in the social system apparently leads co-ed girls to describe a person who is alone as being bored, unhappy, lonely, or afraid. Girls attending the all-girls' school most frequently described such a person as relaxed, thinking, reading, or happy.

In what Coleman (1961b) has referred to as "the competition for adolescent energies," scholastic pursuits seem not to fare as well in the coeducational school. Coeducational students not only were more frequently concerned with matters of popularity and prestige and with nonacademic activities, but were more frequently truant, reported spending significantly less time on homework, and would, if given a free hour, be less inclined to spend it in studying. In what could be considered as a deviation from Coleman's study, the boys at the all-boys' school showed a greater interest than did the co-ed boys in athletics. This is perhaps the result of two factors: There may be fewer ways of achieving status in the all-boys' school; and New Zealand tends to be a male-oriented society with a very strong interest in sports. The all-male environment of the boys' school perhaps reflects the larger male society more than does the society of the coeducational school. In any case, those co-ed students, particularly the girls, who thought of their high school years favorably, tended to describe them as "full of fun and excitement," in contrast to the students at single-sex schools who describe them as "interesting and hard work." It may be that, for many coeducational students, the academic side of school is seen as interfering with the school's ability to provide fun and excitement.

But are there advantages in the coeducational system that outweigh some of these disadvantages? Do students attending a coeducational school like school better? Does coeducation result in a happier, better adjusted adolescent? Unfortunately, the evidence indicates otherwise. Fewer found their high school years interesting and more rated them as dull or unhappy while a minority of co-ed girls thought of them as happy and exciting. A reasonably good indication of the extent to which a person is happy and self-accepting is the extent to which he wishes to change himself. A majority of the adolescents of both sexes in this study would change some things about themselves and in this respect those attending the coeducational school were no different from those attending the single-sex schools.

While there are obviously hazards in generalizing from one society to another, the data obtained in this study are consistent with those obtained by Coleman in his study of adolescents in American high schools, and the differences between the students in coeducational and single-sex schools are consistent with his assumptions about the effects of coeducation on American adolescents. It would seem, then, that one of the more cherished American educational beliefs, our belief in the value of coeducation, is in need of reexamination. We should, perhaps, either change the nature of our educational organization or attempt to alter the social structure and the goals for which students are working in our coeducational schools.

REFERENCES

Ausubel, D. P. "Implications of Preadolescence and Early Adolescent Cognitive Development for Secondary School Teaching." *High School Journal,* 1962, 45, 268.

Braham, M. "Peer-Group Deterrents to Intellectual Development During Adolescence." *Educational Theory,* 1965, **15,** 248–58.

Coleman, J. S. *The Adolescent Society.* New York: The Free Press of Glencoe, 1961. (a)

Coleman, J. S. "The Competition for Adolescent Energies." *Phi Delta Kappan,* 1961, **42,** 231–36. (b)

Piaget, J. *The Origins of Intelligence in Childhood.* New York: International Universities Press, 1952.

Vinacke, W. E. "The Investigation of Concept Formation." *Psychological Bulletin,* 1951, **43,** 16.

ANALYSIS OF STUDY 2

Let us begin with the authors' theoretical frame of reference. After a brief review of the literature, the authors set the stage of the research via an examination of a prominent research study in education by J. S. Coleman. The major question to be investigated is the effect of attendance in a coeducational school on the academic and social life of students. A concise statement of the hypothesis of the study is lacking. The authors chose the New Zealand school system as their research arena for the reasons stated in the fifth paragraph and the "Method" section of the report. They categorized students based on the type of school they attended and their sex (coeducation vs. single-sex and male vs. female). The authors used a questionnaire selected from portions of an instrument used in Coleman's research on the adolescent society. Most survey studies use a questionnaire as the basic data collection device, and the difficulties of using a questionnaire have been discussed earlier. The manner of development of the questionnaire (which questions were selected) and the categorization of schools and students tell us something about the theoretical frame of reference of the researchers.

To examine the collected data, the authors compared students' responses to the parts of the questionnaire based on the type of school they attended and their sex. We cannot tell whether the 1,255 subjects used in the study were all the students in their third and fourth year in the secondary schools used or were selected subjects from a larger population of students. It is important for researchers to describe their subjects and how they were chosen. Another methodological and reporting consideration in a study of this type is that of sampling. How did the number of questionnaires completed relate to the number distributed? Concern with a specific description of the subjects in terms of the pool from which they were chosen and the return rate of questionnaires is important when extending the results of the research to other situations. Were the subjects used different, in terms of school attendance, age, and sex, from similar students who were not surveyed? Were students completing questionnaires different from those not

TABLE 3. Item 9. In the last year have you been truant from school?

Response	Co-ed boys N	Co-ed boys %	Boys N	Boys %	Co-ed girls N	Co-ed girls %	Girls N	Girls %
Yes	155	63.0	263	57.7	102	63.0	146	39.9
No	89	37.0	193	42.3	60	37.0	220	60.1
	$\chi^2 = 2.26$, ns.				$\chi^2 = 24.0, p < .01$.			

completing the questionnaire? If the subjects were all the students in their third and fourth year present at the schools on the day the questionnaire was given, are they different from those not attending the selected schools that day? This point is particularly relevant because one of the questions used relates to school attendance. A possibility exists that students with truancy problems were not even included in the research.

The questions raised in relation to the subjects surveyed must be answered before we can use the results of the study with full confidence. It is important for researchers to describe their methods and procedures carefully and completely. Such a detailed account will permit consumers of research to evaluate and apply the results and researchers to replicate or extend the research.

The statistical treatment of the data is another consideration. The choice made for this study was the chi-square technique. In order to help you understand just what chi-square is designed to accomplish, we have reproduced Table 3 from the study as a departure point to describe chi-square analysis.

The authors present this table to show whether there is any difference in the incidence of truancy among boys and girls in single-sex and in coeducational schools, based on self-reports of truancy within the previous year. The table is arranged according to sex and the type of school attended and to the responses to Item 9 of the authors' questionnaire. The responses show that, in the group of coeducational school boys, 155 said they were truant last year while 89 said they were not truant. A total of 263 boys from all-boy schools reported that they were truant last year and 193 subjects from the same group said they were not truant. These data records are called "observed frequencies."

The chi-square test tells us whether the observed frequencies of one group differ significantly from those in the other group. The statistical calculation for the female group comparison yields a chi-square figure of 24.0 and by referring to a probability table the authors found that this is significant at the 1 percent level. What exactly does this mean?

It means that we would only expect to find a chi-square that large by chance 1 percent of the time if no true difference existed between the groups. Since this seems like a very small probability, we conclude that it was not a chance occurrence, that the difference was a true difference.

We can see from the boys' half of Table 3 that whether they attended a single-sex or coeducational school did not make a difference in their reports of truancy last year. The chi-square is 2.26 and from the probability table this is reported as nonsignificant (ns), that is, the differences are probably due to chance.

Another important point is demonstrated here. In the previous paragraph, we were careful to state "self-reports of truancy" rather than "truancy." This is because the data collected were self-reports from the questionnaires, not school record data. Whenever possible, research should utilize unobtrusive measures.[2] Self-reports should be used only when observed data are not available. They are biased, and if used it should be carefully stated that they are self-reports. From the reported study we do not know about differences on truancy last year, only about self-reports of truancy.

In general, the authors found little evidence to support the notion that coeducation is a powerful influence inimical to the development of adolescent values. The ability to generalize these findings to other adolescents has been tempered by the authors' statements in the "Discussion" section of the study and our questions in this analysis section. The authors point out many questions about generalizability in their report, and this should be done. Many research studies have limitations, and these factors should be detailed in writing the report.

One question still remains unanswered from the research objective explained by the authors at the beginning of their report. The authors state that the theory suggests an influence of coeducation on adolescent values and academic achievement. Yet, no comparisons were made of adolescent achievement differences based on the researchers' categories. We know something about adolescent value adjustments in comparisons by schools and sex but little about academic achievement. Use of school records on achievement could have provided the data needed to make the comparisons.

Do you agree with the authors' conclusions about changes in education based on their findings? How confident could you be in defending the need for such changes? What specific changes could be the focus in your local school setting based on the research reported?

2. Eugene J. Webb, Donald T. Campbell, Richard D. Schwartz, and Lee Sechrest, *Unobtrusive Measures: Nonreactive Research in the Social Sciences,* Chicago: Rand McNally, 1966.

DONALD J. WILLOWER

INTRODUCTION TO STUDY 3

This study by Willower is truly descriptive. The techniques employed, observations and interviews, are standard approaches in developing descriptive data. What makes the study of particular interest, among other things, is the interplay of theory and methodology. In this case, the theoretical stance of the researcher influenced the methods by which the data were collected. Those data in turn were analyzed from the framework of the theory. The author makes this relationship explicit. This study is also an example of sociological/anthropological research in education.

Study 3

The Teacher Subculture and Curriculum Change

DONALD J. WILLOWER

In this paper some ideas about schools and their personnel will be presented and an effort will be made to relate these ideas to some of the problems of curriculum change. The general perspective portrays the school as a small society and gives particular attention to the teacher subculture. The approach is basically sociological. However, our interests go beyond social science. We are concerned with the relationship of theory and practice and with the uses of knowledge. We want to understand schools better because we hope for their improvement. Although its possibilities have seldom been realized, the school is taken to be an agency with the potential for broadening and enhancing human life.

As I understand curriculum as a special area of study, it has usually dealt with school subjects, their aims, their content, and their methods; and students of curriculum have sought to inter-relate school subjects and experiences so that they make sense in terms of an overall school program and in terms of social and individual needs.

Appropriate literatures range across the proper goals of formal education, the various relationships of school and society, the psychology of teaching and learning, instructional media and materials, the organization and placement of school subjects, and the structure of disciplines. There is also a

Excerpted from a paper presented at a Faculty Seminar (May 1968), College of Education, Temple University, and published in *Samplings,* **1,** No. 3 (April 1968), 45–60. Reprinted with permission of the author.

77

body of writing on the processes of curriculum change that, in the main, has tended to emphasize participative techniques.

The approach used here fits none of these literatures very well. Although Waller described the school as a miniature society in a book published in 1932,[1] his work had little impact in the curriculum area, or for that matter, in any of the usual areas of study in education. I will not argue that to view the school in terms of social system concepts is necessarily a truer approach than others; only that it seems to me to be an especially useful way to look at schools, and that the perspective has not been fashionable in the past, and thus, can add to the frameworks available to curriculum researchers.

In examining the school as a small society, our stance will be much like that of the cultural anthropologist observing a primitive society. We will be interested in the school's rituals and celebrations, its traditions and its taboos. We will want to know something of its chiefs and witch doctors, its clans and its totems. While the usual applications of the concepts of cultural anthropology to education treat the school as a socializing agency for the larger society, our primary focus will be the teacher subculture.

We will approach the school with a critical frame of mind. That means that we will question things that often are taken for granted. The obvious and the commonplace may provide important data and we wish to maintain an openness to data. At the same time, we recognize that one looks in a special way for data that are suggested by the theoretical framework he employs and we know that it is the interpretation the investigator imposes upon data that gives it meaning. So we carry theoretical baggage. It consists of familiar concepts such as norms, rules, role expectations, formal and informal structure, latent and manifest functions, and others.

In my portrayal of the school, I will draw upon my own work and that of others. I want to begin with a field study conducted in a single Junior High School. Although it eventually led to a larger scale inquiry that tested hypotheses in a more conventional way,[2] the field study is an example of what has been called qualitative research.[3] Its purpose was to generate hypotheses and develop ideas. We attempted to do this by describing and analyzing the school in essentially social system terms. This was the way we chose to make sense of our data, a substantial amount of which was gathered over the 14-month period that marked the empirical phase of the study.

Our techniques were primarily observation and interview. Observations were made in the faculty lounge, in the corridors, in the cafeteria, in classrooms, in the assembly, and in faculty and administrative meetings. Interviews ranged from those that were quite structured to almost casual conversations. Frequently, interviews were conducted to follow-up on clues and hunches that grew out of earlier observations and interviews. We kept a journal in which we recorded our field notes. It included observational and interview data and our own reactions to the data, often from a common sense perspective but sometimes in more refined theoretical terms. We tried to maintain an ongoing dialogue between the descriptive and the conceptual with explanation as our eventual goal.

One area of special interest was that of principal-teacher relations. The principal was new to the school and we hoped that the phenomenon of succession might serve to highlight and sharpen certain aspects of the social system. It did. Teachers strongly expressed their desire that the new principal not be "weak on discipline;" they wanted to be able to depend upon his backing in confrontations with pupils and, when the occasions arose, with parents.[4] These points were made many times during teacher interviews. Perhaps the principal was more than usually suspect because the teachers were aware that he had a background of training and experience in guidance counseling.

He appeared to sense the teachers' views and he used corporal punishment on a number of occasions although he indicated in interviews that he found it distasteful. A revealing feature was that he often joked with faculty members about "the paddling," and provided humorous anecdotes that were widely quoted among the teachers. Manifestly, paddling was a penalty for rule breaking by students; latently, it provided the principal with an opportunity to dramatize his support of the teachers and thereby gain their approval. He succeeded generally in this but not fully. Thus, near the close of the school year, some of the teachers pointedly noted that he had suspended fewer pupils than his predecessor had during a typical year, an interesting illustration of Gouldner's "Rebecca Myth."[5]

The faculty had its Old Guard. It consisted of older, more experienced teachers with relatively long tenure at the school. They held generally conservative views on teaching and teachers and placed heavy emphasis on pupil control and discipline. A younger group of teachers who generally had been teaching at the school for shorter periods of time had more liberal and permissive sentiments. The older teachers were dominant in the informal structure of the school and they did not hesitate to give advice to their younger colleagues whom they thought of as being lax about maintaining sufficient social distance with regard to pupils.

The flow of communications of this kind was, in the main, in one direction, from the older teachers to the newer teachers, not the reverse. Frequently, the advice was direct and to the point but sometimes it was indirect although no less clear, as when it was remarked that it took longer than usual to settle a class after it had come from Mr. X's room; no one missed the implication that there was a kind of carry over of the chaos that characterized Mr. X's room but which was out of place in an orderly and proper classroom.

The newer teachers clearly recognized the existence of norms in the teacher subculture that required "strictness" and the maintenance of social distance between teachers and pupils. Moreover, they realized that others were apt to equate control and teaching, and even label as poor teachers those using more permissive methods.[6] Therefore, they made substantial efforts to adapt by talking or acting tough with regard to pupils. This kind of on-stage behavior[7] occurred in places of high visibility, that is, in front of colleagues. Here it might be noted that it is especially fruitful to observe behavior in places of high visibility to gather information on norms. People tend to conform in public and sin in secret. The faculty lounges, the assembly, and the cafeteria were locations where teachers were highly visible to their colleagues.

In the faculty lounges, newer teachers were on-stage in what were, in one sense, off-stage locations. The school had separate lounges for men and women teachers. In the men's lounge, the primary topics of discussion were sports and students. The sports talk focused on the national and regional levels and on the school's extensive athletic program. The following kinds of discussion predominated with regard to students: boasting about the uncompromising manner in which a difficult discipline problem had been handled; ridiculing students, especially their answers to teacher questions and tests; and quite aggressive references to students considered to be hopelessly uncooperative. In the women's lounge, a similar although somewhat less pointedly aggressive pattern was followed, but sports were not much discussed. Also, women teachers tended to "gossip" more than the men teachers concerning students. This included more discussion of a student's family, especially of brothers and sisters, and occasionally even parents, who had preceded him at the school.

Newer teachers were frequent participants in these faculty lounge discussions. It was easy for them to join with the group in joking about student shortcomings. To do so required only verbalization and it usually resulted in a sympathetic response from colleagues. Silent acquiescence was the strongest rejoinder we observed. It would have been difficult to take exception to the comments made about students in this setting because of the social pressures involved, and no one did.

Blau and Scott have discussed the "scapegoating" of clients on the part of staff members in a public employment agency.[8] They pointed out that such behavior has several functions. It furnishes an escape valve for the release of aggressive feelings against clients in a relatively harmless form, and it provides social approval from peers which helps to relieve feelings of guilt for not having done a more effective job with clients. While such behavior led to the reduction of staff tensions and increased social support, it also legitimated inconsiderate treatment of clients. These points appear to apply equally well to the teacher behavior just discussed. In addition, it should be noted that it is possible that on-stage behavior, at first inconsistent with underlying attitudes, will eventually lead to changes in attitudes. New attitudes toward clients, in this case, students, may subtly and gradually become internalized as individuals modify their verbalizations, perceptions, and opinions to fit those of the group.

Such considerations have important implications for understanding teacher socialization. They suggest the proposition that the socialization process results in less flexible attitudes toward pupils on the part of teachers, a point we shall return to later.

The cafeteria was another place of high visibility; but it provided a stage primarily for those teachers who were taking their turn at cafeteria duty, a kind of police patrol that had the prevention of disorder as its main assignment. There were several lunch periods beginning fairly early in the school day. Teachers who ate during the earliest lunch period were referred to as "the breakfast clubbers." The teachers ate in a room that was just off the main cafeteria but which afforded a view of at least part of that larger room.

The most dramatic incident of on-stage teacher behavior we observed there illustrates, in rather exaggerated form, the kind of use to which cafeteria duty was put. A young teacher who we know to be considered marginal by many of his colleagues, was on duty along with other teachers. He entered the teachers' lunch room and said simply, "Watch this." He then went into the main cafeteria, hovered near a group of students for a few moments and, on the commission of an expected offense on the part of one of the students, pulled the culprit out of his seat and proceeded to manhandle him. A few of the women teachers appeared to be bothered by the incident but most of the teachers expressed their approval. In the case of this teacher, such staging was of little avail. He soon left teaching "for something better outside of education." While the incident described could not be called typical, cafeteria duty continued to provide an opportunity, especially for some of the newer teachers, to parade their strictness before their colleagues.

The assembly was a place of considerably more tension for newer teachers. Here, it was not so easy to choose one's own battleground. Moreover, visibility was greatly enlarged; more people were present. Furthermore, teachers with homerooms, and this included most of the faculty, were considered to be responsible in a special way for the behavior of their charges. In addition, there was something special about the assemblies themselves. They were ceremonials that presented the public face of the school. Here, students were called upon to identify with the school and to show it in its best and truest light. In the main, this meant good order and good manners as defined in adult terms.

Teachers who felt that their hold on the students was uncertain, and some who preserved a less rigid relationship with students, knew that they would be subjected to the scrutiny of associates and superiors, and they looked forward to assemblies with large measures of dread and small measures of hope. Dread because of the spectre of a public failure; hope because of the possibility of a lucky success, and for some, the opportunity to show a stern demeanor and a proper concern for order, even if things went badly. These occasions furnished special testing grounds where teachers often made valiant efforts to "look good." Thus, in assemblies, some of the most striking performances emanated from the audience.

The adaptations of newer teachers to the prevailing norms for strictness were only partially successful. One younger teacher reported that "no matter how strict you are, they still think you're soft on discipline." Since staging had its personal costs for such individuals, it was all the more frustrating when the strategy failed. Those newer teachers who were highly idealistic appeared to be most distressed. By an idealistic teacher I mean one who has primarily service-oriented motives and a strong commitment to teaching as noble or important work as contrasted with one who has primarily self-oriented motives and views teaching as just a job. Like other teachers, idealistic ones wanted to be accepted by their peers. But the options were limited and the choices hard. When norms for behavior within a social group are repugnant to a member of the group, he can engage in open conflict, withdraw from the group, or somehow adapt, and even this last course may be hazardous and expensive.

Pupil control was given priority in numerous ways in the subculture of the school we observed. I will provide a few more illustrations from our field notes. They range from the attitudes of the teachers toward guidance counseling to the curious case of the teacher who never sat down.

The first concerns the retired principal and occurred before our study but was mentioned frequently in interviews. During the last few years of his tenure, the principal was in poor health and the faculty, in the words of one of the teachers, "carried him;" when possible, they avoided adding to his work load. Instead of sending the more serious discipline cases to the office, the teachers handled them, or quite often, sent them to the guidance counselor. The counselor recognized the undesirability of mixing guidance and punishment but all involved give higher priority to the maintenance of the discipline function. However, this arrangement was never satisfactory from the teachers' standpoint and it ended entirely when the new principal took over. Dissatisfaction stemmed from a belief that the guidance office did not fully support the teachers in discipline matters; instead, it undermined them by redefining the bases of student misbehavior. The teachers considered some students to be just plain troublemakers but the counselor dealt with these students within a more complex, clinical framework that served to contradict the teachers' definition of the situation.

Another interesting situation developed around the early administration of certain final examinations. These examinations were given to all of the students in certain subjects several weeks before the end of the school year to facilitate the accomplishment of necessary paper work. The control function of grades was soon apparent. An unintended consequence of the early examinations was that an important deterrent was removed from the teachers' hands. It was no longer possible to use grades as a threat and it was reported that student motivation dropped substantially. The time was called the "lame duck session" by the teachers and it occasioned considerable griping on their part.

Our third vignette concerns the issue of smoking in the women teachers' lounge. Smoking was permitted in the men's lounge but not in the women's. A few of the bolder women teachers had an occasional cigarette in an out of the way closet that became known as the women's boiler room, but this was not a common practice. It was generally known that the new principal was not as opposed to smoking as his predecessor had been and the smokers among the women teachers made a concerted, and eventually successful effort to have the smoking ban removed. The main argument advanced by those who wanted the prohibition continued was that the students would smell smoke on the women teachers and thereby be encouraged to smoke themselves, perhaps in the lavatories. The point is that these teachers considered the argument based on discipline to be their strongest one; if women teachers smoked regularly at school, it would result in increased rule breaking by students.

Another example concerns the modes of address employed by the teachers. We noted that even teachers who were good friends addressed one another quite formally using the title "mister," "missus," or "miss" along with the last name of the person spoken to. It was interesting to take this simple observation as problematic and to follow up on it. It soon became apparent that formal address was used when students were nearby or likely to be. The presence of students was the crucial factor. If a teacher used another teacher's name when talking with a student, the formal title was always employed. Less formal modes of address were utilized only when students were not present and even then, there was some carry over of the more formal. Of course, the point is that the use of titles functioned to maintain social distance and the superior-subordinate relationship between teachers and pupils.

Our final example concerns the teacher who never sat down. We had a number of interviews with the old principal. In one of them we asked him about faculty informal structure and this elicited some comments about individual teachers. He remarked of one of them that she was "dependable, worth her weight in gold," and added approvingly that, although she had been at the school for many years, he had never seen her sitting down in the classroom. This was considered symbolic of her alertness and good control.

Concern with pupil control was a salient feature of the teacher subculture. But, in educational organizations, control ought to be a means to instructional ends. Yet, instruction itself was seldom an overt concern of the teachers, at least in their interactions with one another. For example, instruction was almost never discussed in the faculty lounges.

Displacement of goals is usually defined as the treatment of a means as an end-in-itself, so that the means replaces the original end or goal.[9] In schools, discipline treated as an end rather than as a means to attention and learning would be an example of goal displacement. Control goals appeared to us to displace instructional goals in a number of ways in the school studied, as our earlier analysis indicates.

Now, two instances of specific structures that failed to contribute to instructional ends as they were intended will be described. The first concerned what were called circles. A circle consisted of those teachers of the four "solid subjects" who taught the same students, along with guidance personnel and the principal who was a member of every circle but did not attend every meeting. The manifest purpose of the circles was better to meet student needs by coordinating the work of teachers, counselors, and administrators with regard to student problems. This was to be accomplished largely in periodic circle meetings. However, the circle meetings actually were used to come to a united front in the grading of students, particularly in the assignment of failing grades. A variety of data led to this conclusion but the following occurrence illustrated it rather well: a circle chairman had some difficulty setting a suitable meeting time for the circle and became anxious because "I don't want to be out on a limb with my F grades." Appropriately enough in terms of its latent functions, the circles met just prior to the close of each marking period.

Our second instance concerns faculty meetings. The old principal instituted what was to be a series of faculty meetings designed to increase each teacher's understanding of the total curriculum. Each department was to be in charge of one meeting during which the objectives, content, and methods of that department's instructional program would be explained and discussed. The first of these meetings was sponsored by the Science Department. It consisted of a film on cancer and a few minutes discussion of science materials. During the film, under cover of darkness, a number of teachers were observed leaving via the rear door of the rather large meeting room. Although the film had been dull, it was generally considered to be a natural way for the science teachers to deal with the unwelcomed responsibility for a faculty meeting. The idea of learning more about the total curriculum died a slow but easy death. It had no mourners. As a last comment on the faculty meetings, we noted that when the new principal presided at his first meeting, he scored heavily with the teachers by remarking that he was "allergic to long meetings." The instances of the circles and the faculty meetings, respectively, show how goal displacement can be accompanied by aversion to risk taking and by ritualism.

Our field notes (and our recollections as well) contain additional events of some interest that occurred during our anthropological inquiry but those that have been presented will suffice for now. Some will be quick to remark that our data are necessarily selective. I agree. But, the integrity of the data was judged by the kind of meaningful integration that could be achieved. In other words, the more important parts of the picture were those that could contribute to the whole portrait. Other pieces of information might have potential significance but until more complete pictures were painted, it remained unrealized. We tried to remain open to all sorts of data and to alternative interpretations, but we were limited to the events that occurred and by our own ingenuity and inventiveness as observers and theorizers. We sought ideas and explanations; discrete bits of information could become useful only in such contexts.

In their studies of societies, anthropologists have used the notions of basic configurations and themes to refer to elements that pervade a culture in a basic way and influence its patterns of norms, structures, and values.[10] In the subculture we examined, pupil control appeared to be a dominant motif.

There is little doubt that the theme approach could be misleading in circumstances where it is employed without sufficient empirical warrant. At the same time, a great deal of research in education has had an especially narrow focus that has ignored the social system of which teachers are a part. In this sense, analysis of the teacher subculture, especially in configuration or in theme terms, tends to redress an imbalance.

The theme of pupil control fitted the general climate of the school we observed as we developed a feel for it. It fitted a great many of our observations, and as has been stressed, enabled us to put them together more coherently. It also fitted the traditional picture of schools as places that pupils seek devoutly to avoid, a view expressed in novels such as *The Adventures of Tom Sawyer* and in what might be called the lore surrounding schools.

Moreover, when the school is considered as an organizational type, additional grounds are added. Carlson has provided a framework for such an analysis based upon whether or not organization-client relationships are mandatory.[11] He notes that, in some service-type organizations, the organization controls the selection of its clients while in others, it does not; in some cases, clients can reject participation in the organization, in others, they cannot. These considerations lead to a four-category classification scheme. Public schools fall in the category of organizations that have no control over client selection and where clients have no choice concerning their participation. That client control should be identified as central in such organizations seems quite reasonable. Indeed, studies of other organizations of the same type, such as prisons and public mental hospitals, often focus on problems of client control.

Prisons and public mental hospitals are, to use Goffman's term,[12] total institutions, and schools are not; also, in prisons and public mental hospitals greater emphasis is given to coercive controls than in schools.[13] Nevertheless, the similarities are instructive, provided they are pursued cautiously. In fact, information in the literature dealing with these similar, if somewhat alien organizations, helped to sharpen certain of the ideas gleaned from the field study.[14]

* * * *

STUDY 3

In providing the research base for understanding schools as social systems, [this] type of work ... appears to have special promise. It blends theoretical ideas and practical illustrations rather well, and it seems basic to the problem of educational change. Numerous studies of this kind would add much to our knowledge of schools.

Educational research has depended rather heavily upon the concepts of learning psychology and on a measurement methodology. This emphasis, so useful in some ways, has resulted in an imbalance in our research efforts. In terms of methodological considerations, more attention should be given to coherence and theoretical meaning. These criteria seem particularly appropriate in a field like education where researchers should seek both to understand phenomena and to present their insights in forms that have relevance for practice.

ENDNOTES TO STUDY 3

1. Willard Waller, *The Sociology of Teaching* (New York: John Wiley and Sons, Inc., 1932). An excellent review of Waller's work can be found in Charles E. Bidwell, "The School as a Formal Organization," *Handbook of Organizations,* ed. James G. March (Chicago: Rand McNally and Co., 1965).
2. The Junior High School study is considered in D. J. Willower and R. G. Jones, "Control in an Educational Organization," *Studying Teaching,* ed. J. D. Rath, et al. (Englewood Cliffs, N.J.: Prentice-Hall, Inc., 1967); D. J. Willower, "Barriers to Change in Educational Organizations," *Theory into Practice,* **2,** (December 1963); and D. J. Willower, "Hypotheses on the School as a Social System," *Educational Administration Quarterly,* **1** (Autumn 1965). The later hypotheses testing work is found in D. J. Willower, T. L. Eidell, and W. K. Hoy, *The School and Pupil Control Ideology* (University Park, Pa.: Penn State Studies Monograph No. 24, 1967).
3. See Barney G. Glaser and Anselm L. Strauss, "Discovery of Substantive Theory: A Basic Strategy Underlying Qualitative Research," *The American Behavioral Scientist,* **8** (February 1965).
4. For similar findings see Edwin M. Bridges, "Teacher Participation in Decision Making," *Administrator's Notebook,* **12** (May 1964) and Howard S. Becker, "The Teacher in the Authority System of the Public School," *Complex Organizations: A Sociological Reader,* ed. Amitai Etzioni (New York: Holt, Rinehart and Winston, Inc., 1961), especially pp. 246–49.
5. Alvin W. Gouldner, *Patterns of Industrial Bureaucracy* (Glencoe, Ill.: The Free Press, 1954), pp. 79–83. The new manager in the gypsum plant Gouldner studied was often compared unfavorably with the former

manager, just as the second wife in the DuMaurier novel was plagued by unfavorable comparisons to the first wife, Rebecca.
6. One investigator has noted that ability to control was often equated with ability to teach. See C. Wayne Gordon, *The Social System of the High School* (Glencoe, Ill.: The Free Press, 1957), especially pp. 42–45.
7. Erving Goffman discusses on-stage behavior in *The Presentation of Self in Everyday Life* (Garden City, N.Y.: Doubleday and Co., 1959).
8. Peter M. Blau and W. Richard Scott, *Formal Organizations* (San Francisco: Chandler Publishing Co., 1962), pp. 84–85.
9. Robert K. Merton, *Social Theory and Social Structure*, 2d ed. rev. (Glencoe, Ill.: The Free Press, 1957), p. 199.
10. For a general discussion see George E. Kneller, *Educational Anthropology: An Introduction* (New York: John Wiley and Sons, Inc., 1965), Chap. 1. See also M. E. Opler, "Themes as Dynamic Forces in Culture," *American Journal of Sociology*, 51 (November 1945).
11. Richard O. Carlson, "Environmental Constraints and Organizational Consequences: The Public School and its Clients" *Behavioral Science and Educational Administration,* ed. Daniel E. Griffiths (Chicago: University of Chicago Press, 1964).
12. Erving Goffman, *Asylums* (Garden City, N. Y.: Doubleday and Co., 1961).
13. Amitai Etzioni, *A Comparative Analysis of Complex Organizations* (New York: The Free Press, 1961).
14. Two excellent treatments of this literature that are now available are Donald R. Cressey, "Prison Organizations," and Charles Perrow, "Hospitals: Technology, Structure, and Goals," both in March, ed., *Handbook of Organizations,* op. cit.

ANALYSIS OF STUDY 3

Willower's study contains a number of interesting facets for the student of educational research, many of which are explicitly discussed by the author. We shall direct your attention to the most salient of these points.

In the first paragraph the author notes that his perspective "protrays the school as a small society and gives particular attention to the teacher subculture." His approach to the problem of studying the school from this perspective is sociological. At the same time, he points out a few paragraphs later, his stance was "much like that of the cultural anthropologist observing a primitive society."

In pursuing this field study, the author makes clear that his concerns are "with the relationship of theory and practice and with the uses of knowledge." He returns to these concerns at the end of his paper in his comments about the imbalance of educational research in favor of "concepts of learning psychology and on a measurement methodology." His feeling is that the approach taken in this study gives greater attention to coherence and theoretical meaning and gives the insights of such research greater relevance to practice.

Returning to the methodology, the author states that he was interested in the "school's rituals and celebrations, its traditions and its taboos. We [wanted] to know something of its chiefs and witch doctors, its clans and its totems." As a special focus of observation, the author chose to concentrate more on the "teacher subculture" and the socializing influences at work there rather than on the student subculture.

Data only have meaning as they are interpreted from some theoretical frame of reference. And, in turn, the data one looks for depend to some extent on one's theoretical frame of reference. The author makes this point explicit when he states, "One looks in a special way for data that are suggested by the theoretical framework he employs and we know that it is the interpretation the investigator imposes upon data that gives it meaning." In keeping with this acknowledgement the author points out that his field study was "qualitative research" that had as a major purpose the generation of hypotheses and the development of ideas about schools. Viewing the school as a social system was seen as the most relevant way to approach this study for those purposes.

All we know of the actual empirical data that formed the basis for the study are the manner and methods by which it was collected and various samples of the data selected to illustrate the generalizations that were made throughout the paper.

The study covered a span of fourteen months; this substantiates the possibility of repeated observations over time, thus adding to the validity and reliability of the data. The techniques were primarily observation and interview. Journals were kept in which field notes were recorded as well as observational, interview data and reactions to the data—sometimes common sense reactions and sometimes theoretical. "We tried to maintain an ongoing dialogue between the descriptive and the conceptual with explanation as our eventual goal."

The bulk of the paper presents the observations and insights that were prompted by this dialogue. Each generalization is accompanied by a selected bit of supporting observational data. Behind each selected bit of data are many more similar bits, but we do not get to see what they are. This raises the question of whether or not the data were selected in a way that would bias the conclusions. Again, the author responds explicitly to this question. He agrees that the data are selective and goes on to say:

> The integrity of the data was judged by the kind of meaningful integration that could be achieved. In other words, the more important parts of the picture were those that could contribute to the whole

portrait. Other pieces of information might have potential significance but until more complete pictures were painted, it remained unrealized. We tried to remain open to all sorts of data and to alternative interpretations, but we were limited to the events that occurred and by our own ingenuity and inventiveness as observers and theorizers.

    Finally, the task of making some comprehensive sense out of the totality of all the data was accomplished through the anthropological notion of "basic configurations and themes ... that pervade a culture in a basic way and influence its patterns of norms, structures, and values." The author identified the dominant motif of the school studied to be that of "pupil control." This theme, in turn, was related by the author to other studies of organizational analysis, as well as the traditional folk wisdom expressed in such novels as The Adventures of Tom Sawyer.[3]

    This paper is distinguished from most of the other research studies in this book by the interesting interplay of methodology and theory which generates insights applicable to educational practice. The author deals with this in his last two paragraphs. His concern with educational change is explicit, and he sees this type of research making maximum contribution to promoting educational change. "Researchers," he says, "should seek both to understand phenomena and to present their insights in forms that have relevance for practice." You can be the judge of whether this author was successful in that effort.

---

[3]. Although not containing the actual data from this study, a related study published as a monograph is D. J. Willower, T. L. Eidell, and W. K. Hoy, *The School and Pupil Control Ideology*, University Park, Pa.: Penn State Case Studies No. 24, 1967.

INTRODUCTION TO STUDY 4

The following correlational study deals with the prediction of college performance by tests and grades with particular emphasis on the prediction of performance in the terms following the initial term of college. It is a good example of predictive research.

Study 4

Prediction of Successive Terms Performance in College from Tests and Grades

ARVO E. JUOLA

Colleges follow an almost universal practice of administering ability tests to new students. These tests are used initially for purposes such as admission, placement, and counseling. The test scores then remain in the files and undoubtedly continue to influence decisions as to whether a given student with marginal initial attainment should be retained in college, be admitted to upper school, and so forth.

In a previous paper (Juola, 1963) the applicability of these freshman-level ability tests to decisions made in later terms was questioned. Here, correlations between ability test scores and attainment in the student's initial quarter in college were found to be in excess of .60. However, these correlations decreased to .30 and lower by the fourth, fifth, and sixth terms. Other data indicated that a portion of this decrease in predictive validity was due to restriction in the range of abilities for the sample of students available in later terms, but even beyond this, the correlations successively decreased term by term.

This tendency is shown in Table 1, which presents correlations between test scores and term grades over a seven-quarter span for a sample of 290 male and 250 female students selected randomly from the total freshman class that entered Michigan State University in Fall, 1960. The test scores reported are for the *MSU Reading Test* and the three subscores and total score of the *College Qualification Tests,* (CQT) Form B (Bennett, et al., 1960). This table shows that the correlations between the CQT—*Total Score,* for example, and the first term grade point average were .52 for males and .50 for females.

Reprinted by permission from *American Educational Research Journal,* 3, 1966, 191–97. Copyright 1966 by the American Educational Research Association.

These predictive validities decrease progressively by term to but .27 and .28 for males and females respectively, by the seventh term. In contrast to this general pattern of decrease in precision of prediction, Table 1 also provides data which show that the cumulative GPA immediately preceding each of these terms provides a considerably better basis for prediction of future grades. The cumulative six-term GPA, for example, correlates .66 with the

TABLE 1. Product Moment Correlation Coefficients between Both Freshmen-Level Ability Tests Scores and Cumulative GPA's and Term GPA's for Each of Seven Successive Terms[a]

	Predicted Grades						
	1st Term GPA	2nd Term GPA	3rd Term GPA	4th Term GPA	5th Term GPA	6th Term GPA	7th Term GPA
Test Score							
MSU Reading Test	.51	.44	.34	.36	.30	.29	.26
	(.51)	(.43)	(.39)	(.35)	(.37)	(.37)	(.30)
CQT-Verbal	.38	.33	.24	.29	.25	.26	.18
	(.38)	(.39)	(.29)	(.36)	(.36)	(.32)	(.22)
CQT-Information	.46	.44	.31	.35	.39	.35	.22
	(.47)	(.40)	(.35)	(.37)	(.34)	(.33)	(.22)
CQT-Numerical	.42	.34	.31	.29	.31	.26	.27
	(.35)	(.32)	(.36)	(.25)	(.24)	(.23)	(.22)
CQT-Total Score	.52	.46	.34	.38	.38	.35	.27
	(.50)	(.46)	(.42)	(.42)	(.40)	(.37)	(.28)
Previous Grades							
1st Term GPA	-	.71	.58	.57	.56	.51	.50
		(.64)	(.55)	(.49)	(.49)	(.49)	(.36)
Cumulative 2-term GPA		-	.71	.61	.62	.56	.57
			(.69)	(.58)	(.59)	(.59)	(.40)
Cumulative 3-term GPA			-	.64	.64	.59	.58
				(.61)	(.62)	(.63)	(.46)
Cumulative 4-term GPA				-	.69	.64	.60
					(.70)	(.69)	(.52)
Cumulative 5-term GPA					-	.68	.63
						(.73)	(.56)
Cumulative 6-term GPA						-	.66
							(.58)

[a]Correlations for males listed 1st; correlations for females appear directly below in parentheses.

STUDY 4

seventh-term GPA for men; the cumulative five-term GPA correlates .68 with the sixth-term GPA; and the cumulative fourth-term GPA correlates .69 with the fifth-term GPA. One can now ask an additional question. Do test scores secured when students were freshmen in college contribute anything to predictions made on the basis of cumulative grades alone?

This problem was first approached by taking the correlation between the cumulative GPA prior to each term and the grade point average for the succeeding term as a zero-order predictor. The "most promising" test score was then combined with the cumulative previous grade index to secure a two-predictor multiple correlation. If test scores are of supplementary value in increasing the precision with which grades at these more advanced levels in

TABLE 2. Zero-order Correlations between Cumulative Previous GPA's and Term GPA's with Two-Predictor Multiple Correlations Using the Cumulative Previous GPA with the Most Relevant Ability Test Scores[a]

	\multicolumn{6}{c}{Predicted Grades}	Gain Mult. R Over Zero-Order r	Test Used for Mult. R
	2nd Term GPA	3rd Term GPA	4th Term GPA	5th Term GPA	6th Term GPA	7th Term GPA		
Previous Grades								
1st Term GPA	.705 (.642)						.008 (.021)	CQT-T CQT-T
Cumulative 2-term GPA		.712 (.689)					.001 (.002)	CQT-T CQT-T
Cumulative 3-term GPA			.642 (.610)				.003 (.008)	CQT-T CQT-T
Cumulative 4-term GPA				.694 (.699)			.003 (.000)	CQT-T CQT-T
Cumulative 5-term GPA					.678 (.730)		.000 (.000)	CQT-T Reading
Cumulative 6-term GPA						.659 (.583)	.005 (.000)	CQT-T Reading

[a]Correlations for males listed 1st; correlations for females appear directly below in parentheses.

college can be predicted, the multiple correlation between the term grade and the composite of the cumulative grades and test scores should be higher than the zero order correlation using only the cumulative previous term grades. Table 2 presents these zero order and multiple correlations.

These data give little support to the utility of the test scores as supplementary predictors of grade point average in more advanced terms in college. While the CQT-total score when coupled with the first-term GPA in the prediction of the second-term GPA, does result in a multiple correlation which is higher than the zero order correlation based on the first-term GPA alone (gain of .008 for males and .021 for females), gains in succeeding terms are less than .01. It would appear that the prediction of the second term GPA may be improved by utilizing test scores along with the first term GPA. After two quarters, however, the cumulative GPA becomes sufficiently stable that test scores made by students when they enter college no longer result in increased precision in prediction.

Additional data on the same question are presented in Table 3 for a sample of 321 men and 308 women, selected randomly from the freshmen who entered Michigan State University in Fall of 1958 and had taken two basic, three-term courses in sequence during their first three terms. As before, correlations between term GPA's and test scores and previous GPA's are provided. Correlations between the term grades and test scores and previous grades are also presented for the two three-term sequence courses, namely *Communication Skills (CS)* and *Natural Science (NS)*. Predictor grades for Table 3 are listed as the first-term grade point average, second-term grade point average, and the cumulative two-term grade point average; the *NS* 181 grade, *NS* 182 grade, and the *NS* 181 grade plus *NS* 182 grade; and finally, the *CS* 111 grade, *CS* 112 grade, and the *CS* 111 plus 112 grade.

As before, previous academic attainment correlates much higher with later academic attainment than do any of the freshman-level ability tests. It is also interesting to observe several proximity and similarity relationships among the predictive coefficients. First, later achievement on a given continuum is predicted best by earlier achievement on that same continuum. For example, the best predictor of the third-term GPA is the cumulative two-term GPA (r = .69 and .77 for males and females, respectively). The best predictor of the *NS* 183 grade is the composite *NS* 181 and *NS* 182 grade (r = .67 and .74) and finally the best predictor of the *CS* 113 grade is the composite 111 and 112 grade (r = .71 and .75). It is also evident that the third-term grade in any of these sequences is predicted best by the term grade immediately prior to that term rather than by a grade in an earlier term, but the cumulative composite is generally superior to either of the term grades.

Table 4 presents multiple correlation gains when the most indicative test score is combined with the cumulative previous grade for each course sequence. The zero order correlations between the cumulative grades and the later term grade is also provided.

STUDY 4

TABLE 3. Correlation Coefficients between Both Test Scores and Previous Grades and Later GPA's and Grades in Specific Courses[a]

	Predicted Grades					
	2nd Term GPA	3rd Term GPA	N.S. 182 Grade	N.S. 183 Grade	C.S. 112 Grade	C.S. 113 Grade
Test Score						
MSU Reading Test	.38	.29	.41	.34	.54	.52
	(.43)	(.42)	(.43)	(.37)	(.48)	(.51)
CQT-Verbal	.36	.24	.35	.20	.53	.55
	(.38)	(.38)	(.41)	(.26)	(.54)	(.51)
CQT-Information	.32	.28	.44	.41	.35	.37
	(.44)	(.41)	(.49)	(.47)	(.49)	(.42)
CQT-Numerical	.21	.28	.29	.58	.18	.16
	(.30)	(.35)	(.31)	(.51)	(.29)	(.27)
CQT-Total Score	.40	.34	.47	.49	.48	.50
	(.51)	(.51)	(.55)	(.55)	(.60)	(.55)
Previous Grades						
1st term GPA	.64	.58	.58	.55	.54	.52
	(.69)	(.71)	(.66)	(.63)	(.58)	(.60)
2nd-term GPA		.66		.52		.58
		(.72)		(.61)		(.68)
Cumulative 2-term GPA		.69		.59		.61
		(.77)		(.67)		(.69)
N.S. 181 Grade	.53	.54	.62	.61	.46	.46
	(.60)	(.58)	(.69)	(.67)	(.55)	(.54)
N.S. 182 Grade		.55		.59		.51
		(.66)		(.69)		(.66)
N.S. 181 plus 182 Grades		.61		.67		.54
		(.68)		(.74)		(.66)
C.S. 111 Grade	.58	.48	.49	.40	.71	.65
	(.67)	(.63)	(.63)	(.52)	(.73)	(.71)
C.S. 112 Grade		.50		.38		.66
		(.64)		(.56)		(.69)
C.S. 111 plus 112 Grades		.53		.42		.71
		(.68)		(.58)		(.75)

[a]Correlations for males listed 1st; correlations for females appear directly below in parentheses.

TABLE 4. Zero-order Correlations between Cumulative Previous Grades with Two-Predictor Multiple Correlations Using the Cumulative Previous Grade and the Most Relevant Test Score[a]

	Predicted Grades						Gain Mult. R Over Zero-Order r	Test Used for Mult. R
	2nd Term GPA	3rd Term GPA	N.S. 182 Grade	N.S. 183 Grade	C.S. 112 Grade	C.S. 113 Grade		
Previous Grades								
1st Term GPA	.64						.01	CQT-T
	(.69)						(.03)	CQT-T
Cumulative 2 Term GPA		.69 (.77)					.00 (.01)	CQT-T CQT-T
N.S. 181 Grade			.62 (.69)				.02 (.04)	CQT-T CQT-T
N.S. 181 plus 182 Grades				.67 (.74)			.08 (.04)	CQT-T CQT-T
C.S. 111 Grade					.71 (.73)		.01 (.03)	Reading CQT-T
C.S. 111 plus 112 Grades						.71 (.75)	.01 (.01)	CQT-V Reading

[a]Correlations for males listed 1st; correlations for females appear directly below in parentheses.

As before, test scores appear to improve the prediction of the second-term GPA but the third-term GPA appears to be predicted about as well by the cumulative GPA prior to the term as by the cumulative GPA together with the best single test predictor. Multiple correlations using the most relevant tests together with previous grades did, however, result in higher multiple correlations in the predictions of *CS* 112, 113 and *NS* 182 grades and markedly higher multiple correlations with *NS* 183 grades. The unusually high increase from the zero order correlation between the two-term *NS* composite grade and the third-term *NS* grade when the CQT *Numerical Test* was added in multiple correlation is partially explained by the first two quarters of this *Natural Science* sequence being devoted largely to the less quantitative biological sciences. Emphasis in the third quarter, however, is on the more highly quantitative physical sciences. Taken together, the data in Table 4 suggest that test scores do aid in prediction of success in specific courses. The degree of supplementary prediction provided is a function of the degree of dissimilarity between previous courses in a sequence and later courses.

This difference in emphasis between previous courses and later ones also suggests a new dimension regarding the applicability of test scores to attain-

STUDY 4

TABLE 5. Multiple Correlation Increments When Based on Previous Grades in a Different Course and Test Scores[a]

	Predicted Grades				Gain Mult. R Over Zero-Order r	Test Used for Mult. R
	N.S. 182 Grades	N.S. 183 Grades	C.S. 112 Grades	C.S. 113 Grades		
Previous Grades						
N.S. 181			.46		.14	CQT-V
			(.55)		(.11)	CQT-T
N.S. 181 plus 182				.54	.08	Reading
				(.66)	(.03)	CQT-T
C.S. 111	.49				.05	CQT-T
	(.63)				(.04)	CQT-T
C.S. 111 plus 112		.42			.24	CQT-T
		(.58)			(.10)	CQT-T

[a]Correlations for males listed 1st; correlations for females appear directly below in parentheses.

ment in latter quarters. While the data reported have presented a rather dismal picture of the longer-term utility of test scores, it now appears that tests may again become useful as indicators of the relative success when students shift their area of concentration to areas in which the relative emphasis is new. This obviously is the case when students shift majors, as from a verbally oriented major to a more quantitative science major. This factor also has obvious implications for advising or counseling, since one may from test scores be able to advise a student in which area he is more apt to be successful.

Additional data on this same question might be adapted from Table 5 by visualizing the prediction of the *NS* 183 grade, for example, from the *CS* 111-112 composite. Here it is clear that supplementing the prediction yielded by the *CS* 111 and 112 composite grade by the CQT *Numerical* score results in a much higher multiple correlation than is provided by the *CS* grades alone—a gain of .24 points for males and .10 for females. The same pattern is also apparent when the *CS* 113 grade is predicted from the *NS* 181 and 182 composite grade. Here again, substantially higher multiple correlations are secured when the CQT verbal score is used along with the previous *NS* 181-182 grades in securing a multiple correlation—gains of .08 and .03 correlation points.

In summary, the data in this paper present both a pessimistic and an optimistic picture of the value of test scores in the prediction of college success beyond the student's initial terms in college. In general, the prediction of a grade point average of students is not enhanced by supplementing previous GPA's with the most relevant test scores. When used with students who are considering a change of major, or are selecting elective courses, however, the test scores may again provide meaningful material for use by counselors and others who are interested in anticipating the relative success to be expected in new areas. The data also indicate that after the student's first term, the best indicator of future attainment in a given area is his previous achievement in that area. To the writer at least, this suggests that rather than concentrating most of our attention on studies of the predictive validities of test scores, perhaps a much more meaningful procedure in understanding college attainment would be to study more fully and to utilize previous achievement measures for purposes such as selection, placement, and guidance of students in later terms in college. A review of the literature (Lavin, 1965) shows that very little appears to have been done in this regard.

REFERENCES

Bennett, George K. et al., *College Qualification Tests, Manual,* New York: The Psychological Corporation, 1960.

Juola, Arvo E. "Freshman Level Ability Tests and Long-range Prediction." Paper presented to the National Council for Measurements in Education, February 1963.

Lavin, David E. *The Prediction of Academic Performance.* New York: Russell Sage Foundation, 1965, p. 58.

ANALYSIS OF STUDY 4

As in all predictive research the purpose of Juola's work was fairly utilitarian: to establish some basis for using the predictive instruments under study. The study can also be understood as descriptive since the correlations shown represent a description of existing patterns of relationships among the test and grade variables. By studying these patterns with a view to their meaning for prediction, a person who uses the tests for predictive purposes can have a better understanding of how to apply the individual data he has for a given student. This would certainly be a valuable piece of research for the counselor who is advising college-bound or in-college students.

The assumptions examined in this study were essentially stated in terms of questions. Test scores of academic aptitude were assumed to predict later performance in academic programs. But to what degree do they predict usefulness? Underlying these questions is a theory that suggests that current performance in specific kinds of tasks will be related to later performance of

STUDY 4

similar kinds of tasks. While this is a very logical, almost self-evident kind of theory, the correlation technique enables the researcher to obtain a precise estimate of the degree to which two tasks are related over time. This in turn reveals the extent to which the theory is substantiated for the particular tasks or variables under study. Tests of academic aptitude, of course, are considered similar to tasks involved in academic study in school or college. And previously performed academic tasks are assumed to be similar to academic tasks to be performed in the future.

The results of the correlations in this study bear out the validity of the assumptions. By calculating the correlations for a sizeable random sample of students over the period of several terms in school, the researcher was able to establish the predictive pattern of the different predictor variables over a period of time.

With no previous college level performance to go on, the test becomes a reasonably useful predictor of success in the first term in college. Thereafter its predictive usefulness declines steadily over successive terms. The cumulative grade point average then becomes much the best predictor of performance in successive terms. We do not, however, know for certain that the use of test scores along with cumulative GPA's would not increase the accuracy of our predictions. So Juola tested this possibility with multiple correlations, examining the extent to which the addition of test scores to the correlation would increase the size of the correlation coefficient over that resulting from correlating previous grades with present grades.

The results, as your reading should have revealed to you, were mixed. Generally, the addition of test scores did not add significantly to the correlations except when certain specialized courses were being predicted. These results suggested to the author that test scores could still be useful to help predict performance in certain types of courses or performance in a new major. But general prediction of success from one term to the next in the same program was best predicted from previous grades alone.

One technical point about correlations in this study is worth noting. In the second paragraph the author states, "Other data indicated that a portion of this decrease in predictive validity was due to restriction in the range of abilities for the sample of students available in later terms. . . ." One of the statistical characteristics of correlation coefficients is that they are affected by the range of distribution on the variables being correlated. The direction of this effect is to lower correlations when the range is restricted and increase correlations when the range is widened. The more homogeneous and restricted the population you are working with, therefore, the smaller will be the correlations obtained when using those populations. As you move across terms in college the population becomes more selective through attrition, and this alone will tend to reduce the size of correlations. But, as Juola points out in his study, the evidence indicates that the decreasing correlations between tests and grades in successive terms cannot be accounted for only on the basis of the more restrictive population in later terms.

Juola opened his report on this research by noting that test scores for students remain on file and invite further use in decisions relative to continuation in college. His data support a much more limited and selective use of these test scores in decisions about students. Such information becomes very valuable in improving the use and curbing the misuse of such test scores. Of course, this study utilized a particular test (the CQT), and in cases where other academic aptitude tests are in use we would need to generalize from these findings pending replication of the study with other tests. There may be some tests that would add more to the prediction from previous grades than does the CQT. But that is conjecture in the absence of further predictive studies.

INTRODUCTION TO STUDY 5

The following study is an excellent example of causal-comparative research, which examines populations and phenomena in such a way as to identify possible causal relationships between the two. In the study comparisons were made on the relation between turnover in superintendencies and turnover in school boards. What makes it a substantive piece of research is the carefully delineated theory that serves as the basis for the collection and analysis of data.

If you have read the analysis of Study 2, you should be familiar with the chi-square statistical technique utilized in this study.

Study 5

School Board Changes and Superintendent Turnover

JOHN C. WALDEN

Until recent years students of educational administration rarely addressed themselves to the political aspects of the role of the superintendent of schools. Largely perceived as playing a nonpolitical role in his position as executive officer for his school board, the superintendent was said to be an administrator only and administration was thought to lie outside the sphere of politics.

Although it is possible to conceptualize the existence of a dichotomy between politics and administration, today it is almost universally recognized that such a separation does not exist in the actual performance of the superintendent's task. By the very nature of his role, the chief school officer is deeply involved in the policy-making process of his school district and, therefore, must play the political game. The superintendent's role is better-defined as a political role with educational underpinning.[1]

Fundamental to the study discussed in this article were certain assumptions regarding relationships among community social environments, community power structures, school boards, and school superintendents.[2] Prevailing among these assumptions was the concept that changes in the socio-economic

---

John C. Walden, "School Board Changes and Superintendent Turnover," *Administrator's Notebook,* **15,** No. 5 (January 1967), 1–4. Reprinted by permission. The *Administrator's Notebook* is published by the Midwest Administration Center of The University of Chicago.

conditions within a community would lead to changes in the values, aspirations, and interests of the body politic and eventually give rise to competition for control of the community's decision-making processes.

The board of education's link to the power structure of a community has been noted by Goldhammer and others and it was assumed that the school board, as one of the formal policy determining bodies of the community, would be one of the focal points for competition among groups for control of the community's decision-making processes.[3] Conflict in the community would result in new groups challenging the old for control of the school board and would be reflected by different groups attaining this control.

The superintendent, playing a role heavily political in nature, would come to be closely identified with the incumbent power group and his position would be vulnerable should they suffer defeat. Perceived as an integral part of the policy-making system of the school district, the superintendent would be threatened by control of that system passing into the hands of a new group, by virtue of a change in the political orientation of the board.

ASSUMPTIONS

School board memberships frequently change, not only at election time, but between elections as well. An attempt was made in this study to differentiate between conflict and nonconflict changes on the school board. It was assumed that vacancies which occurred on the board of education between elections and which were filled through appointment by the remaining board members would not constitute a shift in the political orientation of the board since it is likely that the appointing members would select for a colleague one who shared their political ideology.

Furthermore, it seemed logical to assume that changes in board membership subsequent to uncontested elections would not constitute a shift in the political orientation of the board. It was held that the in-group would not voluntarily abandon its seats on the board and that a new group would have to gain its seats by virtue of a contested election. The defeat of one or more incumbent school board members for reelection was to be considered the clearest evidence of rejection of the old policy-making system. With the focus of the study at this point, an effort was made to determine what this meant in terms of conflict and superintendent turnover.

A further assumption was that time would be a factor both in a superintendent's forming strong political attachments and in the termination of his services. No one can state with precision how long a period of time is necessary for a man to become irrevocably identified with a political structure so that if it is defeated, he too will be pressured into leaving his office. It was decided to remain with the three-year pattern and hypothesize that superintendents appointed three or fewer years before a power shift on the school board might well also survive because they had not been in office long enough to be identified with the defeated power clique.

HYPOTHESIS

Given the foregoing, one would expect to find significantly more turnover in the office of superintendent subsequent to school board elections in which incumbents were defeated than following elections in which no incumbents were unseated. Incumbent defeat might also be described as involuntary turnover on the school board. Therefore, if incumbent defeat signifies rejection of the current policy-making system and, if it is equally valid that the chief school officer is a strong part of that system, then it may be expected that involuntary turnover on the board of education will be followed by involuntary turnover in the office of superintendent.

The nature of turnover was to be the central focus of the study. The initial test would be to determine the significance of turnover subsequent to a change in the composition of the school board. At this point it was desired to examine all those cases of turnover which occurred during the period of the study in order to determine if significantly more involuntary turnover took place in the superintendency subsequent to school board change, defined as the defeat of one or more incumbents for reelection, than when the board had not undergone change. The central hypothesis, then, was:

> When turnover occurs in the office of superintendent, involuntary turnover will be significantly higher when there has been a change in the composition of the school board within the previous three years than when the board has not undergone change during that period.

THE STUDY

All 117 school districts in four Southern California counties which had five-member school boards and which had not undergone any boundary changes between 1956 and 1965 were selected for the study. In each case, school board members were elected by direct vote of the people and all superintendents were appointed to their office by their respective school boards.

Data were gathered on all school board elections and board membership changes for the period of the study. All changes in the office of superintendent were recorded and a questionnaire was employed to determine the nature of turnover in each instance.[4] Interviews were also used to examine each case which, after the initial analysis, apparently deviated from the hypothesis.

The initial analysis of the data on superintendent turnover and school board incumbent defeat left no doubt that a significant relationship existed between the two. Significantly more turnover in the superintendency occurred within three years after an incumbent was defeated for reelection than in those three-year periods following the seating of boards which had not undergone change. A 2 X 2 contingency table based upon the data revealed a chi-square value of 12.88, significant at the .001 probability level.[5]

Turning to the question of the political stability of school districts and incumbent defeat, again a relationship was demonstrated. Superintendents who had assumed office following an incumbent defeat were asked to render a judgment on the stability of the politics of their school districts during their predecessor's tenure. Matching the responses on this question with incumbent defeat gave an indication of the validity of using such a defeat as a reflection of the stability of school district politics. The superintendents' responses were matched with the independently gathered election data and the resultant table clearly linked incumbent defeat to political instability in the school district. The chi-square result was 21.37, again significant at the .001 level.

The data strongly suggested not only that defeat of incumbent school board members for reelections and political instability of school districts were related, but also that incumbent defeat is a reflection of a struggle for power between an emergent power clique and an incumbent one. In short, analysis of these data provided an indication of the validity of the theoretical basis of the study, i.e., changes in value-orientations of the community will in turn lead to a challenge of the incumbent power structure by an emergent group. Incumbent defeat, then, is both a result of and an indicator of this conflict.

The questionnaire was the principal instrument employed to determine the nature of superintendent turnover. After all of the responses were analyzed, each case of turnover was classified as either voluntary or involuntary. Conceptually, involuntary turnover might be characterized as cases when the superintendent was dismissed, asked to leave, was not offered a contract renewal, or left because of conflict with the school board. Voluntary turnover might be described as instances where the chief school officer left the district or retired with no evidence of conflict with his board, or with evidence of support.

The initial analysis of these data matched voluntary-involunatry turnover with the political stability of the school district as described by the superintendent-respondents (Table 1). Significance was once again attained at the .001 probability level. Involuntary turnover was clearly related to political instability. It is of interest to note that in only a single instance did a respondent match voluntary turnover with political instability.

The second contingency table in this series matched voluntary-involuntary turnover as defined by the questionnaire with old school boards (boards

STUDY 5

TABLE 1. School District Political Stability vs. Superintendent Turnover

		Superintendent Turnover[a]	
		Voluntary	Involuntary
School District	S	44	16
Political Stability	U	1	27
		$\chi^2 = 36.18$	N = 87

[a]One respondent did not reply to the question regarding school district political stability.

in which no incumbents had been defeated) and new school boards (boards in which incumbents had been defeated) (Table 2). The chi-square value for this table was 8.818, significance in this instance being attained at the .01 level.

Where school district politics were rather stable with few controversial policy questions to cause divisions among the body politic, school board members suffered few defeats in their bids for reelection and superintendent turnover, when it occurred, was likely to be voluntary. In contrast, where political instability was evident, incumbent defeat frequently occurred, and chief school officer turnover was apt to be involuntary.

Two more tests of the voluntary-involuntary data were made. In these tests, only the clearest cases of voluntary and involuntary turnover were used.[6] This is not to infer that in the remaining instances there was a significant chance for error. This implies only that the cases used in the final analyses had the least possibility of error in judgment on the nature of turnover. Once again, the matching of voluntary-involuntary turnover with the political stability of school districts as judged by the questionnaire respondents produced significance at the .001 level of probability.

Moreover, in the final test, where voluntary-involuntary turnover was matched with old and new school boards (as defined above), significance was

TABLE 2. Old and New School Boards vs. Superintendent Turnover

		Superintendent Turnover	
		Voluntary	Involuntary
School	Old	31	15
Boards	New	15	27
		$\chi^2 = 8.818$	N = 88

TABLE 3. School District Political Stability vs. Selected Cases of Superintendent Turnover

		Superintendent Turnover[a]	
		Voluntary	Involuntary
School District	S	20	11
Political Stability	U	0	22
		$\chi^2 = 22.76$	N = 53

[a] One respondent did not reply to the question regarding school district political stability.

also attained at the .001 level. There seems to be little question, then that incumbent defeat and involuntary turnover in the superintendency are significantly related.

Finally, those cases which did not conform to the hypotheses were examined by interviews. Only a few cases remained truly deviate after all the data were analyzed.

Summary and Implications

Incumbent defeat did appear to signal the representation of an emergent power structure on the school board. There was substantial evidence that incumbent defeat was linked to control of the board by different groups as a result of controversies over policy decisions. This suggests that values were in conflict and that old values, aspirations, and political orientations were being challenged by new ones. In order for the new ones to be heard, thus having an effect upon the decision-making processes of the school district, it seemed necessary to successfully challenge the incumbent power structures and their value-orientations at school board elections.

Further, the data revealed that the chief school officer is perceived as a

TABLE 4. Clearest Cases of Voluntary-Involuntary Turnover of the Superintendency vs. Old and New School Boards

		Superintendent Turnover	
		Voluntary	Involuntary
School	Old	16	10
Boards	New	5	23
		$\chi^2 = 10.83$	N = 54

STUDY 5

policy-maker and as a member of the incumbent decision-making structure. When the incumbent power group was challenged and defeated the superintendent's position became vulnerable. There can be little doubt that the chief administrator operates in a political climate in which his tenure is subject to political decisions.

Finally, those who aspire to the superintendency must realize that they will be required to play the political game and that their fortunes may rise and fall just as do the careers of other political figures whose judgments must meet the challenge of the political market-place.

ENDNOTES

1. Roald F. Campbell, Luvern L. Cunningham, and Roderick F. McPhee, *The Organization and Control of American Schools* (Columbus: Merrill, 1965), p. 214.
2. John C. Walden, "School Board Changes and Involuntary Superintendent Turnover" (unpublished Ph.D. dissertation, Claremont Graduate School, 1966).
3. See for example, Keith Goldhammer, *The School Board* (New York: The Center for Applied Research, Inc., 1964), pp. 20–25. Others who have noted this relationship include Arthur J. Vidich and Joseph Bensman, *Small Town in Mass Society* (Garden City: Anchor, 1960), especially Chapter 7; Ralph B. Kimbrough, *Political Power and Educational Decision-Making* (Chicago: Rand McNally, 1964); and Daniel E. Griffiths, *Human Relations in School Administration* (New York: Appleton-Century-Crofts, 1956), pp. 108–10.
4. The questionnaire was based upon the instrument previously used by the Kammerer group in their city manager study. See Gladys M. Kammerer, et al., *The Urban Political Community: Profiles in Town Politics* (Boston: Houghton Mifflin, 1963), pp. 206–11. Also, Walden, op. cit., pp. 159–61. Specific responses on this instrument were designed in advance to determine the nature of turnover. The respondents, of course, had no knowledge of this.
5. For another discussion of these data, see Robert M. Freeborn, "School Board Changes and the Succession Pattern of Superintendents" (unpublished Ph.D. dissertation, Claremont Graduate School, 1966).
6. When the item designed to answer the question on the nature of turnover did not make it possible to make a clearcut judgment, another item describing the superintendent's relationship with his school board was employed to aid in rendering the decision on turnover. The cases used in Tables 3 and 4 were those in which only the first question was needed to make a judgment. Tables 1 and 2 used all cases. For further discussion of these items see Walden, op. cit., pp. 64–66.

JOHN C. WALDEN

ANALYSIS OF STUDY 5

This study is distinguished by the clarity of the theory upon which it rests. Having established his theory and the resultant links in that theory, the author set about to devise a methodology that would enable him to test his theory. In this particular case the causal-comparative approach was the most appropriate means to make the test.

The theory is described in the first several paragraphs of the study. It begins with the assumption that the superintendent's role is as much political as it is educational. The role is assumed to be a policy-making role as well as an administrative one, and the link between policy-making in public institutions and political processes is clearly well founded.

These assumptions are contrary to much established mythology in education—that the superintendent's role is strictly administrative, that it is separate from politics and policy-making, and that the superintendent merely executes policy established by duly elected or appointed policy-making bodies. When we wish to advance a new explanation for a set of functions over a prevailing explanation, we must seek for the evidence that both explains and supports the new assumptions. It is Walden's theory that provides the basis for testing his contrary assumption because it suggests some causal relationships that should exist if the political model of the superintendency is more realistic than the administrative model.

If the political model of the superintendency is accurate then the superintendency should be as vulnerable to fundamental political changes in a community as other political offices. Walden details his assumptions in this regard and goes on to spell out the kind of evidence that would substantiate his model. These are in the nature of further assumptions such as the one that assumes a relationship between the defeat of an incumbent school board member and the presence of shifting values and political instability in the community. He further assumes that if the superintendency is indeed political then a superintendent who has been in office three years or more before the defeat of an incumbent school board member would be subject to termination because of his identity with the old power structure now giving way to the new.

You can probably see quite readily that having a theory as clearly articulated as this leads directly to the methodological solutions needed to accept or reject the theory, although methodological problems are not always easy to solve simply because a theory is clear and logical. One obvious datum that must be collected is evidence of superintendent turnover, whether the turnover was voluntary or involuntary. Other data needed to test the hypothesis must demonstrate the political stability or instability of the community. The evidence chosen in this case was the defeat of one or more school board incumbents, as opposed to the continuation in office of the incumbents. These two bits of data were then compared in various ways and

STUDY 5

subjected to statistical analysis, and conclusions were reached on the basis of that analysis. Additional data bearing on these comparisons were also collected in the form of questionnaires and interviews, and these were subjected to the analysis. Consistency of results among the various forms of data lent greater reliability to the results.

The chi-square statistic used in this study was appropriate for the kind of data the author gathered. It was essentially discrete data (as opposed to distributed data), in this case in the form of dichotomies that could be tested in 2 × 2 tables. However, the safeguards against inappropriate conclusions using cells with frequencies of 0 and 1 were not used. In each of the tested combinations, the differences in the way the variables were arranged had very low chance probabilities.

On the basis of the analysis of his data, then, Walden concluded that his hypotheses were substantiated and that the superintendency is indeed a highly politicized office subject to the "challenge of the political marketplace."

It is important to remember that causal-comparative studies do not actually establish causation. They do indicate the presence of functional relationships, however. In that sense this study might be said to substantiate the probability that political shifts will affect the incumbency of a superintendent and that superintendents need to take this into account in determining their own functioning. But changes can come about in school systems and other local political structures for varying reasons, not the least of which is rapid growth, so a study like this should not be read as establishing some cause-and-effect relationship.

The significance of the study probably lies in how it helps to clarify in a more functional way the existing role relationships in administering a school district. If a superintendent must, perforce, function as a kind of politician but assumes his role is strictly administrative, he is more likely to be ineffective than if he understands that he is in a political role as well.

V

Experimental research

The basic form of the experiment follows a cause-and-effect model in which the main purpose is to discover the way in which two or more phenomena are functionally related to one another. The relationship is nearly always expressed in probability statements which indicate the extent to which the observed phenomena could have occurred by chance. The experimenter usually introduces some controlled manipulation into the events he is observing and then makes careful observations of what happens as a result of that manipulation. His working model usually includes an expected or anticipated outcome so the data will be interpreted as either supporting or altering his theory.

The major methodological problem for the experimenter is to devise a model that takes into account all of the many events or variables that can have an effect on the relationship he is observing. At the same time the experimenter must set up his experiment and manipulate events in such a way as to prevent the data from being biased or distorted. How this is done is the essence of experimentation.

VARIABLES IN EXPERIMENTATION

A *variable* is anything that can change. Anything appearing in changed amount or quality such as a function, an attribute, a characteristic, and so on, can be called a variable when we wish to call attention to the fact that it is subject to change. Test scores, grades, learning, time of day, experimental conditions, and the like

CHAPTER 5

are examples of typical variables in educational research. The term is an important one to understand because it is applied constantly in any discussion of research as you have already noticed on earlier pages.

Any given variable can be influenced or affected by a multiplicity of other variables. In experimental research there are three important classes of variables which are labeled relevant, independent, and dependent.

Relevant variables. Relevant variables are most likely to affect a given variable we want to study. It is important in an experiment that the relevant variables do not affect one group of subjects differently from any other group in the experiment. The experimenter must either hold these variables constant, that is, keep them from changing, or see that they vary equally and unsystematically for all groups in the experiment.

Independent and dependent variables. In nearly every experiment the investigator has some special variable he wants to manipulate in order to see what happens to another variable as a result of this. The variable that the experimenter manipulates is called the independent variable. The variable that is observed to see what happens to it as a result of this manipulation is called the dependent variable.

A simple example should help to clarify these terms. Suppose we planned an experiment to study the effect of spelling drill on spelling achievement of sixth grade students. In this experiment we will be manipulating the spelling drill and observing the effect of this on spelling achievement. Therefore, spelling drill is the independent variable and spelling achievement is the dependent variable in our experiment. In other words, the spelling achievement in this experiment depends on the manipulation of the spelling drill. However, spelling drill is not the only variable that can affect spelling achievement. Such factors as ability, previous spelling achievement, and spelling instruction (the teacher) will also affect spelling achievement. These are relevant variables, and the experimenter must make sure they do not affect one group differently from the other.

ESTABLISHING CONTROLS IN AN EXPERIMENT

The problem of establishing controls over variables in an experiment is one of the most important aspects of this research method. The major flaws in experimental research almost always stem from inadequate control over the variables.

The physical world is much more easily controlled and manipulated for experimentation than are human beings. Besides this, we are limited in the degree to which we can ethically or morally manipulate human beings. This is one major reason for so much animal experimentation in psychology.

Sometimes important variables can only be inferred or hypothesized from certain behavior, and the experimenter can never be sure how well, if at all, he has controlled this. An example of such a variable would be motivation. We cannot see motivation, and we cannot even measure it very accurately. We can only infer from certain behavior that something we call motivation is present in the person.

To illustrate the way in which variables can be controlled in a simple experiment, we shall return to our example of spelling achievement. In this experiment the manipulation of the independent variable (spelling drill) is a simple matter. We assign spelling drill to one class for a specified amount of time each day and no drill to another class. But to determine whether this makes any difference in spelling achievement, we must hold constant those relevant variables which will also affect achievement. To do this we can make our groups equal at the beginning of the experiment by seeing that the average mental ability and previous spelling achievement of each group is the same. Then we can assign the same teacher to teach each group so that there is no difference introduced as a result of the teacher. Now we can be reasonably confident that if the groups differ on spelling achievement at the end of the experiment the difference will be due to different drill conditions.

BASIC RESEARCH DESIGNS

The means by which controls are introduced into experiments constitutes the design of the experiment. There are many kinds of experimental designs, but most designs are variations of two main types: (1) nonequivalent control group design and (2) factorial design.

Nonequivalent Control Group Design

Nonequivalent control group design is the most common type of experimental design in education. In its simplest form it consists of two groups of subjects which are equated on all the relevant

111

CHAPTER 5

variables. One group, called the experimental group, is exposed to the experimental treatment. The other group, the control group, receives no treatment. If the observed difference between the groups is statistically significant, the difference is attributed to the experimental treatment. If the difference is not statistically significant, it is attributed to chance. (It would be a rare situation to find two groups with numerically equivalent results.) The example of the spelling experiment above illustrates this design.

A few typical variations on this basic design would be as follows:

1. *More than two groups.* An example of this variation would be to expand the spelling experiment to three or more groups. The addition of more groups to the experiment would allow the experimenter to vary the amount of time assigned to spelling drill for the different groups and also to have one group that receives no spelling instruction at all. If we assume that some learning can take place without any instruction at all, then a group with "no treatment" will serve as a useful reference point for assessing the contribution of the treatment received by the other groups.

2. *More than one dependent variable.* We might want to determine the affect of spelling drill on attitude toward spelling lessons, as well as its effect on spelling achievement.

3. *Rotation of two or more groups.* The purpose of such rotation is to have all groups exposed to the experimental treatment or treatments at different times. Our observations will then tell us whether a particular treatment always produced the same change in the dependent variable.

Establishing equivalency. Establishing equivalent groups in an experiment is the crux of experimental control. The basic approach to this problem is randomization. Random selection insures that each member of the population has an equal chance of being chosen for any given group. The assumption is made that differences will tend to distribute evenly between the groups and thus cancel each other out. In this process all the variables which can be used to describe the subjects will distribute themselves in such a way as to make the group means on any variable equivalent. Or, to put it more precisely, the differences in group means will be no larger than what would be expected on a chance basis.

A systematic procedure for randomizing subjects is the use of a table of random numbers. Subjects are assigned numbers which are then located in systematic fashion in the table of random numbers. If you are assigning 100 subjects to two groups, the numbers from 1 to 100 will come up on the table of random numbers in a completely random order. You simply assign the subjects to alternating groups as the numbers come up, with the first number assigned to group A, the second number to group B, the third to group A, and so on.

Another familiar procedure for establishing equivalent groups is matching. Unfortunately, this procedure has appeared deceptively simple to unsophisticated researchers. The procedure itself is more or less self-evident, in that subjects are matched on as many important variables as possible. For example, if IQ is one of the matched variables, you would pair two subjects with the same or nearly the same IQ scores. After this procedure has been followed, you assume that you have two equal groups and proceed with the experiment.

When we begin to examine some of the logic of matching, however, we will discover some contradictions. For one thing, if it is possible to match all the subjects in two groups without discarding any subjects, then the groups would be equivalent before the matching procedure and there would be no point to matching. The process of randomizing all subjects into two groups is simply another way of matching two groups of subjects on all variables. Any differences after an experimental treatment is applied to one group can then be attributed either to random difference occurring by chance or to the effect of the treatment.

What must be done, then, when it seems important to match subjects (such as when very small samples are available) is to randomize the subjects after matching. That is, after matching the pairs of subjects, all subjects are put into the same pool and assigned to groups by random procedures. Unless this is done, the results will be uninterpretable.

The reason for this is a phenomenon known as the regression effect—in simple terms, the tendency for uncorrelated or partially correlated variables to regress toward the mean. Thus, a group that is high on a particular variable will tend to regress down on other variables and vice versa for groups that are low on a particular variable.

The story is told of a school board that asked for the achievement records of the ten highest IQ students in the high school. Upon examination they found that these students were not the ten highest in grades—a result of downward regression since IQ and grades are not perfectly correlated. The school board fired the superintendent because the students were doing poorer than expected. The new superintendent was more sophisticated so after some time he got the jump on the school board by collecting the records of the ten highest achievers in the high school. These students, of course, were not the ten highest in IQ, so he claimed that he had pulled them up beyond expectations. Both cases illustrate regression.

If the nature of one group of subjects tends to pull the group which is matched to them up or down, the matched group will tend to regress in the opposite direction. If a group of "slow readers" has been identified and a second group is matched to it for the purposes of an experiment, the matched group will probably regress upward on other measured variables, unless all subjects are then randomly assigned to groups.

When differences are tested there is no way of knowing how much of the difference was due to simple regression and how much was due to the experimental treatment. *Matching must always be followed by randomization or the results will be distorted and uninterpretable.*

Some experimenters have to work with intact groups for which no random assignment can be made of subjects. Fortunately, there is a statistical technique which enables them to accomplish essentially the same thing that is accomplished through randomization. The statistic is known as *analysis of covariance*, a procedure which enables the researcher to take into account in his data analysis the effect of differences between the groups on the variables he wants held constant. The uncontrolled variables in this case are simply adjusted statistically. You will see an example of the use of analysis of covariance in the study by Cartwright (Study 7).

It is important to keep in mind that randomization remains a basic procedure in any experimental research design for enabling the researcher to extract meaning from his data. Only in this way can he have any confidence that statistically significant differences are due to his independent variable rather than to the operation of variables for which he has not accounted. In the same way, experimenters assign groups to treatments on a random basis, the order of presenting experimental stimuli are randomized, and so on.

Factorial Designs

We turn now to the second major type of experimental design. In contrast to the equivalent group design, the factorial design enables the investigator to observe the effect of more than one independent variable on the dependent variable. In addition to this, the investigator may also observe the interaction of two or

EXPERIMENTAL RESEARCH

Reading Methods Experiment

Teacher 1		Teacher 2	
Group A	Group B	Group C	Group D
Method X	Method Y	Method X	Method Y

Observations
1. Differences due to method: $AC-BD$
2. Differences due to teacher: $AB-CD$
3. Differences between groups: $A-B-C-D$
4. Differences due to the interaction of teacher and method is what remains when No. 1 and No. 2 are subtracted from the between-groups differences, No. 3, or $(A-B) - (C-D)$.

---

more independent variables on the dependent variable. All of these observations, moreover, can be encompassed in a single experiment. The primary vehicle for these observations is a statistical technique called analysis of variance. (ANOVA)

Consider the following problem: What is the effect on reading achievement of two different methods of teaching reading as utilized by two different teachers? In this problem we are interested in observing differences in reading achievement as a result of differences in method of teaching, differences in teachers, and differences resulting from the interaction of teacher and method.[1]

A factorial design for the above experiment would appear as follows: Four groups are drawn from a population of subjects in some way which establishes the equivalency of the groups. We shall label these groups A, B, C, and D. The methods to be utilized in teaching reading to these groups we label X and Y. Teacher 1 will then teach group A by method X and group B by method Y, and Teacher 2 will do the same for groups C and D respectively. At the conclusion of the experiment, the reading achievement of each of the groups is tested and the results are subjected to an analysis of variance.

In this analysis we can combine groups A and C, and B and D to see if the different methods produced different achievement levels. We can then combine groups A and B and C and D to see if

---

[1] Interaction, as the term is used in research, refers to the combined effect of two or more variables which is different from the effect produced by any one of the variables operating alone. A medical analogy may help clarify the concept further. Two different drugs administered separately may have no effect on an ailment, but combined in the same dose their interaction may produce a cure.

CHAPTER 5

the different teachers produced different achievement levels. Finally, by observing the differences between the four groups, after subtracting differences due to method and teachers, we can note the effect on reading achievement of the interaction of the teacher and the method. The table on page 115 may help you visualize this design more clearly.

All of these observations are encompassed in the analysis of variance that the experimenter makes with his reading test data.

STATISTICAL SIGNIFICANCE

Since we rarely find two group results identical, the question arises as to how much difference is significant. The interpretation of differences in educational research rests on probability statements. The statistical analysis usually serves the sole purpose of giving a probability statement on which some interpretation or influence can be based.

Thus, when we say that a difference was "significant at the 5 percent level of confidence," we are only saying that there are five chances in 100 that the difference we observed could have occurred by chance in our sample if there were no true differences between the populations from which they were drawn. Since this is a relatively small probability of chance, we may infer that our difference was not a chance difference but was a difference resulting from our experimental manipulation.

The most typical statistical rule of thumb is to reject the hypothesis of a chance difference when the probability of chance is 5 percent or less. For the consumer of research, the essential point to remember is that the probability statement or level of significance is the most important aspect of the statistical analysis that must be understood. It requires no special statistical knowledge to understand the meaning of this probability figure.

ANALYZING EXPERIMENTAL RESEARCH

Thus far in our discussion of experimental research, we have concentrated on the methodology only and have said little about the substance of experimentation. Experimentation is essentially a method for gathering information in a controlled and objective way. The student of research must have some grasp of the method

EXPERIMENTAL RESEARCH

that is involved for doing this. The studies included in this chapter have been chosen primarily to illustrate different kinds of experimental design, just as the studies in the other chapters were chosen to illustrate other types of educational research. But we must deal with the question of significance, of substance, when we analyze a study, or we reduce the exercise to mere technological nit-picking. The attention to theory that leads to a particular problem being studied is what will enable us to grasp both the importance of experimentation as a method and the problem of experimentation as a means of enlarging our understanding of educational science.

Yet at the same time we are concerned with methodology and with teaching something more about methodology. In each of these experiments, therefore, we shall first examine the methodology in a rather straightforward manner, attempting to clarify what it was the experimenter did in carrying out his experiment. As we move from this concern to that of considering the theory and the significance of the study in the light of the theory, we shall comment further on the relation of these questions to the methodology. Further comments, when appropriate, will be made with regard to the meaning of some important statistics and other experimental techniques that are used in these studies.

Campbell and Stanley have suggested a method to analyze experimental research.[2] Their method of design analysis is organized to determine the validity of the experiments and to aid in making decisions about the conclusions and generalizability of the research. They cite two general sources of invalidity in research designs: threats to internal validity and threats to external validity.

Internal validity threats are focused on possible reasons for the research results that are different from the experimental treatments. The eight major threats to internal validity are:

1. History—events other than the experimental treatments
2. Maturation—processes occuring in the research subjects as a function of the passing of time rather than the treatments
3. Testing—effects of taking a pretest on the posttest scores
4. Instrumentation—effects of changes in the measuring instrument (particularly important in the use of raters and observers)
5. Statistical regression—effects due to the use of extreme groups which will move towards the mean
6. Selection—effects of differential selection on the groups of the experiment

2. Donald T. Campbell and Julian C. Stanley, *Experimental and Quasi-Experimental Designs for Research,* Chicago: Rand McNally, 1963, pp. 5-6.

CHAPTER 5

7. Experimental mortality—effects due to the loss of subjects
8. Selection-maturation interaction—effects due to the method of selection when it interacts with the loss of subjects

External validity threats are concerned with making decisions regarding the representativeness of the findings. Deciding to which other groups or settings the research findings can be generalized is based on an examination of the research design for possible sources of external invalidity. The major threats are:

1. Reactive effect of testing—effects due to the use of a pretest procedure which altered the variable studied
2. Interaction of selection and the dependent variable—effects due to selecting subjects for the experiment based on the availability when considering the variable to be studied
3. Reactive treatment arrangements—effects due to the novelty of the treatment procedures when compared to the usual life routine of the subjects
4. Multiple treatments—effects due to previous treatment procedures on later variables studied

As you read the studies included in this chapter, you should analyze the research in terms of the threats to validity summarized above, as well as in terms of the issues suggested earlier.

WILLIAM J. GNAGEY

INTRODUCTION TO STUDY 6

This study deals with a complex educational phenomenon. Or perhaps it would be more accurate to say that the design of this study involves complex observations. The experimenter chose to conduct his experiment in the natural setting of the classroom. However, you will see that he introduces a number of highly controlled, and therefore artificial, variables into the situation.

Does greater complexity add up to greater comprehensiveness? We shall examine this question in the analysis portion. Meanwhile, this is a rather interesting study and offers a good illustration of the challenges that face an experimenter in devising ways to observe behavior so that a theory can be checked out.

Study 6

Effects on Classmates of a Deviant Student's Power and Response to a Teacher-Exerted Control Technique

WILLIAM J. GNAGEY

The purpose of this study was to further clarify some of the dynamics of discipline in the public school classroom. We were especially interested in the reaction of a misbehaving student (deviant) to a teacher-exerted control technique with respect to its effect upon the behavior of his onlooking nontarget classmates (audience). In addition, we wished to determine the influence of the deviant's status in the class power structure.

Two notable efforts in the area of discipline research have been concerned primarily with the effects of certain types of control efforts upon the

---

William J. Gnagey, "Effects on Classmates of a Deviant Student's Power and Response to a Teacher-Exerted Control Technique," *The Journal of Educational Psychology,* 51, No. 1 (February 1960), 1–8. Copyright 1960 by The American Psychological Association. Reprinted by permission. The present paper represents a portion of the dissertation presented in partial fulfillment of the requirements for the degree of doctor of philosophy at Wayne State University, 1959. The writer wishes to express his thanks to the members of the Education Research Project of Wayne State University: Jacob S. Kounin (doctoral committee chairman), Paul V. Gump, and James J. Ryan. Financial support for the project, of which this is a part, has been provided by the National Institute of Mental Health, National Institutes of Health, Public Health Service, Grant M–1066.

119

deviant himself. Redl and Wineman (1951, 1952) pioneered in this field, reporting the results of a clinical study of ego damaged children. More recently Kounin and Gump (1958) published preliminary findings of a somewhat different nature. They were able to show that a teacher's control effort not only influences the behavior of the deviant who is its target, but significantly affects the behavior of students who are audience to but not targets of the disciplinary action. This phenomenon was called the ripple effect.

One of the factors influencing the ripple effect interested us especially. Kounin and Gump discovered that children who were connected in some way with the deviant or deviancy before the control technique was emitted appeared to have been more influenced than those who had no such previous connection. This raised the question as to what the nature of some of these previous connections might be, other than those of attention or proximity at the time of the deviancy. We believed one might be social power status.

The impact of a powerful group member's behavior upon the other members of the group had previously been studied by Lippitt, Polansky, and Redl (1952) in two camp settings. They concluded that the behavior of a boy was more likely to spread to other members of the group when he had high power than when he had low power. The Lippitt group limited their study of contagion to overt behavior. We were interested in the possibility that the overt reaction of the deviant to the control technique might influence the perceptual behavior of the nontarget audience, as well as their overt actions, and possibly also their learning.

THEORETICAL EXPECTATIONS

Power of the Teacher
Since the Lippitt group found that male members tended to identify more with a high influence peer than with a low influence peer, we believed that if a high-powered deviant submitted to the teacher's control effort, his overt acceptance of the teacher's dominance would spread to the others in the class for whom the deviant was an identifying figure. Likewise, we predicted that a high-powered deviant's attitude of defiance toward the teacher would also spread to his classmates.

The responses of opposite sex members of the class were not clearly predictable. Even if girls should agree with the boys in attributing high power to a certain male deviant, it is doubtful if the identification dynamic would be of the same nature.

Though we expected little contagion from the behavior of the low-powered deviant, we entertained the possibility that the mere success or failure of the teacher to achieve submission from him might be used as a cue by the audience upon which they might base their judgments on the teacher's ability to control the class.

Valence of the Teacher

French (1956) suggests that there are several "bases of power" when considering the influence of a leader over a group. These are: attraction, coercion, expertness, reward, and legitimacy. We hypothesized that any incident which influenced the total power attributed to the teacher by her class might influence their judgment of her power from each of these bases. In other words, we predicted that if the deviant's response tended to cause the audience to raise their appraisal of the teacher's ability to handle the class (i.e., themselves), it might also raise the level of her attractiveness to the group.

Expertness of the Teacher

Following a line of reasoning parallel to that in the paragraph above, we predicted that whatever the experimental incident did to the audience judgment of the teacher's ability to handle the class, this would also be reflected in their judgment of her expertness, another of French's bases of social power.

Fairness of the Control Technique

We anticipated a ripple effect concerning the apparent fairness of the control technique. The attitude of acceptance (submission) or rejection (defiance), conveyed to the audience by means of the deviant's overt response to the control technique, would be spread to others in the audience for whom the deviant was an identifying figure. We believed the effects of the low-powered deviant's response would be negligible, but were uncertain about the responses of members of opposite sex.

Differences in Audience Learning

In appraising defiance and submission as two responses which a deviant might act out, we believed that the former behavior was unusual enough so that the general expectation of the audience—that a student will do what a teacher tells him to—would be disrupted. If this happened, we believed an imbalance tension would result, cutting down the efficiency of recall in the audience. Heider (1946) has discussed balance in some detail.

In addition, we believed that the audience would be in a greater state of tension if the defiant class member had high power, since a greater sensitivity to his actions would be present in those for whom he was an identifying figure.

THE EXPERIMENTAL PROCEDURE

We accordingly devised an experimental design in which the independent variables were (a) the response of the deviant (defiance vs. submission) and (b) the power of the deviant (high power vs. low power). As discussed above,

STUDY 6

TABLE I. Several Characteristics of the Experimental Groups

Group	Number of subjects Boys	Girls	Total	Mean Academic Grade*
High-powered defiant	19	18	37	3.8
High-powered submissive	12	13	25	3.9
Low-powered defiant	18	15	33	3.5
Low-powered submissive	13	22	35	3.2

*Mean academic grade was computed by averaging the grades for all subjects (except art and music) for the preceding grading period. A five-point scale was used: A—5, B—4, C—3, D—2, F—1.

the dependent variables were: (a) power of the teacher, (b) valence of the teacher, (c) expertness of the teacher, (d) fairness of the control technique (as qualitative characteristics of the audience perceptual behavior) and (e) audience learning. In brief, four classes of fifth graders were to be measured before and after the showing of a 10-minute film during which a male classmate, selected and trained secretly beforehand, misbehaved, became the target of a control technique executed by a new teacher, and reacted in a prearranged defiant or submissive manner.

Subjects

Four classes of fifth graders (N = 130) were chosen from schools in the area around North Manchester, Indiana. Since it was our purpose to obtain "classroom reality," we chose intact homerooms which had operated as such from September of 1956 until May of 1957. We felt that the group structure would be more stabilized by the end of the school year than at the beginning. Table I summarizes the size, sex composition, and ability of each group. It was established that none of the differences existing among the average achievement of the groups favored the experimental hypotheses.

Pre-experimental Measurements

The experimenter administered the first questionnaire under the guise of one who was making a study of "how to make school more interesting." The students were provided with a list of their classmates' names, since part of the instrument was a sociogram constructed to measure the social power attributed to each boy by other members of his class. Such items as the following were used:

> When a bunch of kids from this class get together outside of school, which *three boys* nearly always get the others to do what they want to?

Some boys are stronger and tougher than others. If it came to a fight, which *three boys* in this class could win over most of the rest, if they had to?

A second section measured the students' pre-experimental perceptions of the power, expertness, and valence of female teachers in general. Such questions as the following were used:

How well can lady teachers handle the kids in this class?
How much do lady teachers know about showing films?
How well do you like most lady teachers?

Students registered each of their answers by drawing a vertical line across a 100 centimeter horizontal rating scale which had the extreme choices printed at the ends. Scores were ascertained by measuring the number of centimeters between the students' mark and the negative end of the scale.

Selection and Training of Deviants
On a subsequent day, the experimenter and *T* (a female elementary education major) secretly trained the boy who had been selected by means of the sociogram. In each of two classes a high-powered boy was chosen, and in the other two, low-powered boys were selected. Table II summarizes the *attributed power ratio* of each of the boys finally chosen. Other questions helped us avoid choosing deviants who were actively disliked. Each of these boys was secretly trained to play a specific part during the experimental situation in his own group. By means of role-play techniques, they were trained to execute the same deviancy (saying aloud, "Hey, is this film about over?") in each group.

Two of the deviants were trained to react to the control technique in a submissive manner (hanging the head and saying, "Yes ma'am, I'm sorry

TABLE II. Attributed Power Ratios of Deviants by Groups

Group	Girls' Ratings	Boys' Ratings	Combined Ratings
High-powered defiant	.82	.68	.75
High-powered submissive	.70	.75	.72
Low-powered defiant	.16	.03	.09
Low-powered submissive	.01	.03	.02

*Attributed power ratio computed by dividing actual number of power choices received, by most possible.

STUDY 6

ma'am," as each left the room). The other deviants were trained to react in a defiant manner (saying belligerently, "I'll leave the room, but I won't go to the principal's office. The heck with you!" as he left the room).

The Experimental Episode
Some time after the newly trained deviant had returned to his room, the experimenter appeared officially. After the class had been seated in the projection room, the experimenter introduced the teacher by saying, "Yesterday I told you I would bring along a grade-school teacher who would show you a film. This is Miss Robe. She wants to talk to you about the film before she shows it, so I will turn the class over to her." At this, the experimenter left the room.

The teacher then said to the class, "I am very interested in finding out some things about films that we show in school. I have brought one with me today. I want you to watch it quietly, without talking, so that you can rate it accurately when it is over." She then turned out the light and began showing the film.

At a prearranged signal (the teacher scratched her head), the deviant talked aloud in the prescribed manner. The teacher immediately shut off the projector and said in an irritated voice, "Hey you, I told you not to talk. You leave the room and report to the principal's office." The deviant then reacted to this control technique in his prescribed defiant or submissive manner and left the room. The teacher then showed the rest of the film, turned on the light and left the room.

Postexperimental Measurements
Shortly, the experimenter re-entered the room and passed out the final questionnaire which ostensibly rated the film showing, but which also measured the dependent variables. The first part was a rating scale containing questions matched to those on the first instrument. These indicated the change in the dependent variables. The second section of the final measurement was an objective, multiple-choice test over many of the facts presented in the film. Some typical items were: "How many boys were working in the laboratory? (one, two, three, four, five)." "At the end of the film, the boy who held the microscope had: (black hair, red hair, blonde hair, brown hair, white hair)." Scores were ascertained by computing the number of correct responses.

Finally, a fairness question was added. It read: "How fair is it for the teacher to send a person to the principal's office for talking during a film?" The horizontal rating scale technique was used in this item.

Thus the effects of four separate conditions were measured, each one a unique combination of the social power and overt reaction of the deviant, that is, high-powered and defiant, high-powered and submissive, low-powered and defiant, low-powered and submissive. The deviancy, the control technique, the film, and the teacher were all constants in the situation.

RESULTS AND DISCUSSION

With the exception of the questions that measured fairness and learning, scores on all items were derived from the differences between the matched items on the first and second measurements. These change scores were prefixed with a plus or minus sign to indicate the direction in which the subject's answer varied, and where treated by the chi-square test.

Due to an artifact of the measuring device, some of the scores on the premeasurement were seriously restricted from any possibility of shift. We therefore checked back on each apparently significant result to make sure that these frozen scores did not work against the null hypothesis. In cases where they favored the experimental hypotheses, Fisher exact probability test was used.

Power Ascribed to the Teacher

The students of each class were asked to rate how well they thought the teacher "could handle the kids in their class." Students (boys and girls combined) who saw deviants submit to the teacher's control effort rated her as significantly more capable of handling kids in their class than did students who saw deviants defy her ($\chi^2 = 16.55, p < .001$) (see Table III.)

In order to determine whether the power of the deviant influenced the effects on the audience, two other comparisons were completed. Because of the aforementioned possibility of an identification linked contagion effect, we compared male high-powered defiance scores with male high-powered submissive scores and found that boys who saw a high-powered deviant submit thought the teacher could handle the kids in the class significantly better than did boys who saw a high-powered deviant defy ($p = .0096$, Fisher exact test) (see Table III).

TABLE III. Effects of the Deviant's Reaction upon His Classmates' Perception of the Teacher's Power

Subjects	Groups	Scores o and +	−	p	χ^2 (1 df)
All	All Defiant	40	31		
	All Submissive	54	6	16.55	<.001
Male Only	High-powered defiant	11	8		
	High-powered submiss.	12	0		.0095*
Male Only	Low-powered defiant	11	12		
	Low-powered submiss.	12	1		.0524*

*Fisher exact probability.

STUDY 6

When a similar comparison was made between low-powered defiant and low-powered submissive scores, the difference was just below the .05 level of confidence ($p = .0524$, Fisher exact test) (see Table III).

When male and female scores were lumped together, the high-powered defiant vs. the high-powered submissive and the low-powered defiant vs. the low-powered submissive comparisons were both well above the .01 level of confidence.

This might indicate that while all onlookers used the deviant's reaction as a cue to the teacher's success as a disciplinarian, boys were somewhat more sensitive to the cues emitted by the high-powered deviants than those emitted by the low-powered deviants.

Valence of the Teacher

Students were asked to indicate how much they liked the teacher. When male and female scores were lumped together, no significant difference was apparent between students who saw the deviant submit and those who saw deviants defy the teacher. No other comparisons produced significant differences.

Expertness of the Teacher

The students were asked to indicate how much they thought the teacher knew about showing films. Students (boys and girls combined) who saw deviants submit to the teacher's control effort rated her as knowing more about showing films than did students who saw deviants defy her ($\chi^2 = 7.07$, $p < .01$) (see Table IV).

TABLE IV. Effects of the Deviant's Reaction upon His Classmates' Perception of the Teacher's Expertness

Subjects	Groups	Scores o and +	−	χ^2 (1 df)	p
All	Defiant	40	30		
	Submissive	46	12		
				7.07	<.01
All	High-powered defiant	18	19		
	High-powered submiss.	22	1		
				14.10	<.001
All	Low-powered defiant	22	11		
	Low-powered submiss.	23	12		
				.007	>.95

It was found that students who saw high-powered deviants submit rated the teacher as more expert than did students who saw high-powered deviants defy (χ^2 14.10, p <.001). A similar comparison done with those who saw low-powered deviants submit showed no significant difference (χ^2 = .007, p >.95) (see Table IV).

This would tend to support the hypothesis that factors which influence the teacher's total ascribed power tend to influence audience perception of her expertness also. In addition, it would appear that students are more sensitive to cues emitted by high-powered deviants than those by low-powered deviants.

Fairness of the Control Technique

The students were asked to indicate how fair they thought it was for a teacher to send a person to the principal's office. Those (boys and girls combined) who saw deviants submit to the teacher's control effort rated the control technique as significantly fairer than did those who saw defiants defy (χ^2 = 8.96, p <.01) (see Table V).

In addition, while students who saw a high-powered deviant submit rated the control technique as fairer than did students who saw a high-powered deviant defy (χ^2 = 11.09, p <.001), no significant difference was found between students who saw a low-powered deviant submit and those who saw a low-powered deviant defy (χ^2 = .09, p >.80) (see Table V).

This would tend to support the hypothesis that the deviant's attitude tended to spread to his classmates and that the effects were much stronger when he was high-powered than when he had low power.

TABLE V. Effects of the Deviant's Reaction upon His Classmates' Perception of the Fairness of the Control Technique

Subjects	Groups	Scores o and +	−	χ^2 (1 df)	p
All	Defiant	49	19		
	Submissive	49	3		
				8.96	<.01
All	High-powered defiant	19	16		
	High-powered submiss.	23	1		
				11.09	<.001
All	Low-powered defiant	30	3		
	Low-powered submiss.	26	2		
				.09	>.80

STUDY 6

TABLE VI. Effects of the Deviant's Reaction upon His Classmates' Learning of Film Facts

Subjects	Group	N	Mean Score*	S^2	t	p
All	Defiant	70	3.76	.471		
	Submissive	60	4.10	1.31		
					2.07	<.05
Male Only	High-powered defiant	19	3.68	.784		
	High-powered submiss.	12	4.50	1.364		
					2.08	<.05
Male Only	Low-powered defiant	18	4.00	.796		
	Low-powered submiss.	13	4.46	1.603		
					1.14	>.10

*Mean score is average number of items marked correctly on film fact test.

Audience Learning Scores

Scores from the multiple-choice test were used to measure the students' recognition of film facts. Students (boys and girls combined) who saw deviants defy the teacher were able to recognize significantly fewer film facts than were students who saw deviants submit to the teacher's control effort (t = 2.07, df = 129, p <.05) (see Table VI).

In addition, while the boys who saw high-powered deviants submit were able to recognize significantly more film facts than were boys who saw high-powered deviants defy (t = 2.08, df = 30, p <.05), no difference was found between boys who saw low-powered deviants submit and boys who saw low-powered deviants defy (t = 1.14, df = 30, p >.10) (see Table VI).

This would tend to support the hypothesis that a deviant's defiance of a teacher caused enough disruption of the expectations of the other students that they were able to learn fewer facts from the film than those who saw deviants submit. As predicted, this effect appeared to be more pronounced on the male classmates when the deviants had high power than when deviants had low power.

SUMMARY AND CONCLUSIONS

Four classes of fifth graders were shown a science film during which a male classmate misbehaved and became the target of a control technique exerted by a new teacher. The deviants (who were confederates of the experimenter)

were selected on the basis of having high or low power among their peers and were trained to react in either a defiant or submissive manner. Classmates who saw deviants submit to a teacher's control technique perceived the teacher to be more expert and powerful, perceived the control technique to be fairer, and recognized more film facts than did classmates who saw deviants defy. These effects were more pronounced when deviants had high power than when they had low power.

It seems reasonable to conclude that the overt reaction of a male deviant student *does have* some measurable effects on the perceptual behavior and learning performances of his classmates and that these effects are influenced by the social power of the deviant.

REFERENCES

French, J. R. P., Jr. "A Formal Theory of Social Power." *Psychological Review,* 1956, **63**, 181–94.

Heider, F. "Attitudes and Cognitive Organization." *Journal of Psychology,* 1946, **21**, 107–112.

Kounin, J., & Gump, P. "The Ripple Effect in Discipline." *Elementary School Journal,* 1958, **59**, 158–62.

Lippitt, R., Polansky, N., Redl, F., & Rosen, S. "The Dynamics of Power." *Human Relations,* 1952, **5**, 37–64.

Redl, F., & Wineman, D. *Children Who Hate* (Glencoe, Ill.: Free Press, 1951.)

Redl, F., & Wineman, D. *Controls from Within* (Glencoe, Ill.: Free Press, 1952.)

ANALYSIS OF STUDY 6

This study poses a number of interesting possibilities for analysis. It deals, in the first instance, with a rather complex and important aspect of in-school behavior. Secondly, it represents an effort to test a theory, or at least articulate further on a theory. And thirdly, it represents an ingenious and fairly imaginative experimental design. But there are substantial problems on all three counts that call the research into question.

The first thing we can say about the methodology is that it was clearly described in the published report. We might almost say that the description of method was a model of clear and effective research writing, such that further explanatory comments as to what was actually done are not necessary. There are, however, several shortcomings in the experiment as it was designed and conducted that raise questions about the findings.

1. In setting up the experimental situation which involved the training of the deviant boys, you will notice that the teacher in the experiment participated in the training. Here was a possible source of experimental bias if the teacher knew who were the high-powered boys and who were the low-powered boys. Knowing this, she could have subtly influenced pupil behavior in the predicted direction.

2. The measurement problem in any experiment is often a difficult one. The experimenter here had an ingenious, but simple, device which provided for making very fine measurements along a 100-point scale. The exact centimeter measurement was calculated. But then this fine scale was literally abandoned in the analysis since only the direction of the differences on the postexperimental measurements was considered. In other words, whether there was one centimeter difference in a subject's pretest and posttest measure or ninety-nine centimeters difference, the only thing noted was a positive change (+), a negative change (−), or no change (0). These directional shifts were then tested statistically by chi-square which makes no hard assumptions about how a variable is distributed. One can only conclude that a lot of information was lost with this approach. At the same time it is clear that this made the data easier to analyze.

3. Another design problem, possibly a serious one, was the lack of any control group in which the teacher came in the room, made her speech, showed the film without incident, gave the test, and then left. Such a control group would have made it clearer whether or not the differences among the experimental groups were attributable to the experimental incident. We might carry this a step further and suggest that a better test of differences on the learning of the film facts would have been possible if in one group the film had not been interrupted at all, as would be the case with the control group suggested above, and in another group the film was interrupted through a technical accident but with no classroom incident. Without these control groups we do not really know if the learning tested in this experiment would have been any better than it was with the disruptive incidents.

Two aspects of the report raise some additional methodological questions. A count of the number of subjects in Tables III, IV, and V next to the entry of "All Deviant Submissive" should yield totals of 130 each time, to total the number of subjects given by the author. Instead, the numbers are 131, 128, and 120 respectively. Something is obviously wrong somewhere here. There may be a good reason for the variation in these figures but the author never mentions the discrepancy, let alone its cause.

The author also commented in several places that the pupils were more sensitive to the behavior of the high-powered deviants than they were to the low-powered deviants. However, this appears to be an inference arrived at without a direct test. If you examine the tables you will notice that no direct comparisons were made between high-powered and low-powered deviants. How can we be confident that the behavioral cues of the one group elicited a more sensitive response than the other group in the absence of a direct comparison between the two?

While these shortcomings are important for the critical reader to note, they do not necessarily negate either the research effort or the findings. They do suggest ways in which further experiments in the same area could be improved so as to collect less ambiguous data.

Turning now to the theory, we can summarize it as follows: In social situations involving an interaction between two persons with others looking on, the behavior of the two persons will influence both the overt and the perceptual behavior of the onlookers. The social situation on which this theory concentrates, is the classroom, and the two persons now become a student and a teacher. The interaction that is of interest in the theory is that of deviant behavior on the part of the student and the exercise of a control technique on the part of the teacher. Previous research, the author notes, has confirmed the theory that suggests onlookers will be affected (the ripple effect). There was also research evidence to suggest that the effects would differ according to some previous connection that the actor might have had with the audience.

Gnagey's theory suggested to him that the social power status of a student would be a factor in influencing the audience. Furthermore, while previous research had demonstrated effects on overt behavior, Gnagey's theories suggested to him that audience perceptions would be altered by the ripple effect of the interaction. In dealing with perception, we should note, we are dealing with theory. In other words, Gnagey is saying that this student-teacher interaction over a bit of misbehavior would lead the onlookers to alter their opinions of the teacher's fairness, power, expertise, and so on.

The experimental question, then, becomes: Is it so; is that in fact the way it is? The experimenter's job at that point is to create experimental conditions that will represent a legitimate test of his theory, to make observations which either confirm or disprove the model.

Gnagey concludes his report with this sentence: "It seems reasonable to conclude that the overt reaction of a male deviant student does have some measurable effects on the perceptual behavior and learning performances of his classmates and that these effects are influenced by the social power of the deviant." The theory seems to coincide with reality.

At this point, in assessing both the significance of the study and the theory upon which it is based, we must at least raise a question about the reality upon which the test of the theory was based. We come to grips here with a live and difficult problem. If we grant that stringent controls were clamped on nature in this experiment to permit the experimenter to make precise observations which he could measure with reasonable accuracy, can we also grant that the results which support the theory thereby allow us to generalize that theory to the real life situation free of controls? The answer to this is: Yes and No.

Teachers do discipline disruptive or deviant pupils by dismissing them from the room, and these pupils do show a range of reactions from submission to defiance (including "Make me leave"). It is probably also true (certainly this research supports it) that the perceptions of the onlooking pupils are affected by these incidents.

But when we begin to compare realities, we do have to examine once again the basis on which this theory was tested. All the perceptual shifts that were tested had to do with the teacher: the teacher's power, how well she was liked, her ability, and the fairness of the punishment she used. But since the teacher in this experiment was totally new to the pupils and disappeared after the brief experiment, none of the multitude of other variables that might affect the pupil's perception of a teacher were present or measured. The test, therefore, was really only a general one of: Is perception affected? and not really a test of what perceptions were affected, in what direction, and how much. Putting it another way, we cannot generalize from this study to say: When a teacher disciplines a high-powered pupil and he submits to that discipline we can expect that his classmates will see the teacher as "being able to handle kids." In reality, there would be many other variables entering into that perception over a period of time, and any given bit of disciplinary interaction may have no effect at all on the perception of the teacher as it has been developed through numerous interactions, only a few of which have involved discipline.

For the moment, let us note and pass over the probability that the pupils' perceptions of their teacher have a significant effect on their learning.

Turning to audience learning, we have a much more significant and relevant variable. The test of this was a recognition of film facts based on a multiple choice test that asked some rather silly questions such as the color of hair of one of the subjects in the film. The results suggested that witnessing deviant behavior was enough of a disruptive experience to the learning that it had a negative effect on the ability to recognize those facts. We have indicated some of the design deficiencies which still leave this finding in some question. To these we might add a question about the reliability of this test. If the reliability was low, which it might have been, then all scores would have been largely attributable to chance. Yet the argument can be made that if the incident had that much effect on a simple test of immediate recall, it would likely have an effect on more complex learning. From this experiment we simply do not know.

Returning to the theory, now we can raise the question of its comprehensiveness. On its own terms it would appear reasonably comprehensive. It deals with the generalization of effects from one interaction to a number of onlookers. This is obviously of some importance in education. Where the theory purports to focus on the matter of discipline, or specifically a control technique, it seems weakest. As a theory for considering disciplinary activity, it proceeds on the basis of a long-accepted assumption in American education that deviance, especially in the form of disruptive (to the teacher's total *control of the classroom) behavior is not to be tolerated, and the offending pupil must be eliminated from the group.*

We might hope that this experimental support for the ripple effect would at least suggest that the disciplinary theory used to test it is outmoded and detrimental to the learning situation. We could use some theories that would deal more comprehensively than this one does with a wider range of interactions, including discipline, in the learning situation and their effects on more complex learning activities than memorizing film facts.

STUDY 7

INTRODUCTION TO STUDY 7

Study 7 is included to illustrate (1) a published research study which did not report significant findings related to the stated hypotheses of the study and (2) an experimental research project carried out within the school curriculum. The study also provides a clearly stated set of research questions and reports the results in a concise manner.

As you read the study keep in mind the following questions:

1. *What is the theoretical frame of reference of the researcher?*
2. *What specifically is the researcher attempting to establish?*
3. *What were the particular measures taken? What were the dependent variables? How were they collected?*
4. *Were the groups used in the experiment equivalent at the beginning of the experiment? Why or why not?*

When you have completed the reading of Study 7, compare your answers to the questions above with those suggested in the Analysis of Study 7 section.

Study 7

The Relationship Between Sequences of Instruction and Mental Abilities of Retarded Children

G. PHILLIP CARTWRIGHT

Educators are becoming increasingly aware of the importance of dealing with individual differences in children's learning abilities. Of special concern is the problem of finding the best match between children's individual learning styles and instructional procedures. It was the purpose of this research to study the match between sequence of instruction and specific learning abilities of educable mentally retarded adolescents.

Reprinted with permission of the author and publisher from *American Educational Research Journal,* 8, 1, January 1971, 143–50. Copyright 1971 by American Educational Research Association, Washington, D.C.

Several studies (Hamilton, 1964; Jacobs and Kulkarni, 1965; Levin and Baker, 1963; Maurer and Jacobs, 1966; Payne, Krathwohl, and Gordon, 1967; Roe, Case, and Roe, 1962) have dealt with the relationship between sequencing of programed instruction and test performance. In general, these studies have revealed that with normal children and college students there seem to be few real differences in performance between groups of subjects who have been exposed to logical, systematic instructional sequences and subjects who have taken illogical, random, or scrambled sequences of instruction. Although the logical sequencing of programed instruction is intuitively more appealing to educators, there is little evidence that normal children learn more effectively under the ordered than the random sequence.

Wodtke, et al (1967) suggested that verbal ability might interact with type of instructional sequencing (random or ordered) to the effect that low ability students might do better under ordered sequencing. High ability students, on the other hand, might provide their own conceptual organizations to a random sequence and achieve comparable performance with both random and ordered sequencing. Wodtke and his colleagues concluded from their experiments that "... the effects of scrambling a logically ordered instructional program depend on the nature of the learning task and or individual differences in the learners." (Wodtke, et al, 1967, p. 15). These results are consistent with those obtained by Detambel and Stolurow (1956). They found differences in performance following different programed sequences of the same material. Also, the sequence which led to the most rapid learning did not produce scores that correlated with standarized test scores of general mental ability.

Roderick and Anderson (1968) found that a programed instructional sequence led to greater learning than a textbook style summary on a delayed test but not on an immediate test. The findings of the Roderick and Anderson study suggest that careful, systematic sequencing of instruction is necessary to insure retention of the material presented.

The relationship between instructional sequencing and learning abilities of retarded children was the concern of the study reported here. This project focused on the interactions between individual differences and instructional sequences in a sample of educable mentally retarded adolescents.

The hypotheses were as follows:

1. If groups of educable mentally retarded adolescents are given scrambled and systematic sequences of instruction, performance of subjects taking the systematic sequence will be superior to that of subjects taking the scrambled sequence in terms of (a) immediate learning, (b) transfer, and (c) retention.
2. Different aptitudes and abilities are required to achieve equivalent performance on scrambled and systematic sequences of instruction.

STUDY 7

PROGRAMS

The sequences of programed instruction used in this study were adapted from a program designed to teach fractions to normal fifth grade children. The original program, prepared by Smith (1962), was modified by reducing the reading level to that appropriate for the subjects under study. Also, the program was expanded in some places to fill in gaps in the logical arrangement of fractions.

Two sequences of instruction were prepared from the modified Smith program. The systematic version consisted of a total of 612 frames divided into nine sections. A logical, orderly arrangement of frames was maintained by minimizing the changes between frames. Adjacent frames were highly similar and there was a high degree of predictability for following frames.

The scrambled or random sequence was prepared by scrambling the identical 612 frames (within sections) used in the systematic program. The overall sequence of the nine sections was maintained but items within sections were scrambled. The scrambling was random with the exception that adjacent frames were manipulated to eliminate similarity. For example, in the systematic program, 1/2 was compared with 1/3, then with 1/4, then with 1/5, and so on, in sequential order up to 1/10. In the scrambled version, such orderliness was not permitted. Thus, the frame comparing 1/2 with 1/5 might be followed by a frame comparing 1/8 with 1/10, and the latter followed by a comparison of 1/4 and 1/6.

Fifteen teaching machines were constructed to present the programed instructional sequences which were on long rolls of 8 1/2 inch wide paper and were placed inside the machines. The machines were constructed of welded sheet metal with masked plexiglas tops. When a roll of instruction material was locked into the device, students could not roll the paper backward without tearing the paper.

METHOD

Subjects

The subjects were forty educable mentally retarded adolescents, ages 15 to 20, enrolled in special classes for the educable mentally retarded in a large urban high school. Mean chronological age was 17 years 4 months. Mean WISC Full Scale IQ was 71.7 (range 53–83). Mean mental age was 12 years 4 months. In addition to the WISC, the total battery of the California Achievement Test (CAT) was administered prior to the introduction of the programed instruction. Mean grade placement on the CAT was 5.6 (s = 1.2).

Procedure

The forty subjects were randomly assigned to either the scrambled or the orderly sequence of instruction. Four subjects dropped out of the scrambled sequence group prior to completing the sequence but analyses revealed that there were no significant differences between the remaining sixteen subjects and the twenty orderly sequence subjects on chronological age; mental age; Verbal, Performance, and Full-Scale WISC; or any of the CAT subtests.

At the beginning of the study, each student took a 64 item test on general concepts and specific examples of fractions.

The programed instruction sequences were administered during the regular general math period in the students' usual classrooms. Three sessions were held each day with 13 to 15 subjects per session. Subjects attended only one session per day. Orderly sequence and scrambled sequence students worked side by side in each session. The students were not aware that two sequences of instruction were being presented. Approximately two weeks (10 class periods) were required to complete the instruction.

As each student completed the instructional sequence he was re-administered the 64 item pretest. The purpose of this test (hereafter called the posttest) was to test the hypothesis that there would be differences in the two groups on immediate learning.

Approximately 21 days after the posttest the retention and transfer tests were administered. The retention test consisted of 42 items not on the posttest which were included in the programed material. The transfer test consisted of 42 items on fractions that were not taught nor tested during the course of the experiment.

Data Analysis

Means and standard deviations of raw scores were calculated for the posttest, transfer test, and retention test.

Analyses of covariance were performed to determine if there were any statistically significant differences between the means of the two groups on any of the dependent variables. Tests for homogeneity of regression indicated parallel regression lines.

Two separate correlation matrices of IQ, achievement, and dependent variables were computed, one each for the ordered sequence group and the scrambled sequence group. Those instances in which correlation coefficients were significantly different from zero in one group but not the other were noted, and tests of the significance of differences between the correlation coefficients were performed by means of the Fisher Z transformation.

RESULTS

Means, adjusted means, and standard deviations for the two groups on the pretest and the three dependent variables are listed in Table 1.

In Table 2 the results of the covariance analyses are reported. None of the analyses produced F values that were significant with $p<.05$. It was

STUDY 7

TABLE 1. Summary of Learning, Transfer, and Retention Data

	\multicolumn{3}{c	}{Ordered Sequence}	\multicolumn{3}{c}{Scrambled Sequence}
	Mean	Adjusted Mean	SD	Mean	Adjusted Mean	SD
Pretest	30.9		13.7	26.1		10.6
Learning	47.8	46.7	10.9	45.2	46.7	10.8
Transfer	25.9	25.2	8.3	27.0	27.9	5.8
Retention	25.2	24.3	8.6	21.7	22.8	9.9

concluded that the two different sequences of instruction produced equivalent learning, retention, and transfer with the two groups of subjects.

In Table 3 are listed correlation coefficients which were significantly different from zero for one group but not the other. Also, results of the tests for significance of differences between correlation coefficients are reported in Table 3. With $\alpha = .05$, none of the tests revealed significant differences between correlation coefficients. Thus, the results of the correlational analyses, though somewhat provocative, were not statistically significant.

DISCUSSION

The data analyses indicated that subjects taking two different sequences of instruction covering the same content obtained equivalent scores on the criterion tests for immediate learning, retention, and transfer. It appeared that scrambled and ordered sequences of instruction were equally effective.

Support for the suggestion that different aptitudes and abilities are required to achieve equivalent performance from scrambled and systematic presentation can be drawn from inspection of the correlations between the

TABLE 2. Adjusted Analyses of Variances with Pretest as Covariate

Variable	Source	DF	SS	MS	F
Learning	Treatment	1	0.015	0.015	
	Error	33	2564.494	77.712	<1
Transfer	Treatment	1	60.312	60.312	
	Error	33	1324.167	40.126	1.503
Retention	Treatment	1	18.361	18.361	
	Error	33	1821.748	55.204	<1

TABLE 3. Correlation Coefficients Significantly Different from Zero and Tests of Difference Between Correlation Coefficients

Dependent Variables	Individual Difference Variables	Ordered Sequence Group	Scrambled Sequence Group	Z	P
Learning:					
Posttest	IQ	.187	.614	1.428	0.76
Posttest	Tot. Lang.	.411	.634	.844	.200
Posttest	Read. Comp.	.511	.457	.193	.423
Posttest	Arith. Fund.	.738	.414	1.371	.085
% Max. Gain[2]	Mental Age	−.010	.513	1.566	.059
% Max. Gain	IQ	.130	.605	1.547	.061
% Max. Gain	Tot. Lang.	.239	.557	1.045	.148
% Max. Gain	Arith. Reas.	.531	.455	.271	.393
% Max. Gain	Arith. Fund.	.452	.175	.841	.201
	Tot. Arith.	.509	.331	.592	.277
Transfer:					
Raw Score	Read. Vocab.	.620	.415	.768	.221
Raw Score	Read. Comp.	.593	.355	.844	.220
Raw Score	Tot. Read	.634	.434	.768	.221
Raw Score	Arith. Reas.	.508	.477	.109	.457
Raw Score	Arith. Fund.	.544	.234	1.010	.156
Raw Score	Tot. Arith.	.550	.371	.622	.267
Raw Score	Tot. Lang.	.516	.243	.578	.282
Raw Score	Tot. Battery	.595	.376	.787	.215
Retention:					
Raw Score	Arith. Fund	.671	.441	.923	.178
Raw Score	Tot. Lang.	.505	.404	.345	.365

[1] All underlined correlation coefficients in this table are significantly different from zero with $p < .05$.

[2] Percent maximum possible gain. This measure was calculated by dividing the difference between a student's pretest and posttest score by the difference between his pretest score and the total number of questions on the posttest.

dependent variables and the measures of general and specific aptitudes and abilities (Table 3). These data suggest that different educational requirements were placed on the learners in the two different sequences. Different kinds of skills or abilities were used to achieve equivalent performances. Most notable was the fact that with students taking the scrambled sequence the general ability measures (IQ, MA, Total Language) tended to correlate significantly with criterion variables. The reverse was true with the ordered sequence group; specific, not general abilities, tended to correlate highly with criterion variables. These findings suggest that an unsystematic program or sequence of instruction places more demands on the general intellectual abilities of the students. A systematic, ordered program, does not demand the same general abilities but requires that the student make use of more specific intellectual or learning abilities. These ideas are, of course, highly speculative and are not strongly supported by the data from the present study.

Overall, the findings of this study do not provide strong support for the theory that sequences of instruction should be matched to children's profiles of general and specific abilities.

REFERENCES

Detambel, M. H., & Stolurow, L. M. "Stimulus Sequence and Concept Learning." *Journal of Experimental Psychology,* 1956, **51,** 34–40.

Hamilton, N. R. "Effects of Logical Versus Random Sequencing of Items in an Auto-Instructional Program Under Two Conditions of Overt Response." *Journal of Educational Psychology,* 1964. **55,** 258–66.

Jacobs, P. I., & Kulkarni, S. "A Test of Some Assumptions Underlying Programed Instruction." *Psychological Reports,* 1966, **18,** 103–10.

Levin, G. R., & Baker, B. L. "Item Scrambling in a Self-Instructional Program." *Journal of Educational Psychology,* 1963, **54,** 138–43.

Maurer, M. H., & Jacobs, P. I. "Effects of Variation in a Self-Instructional Program on Instructional Outcomes." *Psychological Reports,* 1966, **18,** 539–46.

Payne, D. A., Krathwohl, D. R., & Gordon, J. "The Effect of Sequence on Programmed Instruction." *American Educational Research Journal,* 1967, **4,** 125–32.

Roderick, M., & Anderson, R. C. "Programmed Introduction to Psychology Versus Text-Book Style Summary of the Same Lesson." *Journal of Educational Psychology,* 1968, **59,** 381–87.

Roe, K. V., Case, H. W., & Roe, A. "Scrambled Versus Ordered Sequence in Auto-Instructional Programs." *Journal of Educational Psychology,* 1962, **53,** 101–04.

Smith, L. M. *Programed Learning in Elementary School: An Experimental Study of Relationships Between Mental Abilities and Performance.* USOE Title VII, Project No. 711151.01, Technical Report No. 2. Urbana: Training Research Laboratory, University of Illinois, August 1962.

Wodtke, K. H., Brown, B. R., Sands, H. R., & Fredericks, P. *Scrambled Versus Ordered Sequencing in Computer-Assisted Instruction.* Final Report—R8, July 1967. Computer Assisted Instruction Laboratory, Penn State University, University Park, Pennsylvania.

G. PHILLIP CARTWRIGHT

ANALYSIS OF STUDY 7

Much of the current discussion in education centers around the topic of prescribing individual instructional techniques for particular students with specific abilities and achievement levels in conjunction with categorized portions of the curriculum. Study 7 is based on a belief in this theoretical framework as opposed to an open concept of learning permitting students to sort out their own instructional programs. Cartwright is attempting to select instructional programs in conjunction with the ability and achievement levels of educationally retarded students.

Based on this theory and previous research, Cartwright has developed two major hypotheses. Specifically, he is to research effects of two types of math instructional sequences (ordered and scrambled) on three measures of learning (immediate, transfer, and retention). He states his two hypotheses clearly. The first hypothesis is a directional one: he predicts from theory and research that systematic, ordered instructional sequencing is superior to the scrambled type. The second hypothesis is nondirectional: he claims that there will be a difference without stating the direction of the difference.

The design is an example of a nonequivalent control group. After selecting a sample of forty students for the study, Cartwright randomly assigned them to treatment groups—a method to establish equivalency. The author further established equivalency with the groups by using an analysis of covariance statistical procedure to test his first hypothesis. The dependent variables of immediate, transfer, and retention learning were all adjusted in terms of the pretest scores of the students. Thus, any differences in the groups on the basis of previous skills and learning related to the three dependent variables used were controlled. We can question whether the particular assumptions of analysis of covariance were met since the author did not attend to this concern. The research article should report such information when a statistical procedure has some particularly difficult assumptions to meet.

Another possible deficiency is: Were the three dependent variables significantly correlated with each other? The report does not furnish this information. If they were correlated, the researcher would have been correct in using a multivariate analysis of variance or a repeated measure procedure. Again, we do not have the necessary information to make this decision.

The results of the research do not support either of the hypotheses. Sequenced instruction was not better than scrambled instruction on any of the three measures collected. While several significant correlations between ability and achievement levels and the dependent variables are reported in Table 3, none were significant for both groups, and the correlations between the groups were not significant. The second hypothesis was also not accepted.

Although attempts are made in the last portion of the report to

STUDY 7

interpret the research as supporting via suggestion the hypotheses and theory, the last sentence reports the findings. No strong support for the theoretical frame of reference was investigated in this study. The data tell the story and this is the rationale for the entire research process.

The article is an example of a clearly written and concise research study. The author was straightforward in stating the theory, reviewing the previous research, identifying the hypotheses, reporting the methods and procedures, and presenting the results. The design was accurate for the research problem. While there may be problems associated with the statistical procedures used, we do not have the necessary information to make these decisions. We just raise the questions to illustrate the need to be precise in completing, reporting, and consuming educational research.

INTRODUCTION TO STUDY 8

Lepper's study is included here as an example of a factorial design research project. It examined a complex question and used imaginative methods to investigate it. While the previous study used math testing scores, Lepper investigates concepts such as honesty and temptation.

As you read the study, note carefully what the researcher is seeking and the procedures he used to examine his research questions. It is a detailed account, and we suggest that you read it slowly and with care, referring back to previous paragraphs of the report if you find that you have lost the researcher's train of thought.

Study 8

Dissonance, Self-Perception, and Honesty in Children[1]

MARK R. LEPPER

Several years ago, Freedman and Fraser (1966) published an intriguing demonstration of a phenomenon they called the "foot in the door" effect—the proposition that a person's compliance with an initial small and perhaps trivial request might increase the probability of his subsequent compliance with a larger and more substantial demand. In this study, two undergraduate experimenters contacted suburban housewives in their homes, first with a small request and later with a larger, more consequential request. The initial request, moreover, varied in both the sort of action requested and the issue involved. The housewives were first asked either to place a small sign in their window or to sign a petition on the issue of either safe driving or keeping California beautiful, and virtually all subjects, in each case, complied. Two weeks after their first contact, a second experimenter returned to each home to make a larger request, asking all subjects to place a large, unattractive billboard promoting auto safety on their front lawns for several weeks. All subjects who had been contacted originally were seen this second time, and the performance of those subjects receiving each of these four initial requests was compared to that of a control group not contacted prior to the final request.

Reprinted with permission of the author and publisher from *Journal of Personality and Social Psychology,* Vol. 25, No. 1 (January 1973), 65–74. Copyright 1973 by The American Psychological Association.

STUDY 8

Remarkably, this study succeeded in demonstrating a foot-in-the-door effect of fascinating and unexpected generality. Each of the four prior request conditions produced significantly greater compliance with the large final request than the control condition which had not been previously contacted, and the differences among the four request conditions were minimal. Even the simple action of signing an innocuous petition, passed by a first experimenter, to "Keep California Beautiful" increased the subsequent probability of the subject's agreeing to place a large billboard reading "Drive Safely" on her lawn, when asked to do so by a second, unrelated experimenter.

To explain this unexpected generality of their foot-in-the-door effect, Freedman and Fraser (1966) offered the following speculation:

> What may occur is a change in the person's feelings about getting involved or about taking action. Once he has agreed to a request, his attitude may change. He may become, in his own eyes, the kind of person who does this sort of thing, who agrees to requests made by strangers, who takes action on things he believes in, who cooperates with good causes [p. 201].

In essence, they suggested, the generality of the effect of initial compliance might have stemmed from a two-stage process in which, as a result of performing an initial action, (a) the person's perception of his own dispositions and attitudes toward such actions is changed and (b) the likelihood that the person will perform other similar and even more consequential actions when subsequently given an opportunity is increased by these changes in his self-perceptions.

Despite its intuitive plausibility, Freedman and Fraser's account of their data has remained largely speculative and has received little further research attention. Recent theoretical analyses of the self-perception process (Bem, 1965, 1967; Kelley, 1967), however, suggest a broader theoretical context for Freedman and Fraser's hypothesis by implying precisely that people's perceptions of their own attitudes and dispositions will frequently be affected by observation of their own overt actions.

Essentially, this self-perception analysis proposed by Bem and by Kelley rests on two assertions that present self-perception processes as a special case of more general person-perception processes. The first assertion is that people will ascribe attitudes, traits, and dispositions to others from an observation of the others' overt behavior and its controlling circumstances. To the extent that external pressures are perceived as great, one will attribute another's actions to his environment; while to the extent that external pressures toward action appear weak, one will attribute another's actions to characteristics of that other. The second assertion is that a person may also come to "know" his own attitudes and dispositions, in part, through an identical process of drawing inferences about his own attitudes and dispositions—the sort of person he must be to have behaved as he did—from the actions he observes himself taking and the conditions under which they occurred.

With this self-perception theory, it is possible to account for a variety of phenomena, including the large dissonance literature on "insufficient justification" (cf. Aronson, 1966). In these studies, subjects are induced to engage in some unpleasant or inconsistent behavior under conditions of either high and clearly adequate or low and psychologically "insufficient" external justification for the behavior; the typical dissonance result is that subjects given low extrinsic justification for the behavior they have been induced to undertake come to believe that these actions were intrinsically justified. In a self-perception analysis, this outcome is the result of a simple inference process: In the low justification conditions, the subject infers from the lack of external pressure that he must have wished to behave as he did; while in the high justification conditions, he infers that he was forced to behave as he did by the external pressures in the situation.

Similarly, one can construct a self-perception account of the Freedman and Fraser (1966) study—the person observes himself taking action on a good, if innocuous, cause without any obvious external pressure and infers that he must be the kind of person who becomes involved with such causes—and, viewing this experiment from a self-perception perspective, he has two theoretical consequences. First, this account stresses the importance of the amount of external pressure used to induce initial compliance, proposing that changes in self-perceptions and a resultant increase in subsequent compliance should occur only when initial pressure is minimal, as in the Freedman and Fraser study. In fact, the self-perception account additionally suggests the possibility of an "overjustification" effect (Lepper, Greene, & Nisbett, in press; Nisbett & Valins, 1971). That is, if external justifications were perceived as clearly "oversufficient," the subject might infer that he is the sort of person who behaves as he did only when there is a great deal of external pressure, and he might be actually less likely to comply subsequently in situations involving lower extrinsic justification. Equally important, a self-perception analysis suggests that foot-in-the-door effects may occur in a wide variety of situations, including the various insufficient justification paradigms.

Consider, for example, the classic "forbidden toy" paradigm of Aronson and Carlsmith (1963). Children are asked not to play with an attractive toy under either mild or severe threat of punishment for transgression. Following a period in which all children resist temptation, children under mild threat have been shown repeatedly to devalue the prohibited activity—on both verbal derogation (Aronson & Carlsmith, 1963; Carlsmith, Ebbesen, Lepper, Zanna, Joncas, & Abelson, 1969; Lepper, Zanna, & Abelson, 1970;

STUDY 8

Ostfeld & Katz, 1969; Turner & Wright, 1965) and behavioral avoidance (Freedman, 1965; Pepitone, McCauley, & Hammond, 1967) measures, up to 6 weeks after the initial session.

The implication of the above analysis for this situation is that compliance with an initial prohibition under mild threat may produce changes in a child's self-perceptions that would lead to increased compliance with later adult demands in other, different resistance to temptation situations. That is, one plausible inference that a child might draw from his behavior of not playing with the forbidden toy, under low justification conditions, would be that he is a particularly "good" boy—at least one who complies with adult prohibitions and is able to resist temptation in such situations. On the other hand, if the external justification for the child's initial resistance to temptation were high, as under severe threat, an increase in subsequent resistance would not be expected; and, instead, an opposite, "overjustification," effect might be obtained, leading to decreased resistance to temptation.

The major purpose of the present study, then, was to examine this hypothesis by inducing children in a first session not to play with an attractive toy, under either mild or severe threat, or by exposing them to a control procedure with no prohibition and then placing them subsequently in a different resistance to temptation situation. As in the Freedman and Fraser study, the initial request in the forbidden toy setting was designed to produce compliance by all subjects, while the second resistance to temptation situation involved attractive rewards for noncompliance and was designed to produce overt compliance by only some of the subjects. The major prediction of this study was that children complying with the initial prohibition under mild threat would show greater subsequent resistance to temptation than children complying under severe threat or than control subjects, and that control subjects would show at least as much, and possibly more, subsequent resistance to temptation than severe threat subjects.

In addition, the present study had two secondary purposes. First, it attempted to provide evidence for the postulated mediation of any resistance to temptation effects by changes in the child's self-perceptions. To this end, half of the subjects in each condition were given a self-description task designed to measure self-perceptions following the initial forbidden toy situation, as well as measures of the subjects' attitudes about transgression. For the remaining subjects, these measures were not included, to allow an assessment of the possible reactivity of these intervening measures with later resistance to temptation. Second, the study also attempted to test the "hydraulic" assumption implicit in many discussions of dissonance and self-perception processes—the assumption that when a person may plausibly justify or account for his behavior in a number of ways, his acceptance of any single explanation or resolution will tend to reduce his acceptance of other, possibly alternative resolutions. In effect, the various alternative justifications available in most insufficient justification situations are often viewed as being somewhat mutually exclusive (Brehm & Cohen, 1962; Lepper, Zanna, & Abelson, 1970; Steiner, 1968). To test this proposition, half of the subjects in each condition were told, prior to the initial temptation period, that their peers had also found the to-be-forbidden toy highly attractive. Presumably, this manipulation should serve to prevent the usual derogation of the forbidden toy, which should be reproduced under standard mild threat conditions. If the hydraulic model were correct, one would predict both greater subsequent resistance to temptation in the mild threat conditions when this "attitude stabilizing" information was provided and a negative correlation between derogation of the prohibited toy and later resistance to temptation.

METHOD

Overview

Second-grade children served as subjects in two experimental sessions, several weeks apart. In the first session, the child indicated his relative preferences for six attractive toys. Following this ranking in the attitude stabilization conditions, the experimenter informed the child that most of his peers had agreed with his ratings of the toys, while in the standard conditions, no such remark was made. Orthogonal to this manipulation, two groups of children were induced not to play with their second-favorite toy during a short temptation period under either mild (high dissonance) or severe (low dissonance) threat of punishment for transgression. In a third, control, group, no prohibition was made, and the child was allowed to play with all of the toys.

At the end of this temptation period, a second "blind" experimenter asked the child to rerank the six toys, providing the traditional dissonance measure of derogation of the forbidden toy. In addition, half of the children in each condition were given a self-description task to assess changes in the child's self-perceptions postulated to mediate any behavioral effects on the measure of resistance to temptation. The remaining children in each condition were asked instead to play with a set of multicolored plastic tiles for an equivalent amount of time.

Three weeks later, the child was brought to a different room by a third, also "blind," experimenter to assess the child's resistance to temptation in a different situation designed to elicit overt transgression from some of the children. In this session, the child played a simple bowling game in which he could win a small prize only by falsifying his score. The score that the child reported earning in the experimenter's absence served as the measure of resistance to temptation in this new situation.

Subjects and Experimenters

The subjects were 129 second-grade children, with a mean age of 7½ years. The subjects were obtained from two predominantly middle-class schools and

STUDY 8

were randomly assigned to conditions. The sample included 66 males and 63 females, distributed about equally across conditions. Twelve subjects in each of the six cells received the intervening process measures, while an additional 9 or 10 subjects per cell did not receive these measures. Data from an additional 6 subjects, distributed across conditions, were discarded due to equipment failure in Session 2. Inclusion of their data in Session 1, however, does not alter the significance of the results obtained.

The study involved three experimenters. A male graduate student served as Experimenter 1 throughout, delivering the manipulations; and two female research assistants served as Experimenter 2 and Experimenter 3, collecting the dependent measures. Throughout the study, both Experimenter 2 and Experimenter 3 remained blind to the conditions of the subjects and unaware of the experimental hypothesis.

Session 1

Experimenter 1 brought each child individually to the experimental room and demonstrated to the subject six attractive toys—a battery-operated airplane, a Tonka bulldozer, a gyroscope, an Etch-A-Sketch, a mechanical dog, and a small battery-powered robot. The toys were placed on a table, and the subject was asked to rank them by a method of elimination. The subject was first asked to indicate his favorite toy of the six, then his favorite of the remaining five, and so forth, until he had indicated his relative preferences for all six toys (cf. Turner & Wright, 1965).

Attitude stabilization manipulation. When the subject had completed the ranking procedure in the attitude stabilization conditions, Experimenter 1 mentioned casually, "Gee, you know, most of the other boys [or girls] liked the toys just the way you did. They liked the *first-ranked toy* best of all. Then they liked the *second-ranked toy* next best, and then the rest of the toys." This manipulation was restricted to same-sex peers to maintain its plausibility in the face of clearly differential attractiveness of some of the toys to the male and female subjects. For subjects in the standard conditions, this comment was omitted.

Dissonance manipulation. At this point, Experimenter 1 "remembered" aloud that he had some important work to do and would have to leave the subject alone for a few minutes. As Experimenter 1 rose to leave, in the mild (or the severe) threat conditions, he picked up the subject's second-favorite toy and told the subject,

> Now while I'm gone, you can play with all of the toys except the *second-ranked toy.* It would be wrong to play with the *second-ranked toy,* and if you play with it, I would be a little bit annoyed (or very upset and very angry) with you.

Experimenter 1 then placed the forbidden toy at the far end of the table, reiterating "Now remember, I don't want you to play with the *second-ranked toy,* and if you play with it, I would be a little bit annoyed (or very upset and very annoyed) with you, so I'm going to leave it down here." In the two threat conditions, when the prohibited toy was placed on the table, it was aligned with two fine lines out of the subject's sight. This procedure, validated by covert observations in previous studies (Carlsmith et al., 1969), allowed Experimenter 1 to determine whether the subject had played with the toy in his absence. No child in either threat condition actually transgressed.

In the control condition, no prohibition was given. The subject was told instead that he could play with all the toys.

Intervening process measures. At the end of the temptation period, Experimenter 1 returned, replaced all the toys in the center of the table, and signaled to Experimenter 2. Experimenter 2 entered the room and was introduced by Experimenter 1, who then departed, leaving Experimenter 2 alone with the subject. Experimenter 2 asked the subject to rank the toys again, using the same procedure as before. Derogation scores thus ranged from 1 (enhancement of the toy) to 6 (maximal derogation of the toy).

For the subjects who were to receive further intervening measures, Experimenter 2 next presented the self-perception measure. Five placards, labeled from "Very much like me" to "Not at all like me," were placed in order facing the subject and were read aloud to him. The subject was then presented with 12 adjectives—4 chosen to fall on a dimension of honesty-dishonesty and an additional 8 chosen to fall on a more general positive-negative continuum—printed on individual 3 X 5 inch cards. Each adjective was read to the subject, who was then asked to place the card in the most appropriate category. Each item was scored on a 5-point scale from 1 (dishonest/negative) to 5 (honest/positive), and the 4 "honesty" items and the 8 general "self-concept" items were each summed to yield two self-perception scores for each subject. At the completion of this procedure, Experimenter 2 removed these materials and showed the subject an ordered series of five male face sketches, which ranged in expression from a broad smile to a slight frown. To measure liking for Experimenter 1, the subject was asked to point to the face that was most like the man who had shown him the toys. Finally, to assess the subject's attitudes toward moral offenses, Experimenter 2 presented the subject with two brief stories of children yielding to temptation. After each story, the subject was shown a visual scale of five ordered squares (cf. Walster, Berscheid, & Barclay, 1967), was instructed in its use, and was asked to indicate (a) how bad he thought the protagonist was to act as he did and (b) how bad he thought the protagonist felt about what he had done.

For the other subjects, these intervening process measures were not administered, since it was felt that these measures might be reactive with the subsequent resistance to temptation measure. In these conditions, the subject was simply asked to make a design with a set of multicolored plastic tiles and was allowed to work at this task for a period of time equivalent to that

STUDY 8

required by the other subjects to complete the intervening process measures.

In all cases, when Experimenter 2 was finished, she signaled Experimenter 1, who returned and accompanied the child back to his classroom, thereby terminating the first session.

Session 2

Approximately 3 weeks after the initial session (mean interval = 19.2 days, median interval = 18 days), each subject was brought individually by Experimenter 3 to a second experimental room to play a bowling game. This game consisted of a 3-foot, felt-covered alley down which a steel ball bearing could be rolled. At the end of the alley was a vertical scoreboard containing three colored lights numbered 1–3. When the ball was thrown down the alley, a microswitch activated one of the lights in a preprogrammed sequence.

The subject was informed that these lights indicated how good each shot was and that the number next to each light represented the number of "points" that each shot was worth. The subject was given a board containing holes into which marbles could be fit and a box of marbles, and Experimenter 3 demonstrated to the subject how the marble board could be used to keep score. The subject was given several practice shots to be certain that he understood the rules of the game and how to keep score. The subject was then shown a tray of small prizes (e.g., a small flashlight, an Old Maid game, a magnifying glass, a tiny doll, etc.) that he could win if he did especially well on the bowling game. Experimenter 3 indicated that if the subject were able to fill a section of the board containing 35 spaces, he would win one of the prizes, and that if he did even better than that, he might possibly win additional prizes.

So that the subject could concentrate on the bowling game, Experimenter 3 suggested that she would go into the next room. The subject was instructed to play the game until it turned itself off and to keep his score on the marble board, so that Experimenter 3 could tell if he won any prizes.

TABLE 1. Mean Final Rankings of the Forbidden Toy

	Threat condition		
Stabilization condition	Mild	Control	Severe
Standard (no stabilization)	3.27_a	2.29_b	2.09_b
n	22	21	22
Attitude stabilization	2.41_b	2.38_b	2.00_b
n	22	21	21

Note. Higher means indicate greater derogation. Cells not sharing common subscripts differ at the .01 level by Newman-Keuls procedure.

TABLE 2. Mean Resistance to Temptation Scores

Stabilization condition	Threat condition		
	Mild	Control	Severe
Standard (no stabilization)	34.82	36.48	38.86
n	22	21	22
Attitude stabilization	33.36	35.81	37.52
n	22	21	21

Note. Lower means indicate greater resistance to temptation.

Experimenter 3 then left the room, telling the subject to come and get her when he was finished with the game.

The game was constructed to give each child a total score of 33 points—2 points short of the score presumably necessary to win a prize. Hence, the score that the subject claimed provided a measure of his resistance to temptation in this second situation, and when the subject fetched Experimenter 3 from the next room, she recorded the score he claimed to have earned. In fact, each child was awarded a prize, and at the completion of the study, the chosen prizes were distributed to all subjects. The subject was asked not to tell his classmates about the session, and he was returned to his classroom by Experimenter 3.

RESULTS

Preliminary analyses revealed (a) no significant effects of sex of subjects or interaction of sex with experimental conditions and (b) no significant effects on the final resistance to temptation data of whether or not the subjects had received the additional intervening measures at the end of the first session. For subsequent analyses, therefore, the data were collapsed across these two dimensions.

Derogation of the Forbidden Toy

The mean rerankings of the toy which had been initially ranked second, and which had been forbidden in the two threat conditions, are presented in Table 1, where the predicted pattern of results—derogation occurring only in the mild threat-standard condition—is evident. Since this pattern may best be described by individual comparisons among the groups, a Newman-Keuls procedure for multiple comparisons (Winer, 1962) was employed to test the significance of the results. This analysis indicated that the mild threat-standard group did produce significantly ($p < .01$) more[2] derogation of the forbidden toy than all of the remaining conditions, which did not differ significantly from each other.

These results suggest that the necessary conditions for an appropriate test of the predictions concerning later resistance to temptation were met. Conditions of "insufficient" justification seem to have been created under mild threat, producing the traditional dissonance effect in the standard condition, but this derogation of the forbidden toy under mild threat was effectively inhibited by the attitude stabilization manipulation.

Resistance to Temptation

The mean resistance to temptation scores—the number of "points" that the subjects claimed to have earned on the bowling game approximately 3 weeks after the initial session—are presented in Table 2. For this measure, a score of 33 represented an objectively accurate claim, and a score of 35 represented the minimal score necessary to win a prize.[3] These data were subjected to a 3 × 2 unweighted-means analysis of variance, which appears in Table 3. In this analysis, as hypothesized, threat level had a highly significant effect on later resistance to temptation ($F = 6.00$, $df = 2/123$, $p < .005$), while neither the attitude stabilization manipulation nor the interaction of this manipulation with threat level had significant effects on later behavior.

Clearly, this significant effect of threat level on resistance to temptation some weeks later, in a different setting and with a different experimenter, is consistent with the major prediction of this study. Subjects in the mild threat conditions showed significantly greater resistance to temptation than did subjects in either the severe threat ($t = 3.35$, $df = 85$, $p < .01$) or the control ($t = 1.99$, $df = 84$, $p < .05$) conditions, while the subjects in the severe threat conditions tended to show less resistance to temptation than the control subjects ($t = 1.66$, $df = 83$, $p < .10$). In short, the subjects who complied with the first experimenter's initial request not to play with one of a number of attractive toys under conditions of "insufficient" justification subsequently showed increased compliance with the rules set by a second experimenter for the bowling game, while the subjects who complied with the initial request

TABLE 3. Analysis of Variance on Resistance to Temptation Scores

Source	df	MS	F
Threat level (A)	2	180,86	6.00*
Stabilization (B)	1	42.91	1.42
A × B	2	1.94	<1
Within-cell error	123	30.12	

*$p < .005$.

TABLE 4. Mean Self-Ascribed Honesty Scores

Stabilization condition	Threat condition		
	Mild	Control	Severe
Standard (no stabilization)	16.50	15.33	14.92
Attitude stabilization	17.50	15.92	16.33

Note. n = 12 subjects per cell. Higher means indicate greater self-ascribed honesty.

under conditions of "oversufficient" justification tended to show decreased compliance with this later implicit request.

However, while the data provide support for the major hypothesis of the study, they produced no evidence for a "hydraulic" model, in which derogation of the toy and subsequent resistance to temptation would be viewed as mutually exclusive responses in this situation. The prevention of derogation of the forbidden toy under mild threat in the attitude stabilization condition did not produce the increased resistance to temptation that a hydraulic account would predict; nor was there any significant correlation between derogation and resistance, either within the mild threat-standard cell or across all conditions.

Intervening Process Measures

Given these effects of threat level on resistance to temptation—increased resistance following mild threat and a tendency toward decreased resistance following severe threat—it is possible to examine the intervening process measures obtained from half of the subjects for evidence concerning the mediation of these behavioral effects.

Table 4 presents the mean self-perception scores for the subjects along the "honesty-dishonesty" dimension, where a score of 20 represents maximal self-ascribed honesty. Clearly, these data bear only a partial resemblance to the resistance to temptation data; and, in fact, a 3 X 2 analysis of variance on these data yielded no significant effects for either manipulation or their interaction. An examination of the more specific, predicted comparison of the mild threat condition with the control and the severe threat conditions, however, did yield weak support for the hypothesized mediational role of self-perceptions related to honesty. Specifically, this comparison indicated a tendency toward higher self-ascribed honesty scores in the mild threat conditions than in the severe threat and control conditions combined (t = 1.80, df = 70, p < .10)—a pattern consistent with the significantly increased resistance to temptation obtained under mild threat. It should be noted, however, (a) that these data were obtained from only 72 of the subjects in this study and (b) that these results were severely attenuated by the data from a single aberrant subject in the mild threat condition, whose score fell 3.7 standard deviations below the mean of the remaining 23 scores in this condition. Were this subject's data deleted from the analysis, the mild threat condition would differ significantly from both the severe threat ($t = 2.39$, $df = 46$, $p < .05$) and the control ($t = 2.11$, $df = 46$, $p < .05$) conditions.

In addition to the self-ascribed honesty measure, this study also included several measures designed to assess possible alternative mediating processes that might have accounted for the obtained resistance to temptation effects—self perceptions along a more general "positivity" dimension, attitudes toward transgression, perceptions of the consequences of transgression, and liking for the first experimenter. Analyses of variance performed on each of these four auxiliary measures yielded no significant effects, and none of these measures showed a significant correlation with later resistance to temptation. Hence, these additional data, while not conclusive, provide no evidence for the mediation of the obtained resistance to temptation effects by any of these variables.

DISCUSSION

The major results of this study, then, provide a clear conceptual analogue to Freedman and Fraser's (1966) foot-in-the-door effect in a radically different paradigm involving young children's compliance with adult prohibitions in the face of temptations not to comply. Theoretically, it was argued, the effects in both these studies could be seen as the result of a process of self-perception in which the subject observes his initial actions in the face of minimal external pressures and infers that he must be the kind of person who typically engages in such actions. Such a change in self-perceptions was hypothesized to mediate the increased subsequent compliance with larger future requests. Thus, in the Freedman and Fraser paradigm, the housewife infers that she is an "activist," in the sense of one who takes action on noncontroversial sorts of issues when requested; and in the present study, the child infers that he is a "good boy," at least in the sense of one who abides by adult rules in unfamiliar situations.

While these presumed changes in self-perceptions seem to show an unexpected generality in their effects on subsequent compliance in new situations, however, it also seems likely that these changes are, in another sense, relatively specific. In both studies, it seems probable that the two compliance situations were psychologically related, although temporally separated and involving different experimenters. Indeed, one might expect that the second setting in these studies immediately recalled the earlier situation for the subject, turning his attention to his previous behavior and suggesting the relevance of his initial actions for his behavior in this second situation. Certainly there is ample literature documenting the general stability of a person's global self-concept or self-esteem (Coopersmith, 1967; Wylie, 1961) to suggest that the brief experiences of the sort involved in these studies would be unlikely to alter dramatically the subject's general self-concept. More specific self-perceptions, on the other hand, with behavioral implications for only a limited set of psychologically related situations might well be substantially more liable to change and experimental manipulation.

In an attempt to assess the changes in self-perceptions presumed to mediate the resistance to temptation effects directly, this study included a measure of the subjects' self-descriptions along an honesty-dishonesty dimension, which provided only weak support for the hypothesis. That these results were weaker than the resistance to temptation data that they were presumed to mediate may simply be a function of the lesser reliability of the self-perception measure, the social-desirability constraints inherent in this measure, and the fact that only half of the subjects received these measures.

At the same time it may be worth noting that a number of previous self-perception studies have obtained results conceptually analogous to the present data—namely, behavioral effects consistent with a self-perception hypothesis with little evidence of postulated changes in self-perceptions. Thus, Valins and Ray (1967) produced decreased avoidance of snakes among snakephobics without changes in reported fear of snakes; Davison and Valins (1969) produced increased shock tolerance without changes in reported painfulness of the shocks; and Storms and Nisbett (1970) produced reports of earlier sleep onset among insomniacs without any differences in subjective reports of suffering.

Taken together, these data suggest the possibility of a more fundamental source of discrepancy between the verbal self-perception and behavioral resistance to temptation measures obtained in this study. Perhaps, as Nisbett and Valins (1971) have suggested, changes in self-perceptions will remain tentative for a subject until he has been provided an opportunity to validate these changes behaviorally. Alternatively, the implications of one's previous actions may become fully apparent only when one is subsequently placed in a similar situation that requires further related action. In any case, these results indicate a need for further study of the mediational role of self-perceptions in producing behavioral effects.

Regarding the common hydraulic assumption—that alternative modes of explanation or justification should tend to be negatively correlated—the results of this study were unequivocally negative. Although the derogation data indicated that the conditions presumably necessary for a test of this assumption were met, the mild-standard and mild-stabilization conditions did not differ in subsequent resistance to temptation. Nor was there any correlation of the two measures either across conditions or within the mild-standard condition. Since the hydraulic prediction was relatively straightforward, these negative data are slightly puzzling. Presumably, if the child in this situation is motivated to seek an explanation of his behavior, the child under mild threat could infer that he complied with the prohibition either because he happened to be the sort of person who consistently acts that way or because he happened to dislike the toy that was forbidden anyway. Thus, if the child were to decide, for example, that his behavior was simply the result of his clear dislike of the forbidden toy, there would be no reason for him to draw any additional inferences about the sort of person he is, and vice versa. Clearly, such was not the case. Possibly the attitude stabilization manipulation, instead of actually preventing derogation under mild threat, simply prevented the children from reporting derogation; perhaps the children actually derogated the toy in the mild-stabilization condition but simply did not report a change for fear of appearing "different" than their peers. In any case, these data failed to clarify the predictive problem posed by the simultaneous availability of multiple attributions in this setting.

Throughout, this study has been discussed in terms of children's compliance with implicit and explicit adult demands; but it should also be clear that the present data support Freedman's (1965) contention that a strategy of moral training involving minimally sufficient pressure will, in the long run, prove more effective than a strategy involving more powerful, but effectively unnecessary, pressure. Such a strategy, as the present results indicate, can successfully produce not only behavioral avoidance of the forbidden activity in subsequent situations but also increased resistance to temptation in later related, but quite independent, situations as well.

Whether children's resistance to temptation in such situations is best characterized as indicative of "compliance" or "honesty," however, is perhaps a moot point, given the particular subject population employed. Certainly Kohlberg's (1964, 1969) analysis of and normative data on the development of moral judgments suggests that a child's "morality" this early in life consists precisely of an orientation toward obedience to authority figures and the avoidance of possible punishment. In any case, the notion that a child's resistance to temptation may be importantly governed by his rather specific perceptions and expectations of himself, based in part on his previous patterns of behavior, seems to be a proposition worthy of further study.

END NOTES

1. This article is based on a dissertation submitted to the Department of Psychology, Yale University, in partial fulfillment of the requirements of the PhD degree. The author wishes to express his indebtedness to the members of his advisory committee—Robert P. Abelson, Charles A. Kiesler, and Susan Harter—for their helpful advice and encouragement throughout the study and to Katherine Shultz and Joan Wasserman for their exemplary performance as experimenters and commiserators in this project. Appreciation is also due to John Mulrain and Richard Belfonti,

the principals, and to the teachers of the Center Elementary School in Woodbridge, Connecticut, and the William Douglas Elementary School in North Branford, Connecticut, where the study was conducted.
2. All p values reported in this study are based on two-tailed tests of significance.
3. Although the bowling game was designed to yield an objective score of 33 for each subject, a few subjects claimed scores below 33. These errors seemed typically to result either from simple scoring errors by the subject or from "mistreatment" of the experimental apparatus by the subject, which could cause the subject to lose a trial. Since these errors were distributed across conditions and were not instrumental to the subject, the data were analyzed as reported by the subject. Replacing those scores with scores of 33, however, does not change the pattern or the significance of the findings reported above.

REFERENCES

Aronson, E. "The Psychology of Insufficient Justification: An Analysis of Some Conflicting Data." In S. Feldman (ed.), *Cognitive Consistency.* New York: Academic Press, 1966.

Aronson, E., & Carlsmith, J. M. "Effect of Severity of Threat on the Valuation of Forbidden Behavior." *Journal of Abnormal and Social Psychology,* 1963, **66,** 584–88.

Bem, D. J. "An Experimental Analysis of Self-Persuasion." *Journal of Experimental Social Psychology,* 1965, **1,** 199–218.

Bem, D. J. "Self-Perception: An Alternative Interpretation of Cognitive Dissonance Phenomena." *Psychological Review,* 1967, **74,** 183–200.

Brehm, J. W., & Cohen, A. R. *Explorations in Cognitive Dissonance.* New York: Wiley, 1962.

Carlsmith, J. M., Ebbesen, E. B., Lepper, M. R., Zanna, M. P., Joncas, A. J., & Abelson, R. P. "Dissonance Reduction Following Forced Attention to the Dissonance." *Proceedings of the 77th Annual Convention of the American Psychological Association,* 1969, **4,** 321–22. (Summary)

Coopersmith, S. *The Antecedents of Self-Esteem.* San Francisco: Freeman, 1967.

Davison, G. C., & Valins, S. "Maintenance of Self-Attributed and Drug-Attributed Behavior Change." *Journal of Personality and Social Psychology,* 1969, **11,** 25–33.

Freedman, J. L. "Long-Term Behavioral Effects of Cognitive Dissonance." *Journal of Experimental Social Psychology,* 1965, **1,** 145–55.

Freedman, J. L., & Fraser, S. C. "Compliance Without Pressure: The Foot-in-the-Door Technique." *Journal of Personality and Social Psychology,* 1966, **4,** 195–202.

Kelley, H. H. "Attribution Theory in Social Psychology." *Nebraska Symposium on Motivation,* 1967, **15,** 192–238.

Kohlberg, L. "Development of Moral Character and Moral Ideology." In M. Hoffman & L. Hoffman (eds.), *Review of Child Development Research.* New York: Russell Sage Foundation, 1964.

Kohlberg, L. "Stage and Sequence: The Cognitive-Developmental Approach to Socialization." In D. A. Goslin (ed.), *Handbook of Socialization Theory and Research.* New York: Rand McNally, 1969.

Lepper, M. R., Greene, D., & Nisbett, R. E. "Undermining Children's Intrinsic Interest with Extrinsic Rewards: A Test of the Overjustification Hypothesis." *Journal of Personality and Social Psychology,* in press.

Lepper, M. R., Zanna, M. P., & Abelson, R. P. "Cognitive Irreversibility in a Dissonance Reduction Situation." *Journal of Personality and Social Psychology,* 1970, **16,** 191–98.

Nisbett, R. E., & Valins, S. "Perceiving the Causes of One's Own Behavior." In E. E. Jones, D. E. Kanouse, H. H. Kelley, R. E. Nisbett, S. Valins, & B. Weiner (eds.), *Attribution: Perceiving the Causes of Behavior.* New York: General Learning Press, 1971.

Ostfeld, B., & Katz, P. A. "The Effect of Threat Severity in Children of Varying Socioeconomic Levels." *Developmental Psychology,* 1969, **1,** 205–10.

Pepitone, A., McCauley, C., & Hammond, P. "Change in Attractiveness of Forbidden Toys as a Function of Severity of Threat." *Journal of Experimental Psychology,* 1967, **3,** 221–29.

Steiner, I. D. "Responses to Inconsistency." In R. P. Abelson, E. Aronson, W. J. McGuire, T. M. Newcomb, M. J. Rosenberg, & P. H. Tannenbaum (eds.), *Theories of Cognitive Consistency: A Sourcebook.* Chicago: Rand McNally, 1968.

Storms, M. D., & Nisbett, R. E. "Insomnia and the Attribution Process." *Journal of Personality and Social Psychology,* 1970, **16,** 319–28.

Turner, E. A., & Wright, J. "Effects of Severity of Threat and Perceived Availability on the Attractiveness of Objects." *Journal of Personality and Social Psychology,* 1965, **2,** 128–32.

Valins, S., & Ray, A. A. "Effects of Cognitive Desensitization on Avoidance Behavior." *Journal of Personality and Social Psychology,* 1967, **7,** 345–50.

Walster, E., Berscheid, E. & Barclay, A. M. "A Determinant of Preference Among Modes of Dissonance Reduction." *Journal of Personality and Social Psychology,* 1967, **7,** 211–16.

Winer, B. J. *Statistical Principles in Experimental Design.* New York: McGraw-Hill, 1962.

Wylie, R. *The Self-Concept.* Lincoln, Neb.: University of Nebraska Press, 1961.

ANALYSIS OF STUDY 8

The research is based on a simply stated theory which suggests that individuals will comply with the wishes of others more readily if the first exposure to those others is in an environment of minor rather than severe threat. The development of attitudes and values of students is fostered in appropriate directions through educational environments that do not pose severe threat. The author completed his research from this theoretical frame of reference with the design, treatments, data collection, and analysis procedures based on the theory.

The study is an example of complete and careful research reporting. Lepper is explicit in his description of what was done, and the research can be replicated from the information included in the study. At times the reporting appears overbearing but this is necessary with complex studies. It is a more comprehensive theory and design than the previous study and the reporting must, therefore, be exacting in its detail.

The independent variables in the major portion of the study were the types of threat (severe, mild, and none) and the feedback or attitude stabilization type (peer agreement and none). Three major dependent variables were collected: temptation scores, honesty, and change in toy ranking. The "Overview" section of the study reports the general procedures used:

1. The children ranked the six toys.
2. One-half were told that their ranking was just like other girls (or boys) while the other one-half were not given any feedback on their ranking.
3. One-third were presented with severe threat, one-third were presented with mild threats, and one-third were presented with no threats regarding playing with the second ranked toy.

Graphically, the procedure design would be:

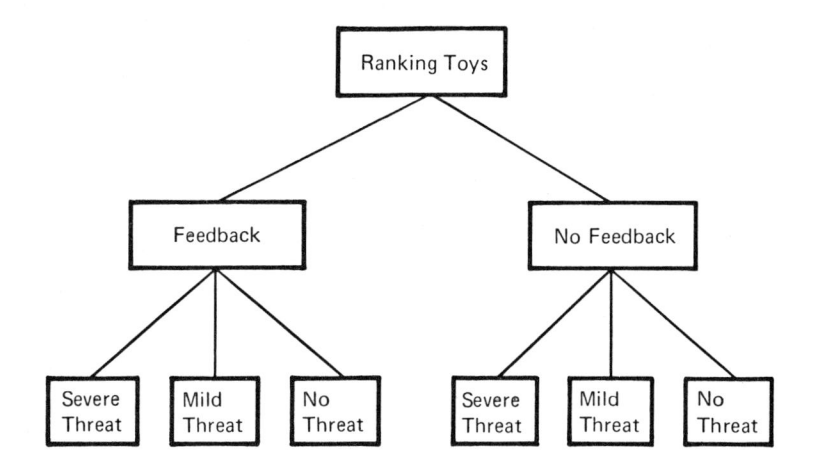

STUDY 8

For data collection purposes, the major portion of the study had a 3 X 2 matrix that graphically would be:

	Threat Level		
	Severe	Mild	None
Feedback — None			
Feedback — Peers			

The data collected were placed in one of the six cells above based on the type of experimental procedure the student received.

To illustrate how this data matrix was used in the analysis, Table 3 is reproduced. Remember that there were three types of threat and two types of stabilization or feedback. Notice in Table 3 that in the second column for degrees of freedom (df) there is a 2 for the row "Threat level (A)" and a 1 for the row "Stabilization (B)." In an analysis of variance the degrees of freedom for each of the independent variables are one less than the number of types (or levels) of each variable. From the fourth column of Table 3 (column F) we can tell whether any of the levels of the particular independent variable were significantly different from each other. Table 3 reports that, in relationship to the temptation scores there were significant differences between the levels of threat (significant at beyond the .005 level), there were no significant differences between the two levels of attitude stabilization and no significant interaction between types of threat and type of stabilization. In essence, the type of threat the student received affected the resistance to temptation score of the individual.

TABLE 3. Analysis of Variance on Resistance to Temptation Scores

Source	df	MS	F
Threat level (A)	2	180.86	600*
Stabilization (B)	1	42.91	1.42
A X B	2	1.94	<1
Within-cell error	123	30.12	

*$p < .005$.

The analysis procedures used compared the data of groups. However, the author took an important step in the second paragraph of the "Intervening Process Measures" section when he reported an examination of the individual subjects within the groups. Taking the group mean scores, he only could report a "tendency towards higher self-ascribed honesty scores in the mild threat conditions." However, on inspecting the individual scores in the mild threat group, one individual was found to have a score significantly different from the others in the group. When removing this individual's score from the group, the report is of a significant difference rather than a tendency. Part of research is a careful examination of your data to fully explain and discuss your results. We know more about the theoretical realm because this author took the necessary steps to investigate his data carefully.

A research model is also found in the "Discussion" section of the study. The theoretical perspective is tied in with the research results and ample projected reasons for the results are provided. Research is important, and a constant tie to the theoretical reference points is imperative.

Finally the last paragraph of the study is a good summary and statement of "where we are" in relationship to theory and practice. While not typical of research in education, the issues investigated and the research procedure employed have much to suggest to education. We are, after all, involved with children.

STUDY 9

INTRODUCTION TO STUDY 9

In this study by McAllister and his colleagues, we have a test of the efficacy of a theory as applied to a practical problem in a real life situation. Insofar as the test was successful, it lends further validity to a theory of B. F. Skinner by demonstrating the utility of the principles of learning applied in the classroom.

The study provides an interesting example of how Skinner's stimulus-response (S-R) theory of learning was tested in the reality of the classroom. Some significant differences between this study and many other S-R experimental studies should be noted: (1) the setting was a real classroom in a school, not a laboratory, (2) the experimental subjects were all the students in the class, not small samples from different classes, (3) the subjects were high school juniors and seniors rather than elementary school children, and (4) the teacher was a regular classroom teacher instead of an experimenter.

Study 9

The Application of Operant Conditioning Techniques in a Secondary School Classroom

L. W. McALLISTER
J. G. STACHOWIAK
D. M. BAER
L. CONDERMAN

Numerous studies have reported the effectiveness of operant conditioning techniques in modifying the behavior of children in various situations. Harris, Wolf, and Baer (1964), in a series of studies on preschool children, described the effectiveness of contingent teacher attention in modifying inappropriate

Reprinted by permission from *Journal of Applied Behavior Analysis,* **2, 4,** Winter 1969, 277–85. Copyright 1969 by the Society for the Experimental Analysis of Behavior, Inc.

This study is based upon a dissertation submitted by the senior author to the Department of Psychology, University of Kansas in partial fulfillment of the requirements for the degree of doctor of philosophy. The authors express appreciation to Mr. William Medley, Principal, and Mr. Max Stalcup, Head Guidance Counselor, at Lawrence (Kansas) Senior High School for their assistance and cooperation in the conduct of the study. Reprints may be obtained from Loring W. McAllister, Western Mental Health Center, Inc., 438 West Main Street, Marshall, Minnesota 56258.

behavior. Hall and Broden (1967), Patterson (1965), Rabb and Hewett (1967), and Zimmerman and Zimmerman (1962) have demonstrated the usefulness of teacher-supplied contingent social reinforcement in reducing problem behaviors and increasing appropriate behaviors of young children in special classrooms. Becker, Madsen, Arnold, and Thomas (1967); Hall, Lund, and Jackson (1968); and Madsen, Becker, and Thomas (1968) extended these techniques into the regular primary school classroom and demonstrated their effectiveness there. In all of the above studies, only a limited number of children were studied in each situation, usually one or two per classroom.

Thomas, Becker, and Armstrong (1968) studied the effects of varying teachers' social behaviors on the classroom behaviors of an entire elementary school classroom of 28 students. By observing 10 children per session, one at a time, they demonstrated the effectiveness of approving teacher responses in maintaining appropriate classroom behaviors. Bushell, Wrobel, and Michaelis (1968) also applied group contingencies (special events contingent on earning tokens for study behaviors) to an entire class of 12 preschool children.

There has been an effort to extend the study of teacher-supplied consequences to larger groups of preschool and elementary school subjects in regular classrooms, but no systematic research investigating these procedures has yet been undertaken in the secondary school classroom. Cohen, Filipczak, and Bis (1967) reported the application of various non-social contingencies (earning points, being "correct," and taking advanced educational courses) in modifying attitudinal and academic behaviors of adolescent inmates in a penal institution. But there is no record of investigations into the effects of teacher-supplied social consequences on the classroom behavior of secondary school students in regular classrooms.

At present, the usefulness of contingent teacher social reinforcement in the management of student classroom behaviors is well documented on the preschool and primary elementary school levels, particularly when the investigation focuses on a limited number of children in the classroom. Systematic replication now requires that these procedures be extended to larger groups of students in the classroom and to students in the upper elementary and secondary grades. The present study sought to investigate the effects of teacher-supplied social consequences on the classroom behaviors of an entire class of secondary school students.

METHOD

Subjects

Students. The experimental group was a low-track, junior-senior English class containing 25 students (12 boys and 13 girls). At the beginning of the study the ages ranged from 16 to 19 yr (mean 17.11 yr); I.Q.s ranged from 77 to 114 (mean 94.43). Approximately 80% of the students were from lower-class families; the remainder were from middle-class families. The control group was also a low-track, junior-senior English class of 26 students (13 boys and 13 girls). The ages ranged from 16 to 19 yr (mean 17.04 yr); I.Q.s ranged from 73 to 111 (mean 91.04). About 76% of these students were from lower-class families, 16% were from middle-class families and 4% were from upper-middle to upper-class families. The experimental class met in the mornings for a 70-min period and the control class met in the afternoons for a 60-min period.

Teacher. The teacher was 23 yr old, female, middle class, and held a Bachelor's degree in education. She had had one year's experience in teaching secondary level students, which included a low-track English class. She taught both the experimental and control classes in the same classroom and utilized the same curriculum content for both. She stated that she had been having some difficulties in controlling classroom behavior in both classes and volunteered to cooperate in the experiment in the interest of improving her teaching-management skills. She stated that she had been able to achieve some rapport with these students during the two months that school had been in session. She described the students, generally, as performing poorly in academic work and ascribed whatever academic behaviors she was able to observe in them as being the result of her rapport with them. She stated that she was afraid that she would destroy this rapport if she attempted to exercise discipline over inappropriate classroom behaviors.

Procedures

The basic design utilized was the common pretest-posttest control group design combined with the use of a multiple baseline technique (Baer, Wolf, and Risley, 1968) in the experimental class.

Target behaviors. Both classes were observed for two weeks to ascertain general occurrence rates of various problem behaviors that had been described by the teacher. Inappropriate talking and turning around were selected as target behaviors because of their relatively high rate of occurrence. Inappropriate talking was defined as any audible vocal behavior engaged in by a student without the teacher's permission. Students were required to raise their hands to obtain permission to talk, either to the teacher or to other students, except when general classroom discussions were taking place, in which cases a student was not required to obtain permission to talk if his statements were addressed to the class and/or teacher and were made within the context of the discussion. Inappropriate turning was defined as any turning-around behavior engaged in by any student while seated in which he turned more than 90 degrees in either direction from the position of facing the front of the room. Two exceptions to this definition were made: turning behavior observed while in the process of transferring material to or from the book holder in the bottom of the desk was considered appropriate, as was any turning that took place when a student had directly implied permission to turn around. Examples of the latter exception would be when the class was asked to pass papers up or down the rows of desks, or when students turned to look at another student who was talking appropriately in the context of a recitation or discussion.

Observation and recording. Behavior record forms were made up for recording observed target behaviors in both classes. A portion of the form is illustrated in Fig. 1. The forms for the experimental class contained 70 sequentially numbered boxes for each behavior; the forms for the control class contained 60 sequentially numbered boxes for each behavior (covering the 70- and 60-min class periods, respectively). The occurrence of a target behavior during any minute interval of time (e.g., during the twenty-fifth minute of class time) was recorded by placing a check mark in the appropriate box for that interval (e.g., box 25) beside the behavior listed. Further occurrences of that behavior during that particular interval were not recorded. Thus, each time interval represented a dichotomy with respect to each behavior; the behavior had or had not occurred during that interval of time. A daily quantified measurement of each behavior was obtained by dividing the number of intervals that were checked by the total number of intervals in the class period, yielding a percentage of intervals in which the behavior occurred at least once. Time was kept by referral to a large, easily readable wall clock whose minute hand moved 1 min at a time.

Behaviors were recorded daily during all conditions by the teacher. Reliability of observation was checked by using from one to two additional observers (student teachers and the senior author) who visited the classes twice per week. Students in this particular school were thought to be quite accustomed to observers, due to the large amount of classroom observation done there by student teachers from a nearby university. Except for the senior author and teacher, other observers were not made aware of changes in experimental conditions. Reliability was assessed by comparing the behavior record forms of the teacher and observers after each class period in which both teacher and observers recorded behavior. A percentage of agreement for

Minute No.	1	2	3	4	5	6	7	8	9	10	11	12	13	14	15	16	17	18	19	20	21
Talking																					
Turning																					

FIGURE 1. Portion of behavior record form used to record incidence of target behavior.

each target behavior was computed, based on a ratio of the number of intervals on which all recorders agreed (i.e., that the behavior had or had not occurred) to the total number of intervals in the period. Average reliability for talking behavior was 90.49% in the experimental class (range 74 to 98%) and 89.49% in the control class (range 78 to 96%). Average reliability for turning behavior was 94.27% in the experimental class (range 87 to 98%) and 90.98% in the control class (range 85 to 96%).

In addition, two aspects of the teacher's behavior were recorded during all conditions by the observers when present: (a) the number of inappropriate talking or turning instances that occasioned a verbal reprimand from the teacher, and (b) the number of direct statements of praise dispensed by the teacher for appropriate behaviors. These behaviors were recorded by simply tallying the number of instances in which they were observed on the reverse side of the observer's form. Reliability between observers was checked by computing a percentage of agreement between them on the number of instances of each type of behavior observed. Average reliability for reprimand behavior was 92.78% in the experimental class (range 84 to 100%) and 94.84% in the control class (range 82 to 100%). Average reliability for praise behavior was 98.85% in the experimental class (range 83 to 100%) and 97.65% in the control class (range 81 to 100%).

Baseline Condition. During the Baseline Condition, the two target behaviors and teacher behaviors were recorded in both the experimental and control classes. The teacher was asked to behave in her usual manner in both classrooms and no restrictions were placed on any disciplinary techniques she wished to use. The Baseline Condition in the experimental class was continued for 27 class days (approximately five weeks) to obtain as clear a picture as possible of the student and teacher behaviors occurring.

Experimental Condition I. This first experimental condition began in the experimental class on the twenty-eighth day when the teacher initiated various social consequences contingent on inappropriate talking behavior aimed at lowering the amount of this behavior taking place. The procedures agreed upon with the teacher for the application of social consequences were as follows:

(1) The teacher was to attempt to disapprove of all instances of inappropriate talking behavior whenever they occurred with a direct, verbal sternly given reproof. Whenever possible, the teacher was to use students' names when correcting them. The teacher was instructed not to mention any other inappropriate behavior (e.g., turning around) that might also be occurring at the time. Examples of reprimands given were: "John, be quiet!", "Jane, stop talking!", "Phil, shut up!", "You people, be quiet!" It was hypothesized that these consequences constituted an aversive social consequence for inappropriate talking.

(2) The teacher was asked not to threaten students with or apply other consequences, such as keeping them after school, exclusion from class,

sending them to the Assistant Principal, etc. for inappropriate talking or for any other inappropriate behavior.

(3) The teacher was to praise the entire class in the form of remarks like: "Thank you for being quiet!", "Thank you for not talking!", or "I'm delighted to see you so quiet today!" according to the following contingencies: (a) During the first 2 min of class, praise at the end of approximately each 30-sec period in which there had been no inappropriate talking. (b) During the time in which a lecture, recitation, or class discussion was taking place, praise the class at the end of approximately each 15-min period in which no inappropriate talking had occurred. (c) When silent seatwork had been assigned, do not interrupt the period to praise, but praise the class at the end of the period if no inappropriate talking had occurred during the period. (d) At the end of each class make a summary statement concerning talking behavior, such as: "Thank you all for being so quiet today!", or "There has been entirely too much talking today, I'm disappointed in you!", or, "You have done pretty well in keeping quiet today, let's see if you can do better tomorrow!"

The concentration of praising instances during the first 2 min of class was scheduled because the baseline data revealed inappropriate talking as particularly frequent at this time.

Although the teacher continued to record instances of turning behavior, she was instructed to ignore this behavior in the experimental class during Experimental Condition I. In effect, baseline recording of turning behavior continued during this Condition. No changes were made in the teacher's behavior in the control class.

Experimental Condition II. After Experimental Condition I had been in effect in the experimental class for 26 class days and had markedly reduced talking behavior (see Results), Experimental Condition II was put into effect on the fifty-fourth day of the study. In this condition, the contingent social consequences for talking behavior in the experimental class were continued and, in addition, the teacher initiated the same system of contingent social consequences for turning behavior, with the aim of reducing the amount of this behavior occurring. This subsequent provision of similar consequences, first for one behavior and then for another, constitutes the multiple baseline technique.

The procedures agreed upon for providing reprimands for inappropriate turning behavior were the same as those for talking behaviors, except that the teacher referred to "turning" instead of "talking" in her reproofs. She could now also mention both behaviors in her reproof if a student happened to be doing both. The procedures regarding the application of praise contingent on not turning around were also the same as before, except that the higher frequency of praising during the first 2 min of class was not used. Also, the teacher could now combine her positive remarks about not talking and not turning if such were appropriate to existing conditions. Finally, since inappro-

STUDY 9

priate talking behavior had been reduced considerably by this time, the procedure of praising every 30 sec during the first 2 min of class was dropped. As before, no changes were made in the teacher's behavior in the control class.

RESULTS

Because data were not collected on individual students, it is not possible to specify exactly how many students were involved in either inappropriate talking or turning behavior. The observers and teacher agreed that over one-half of the students in both classes were involved in inappropriate talking behavior and that about one-third of the students in both classes were involved in inappropriate turning behavior.

Talking Behavior

Figure 2 indicates the daily percentages of intervals of inappropriate talking behavior in the experimental and control classes throughout the study. During the Baseline Condition in the experimental class and the equivalent period in the control class (Days 1 through 27), the average daily percentage of inappropriate talking intervals was 25.33% in the experimental class and

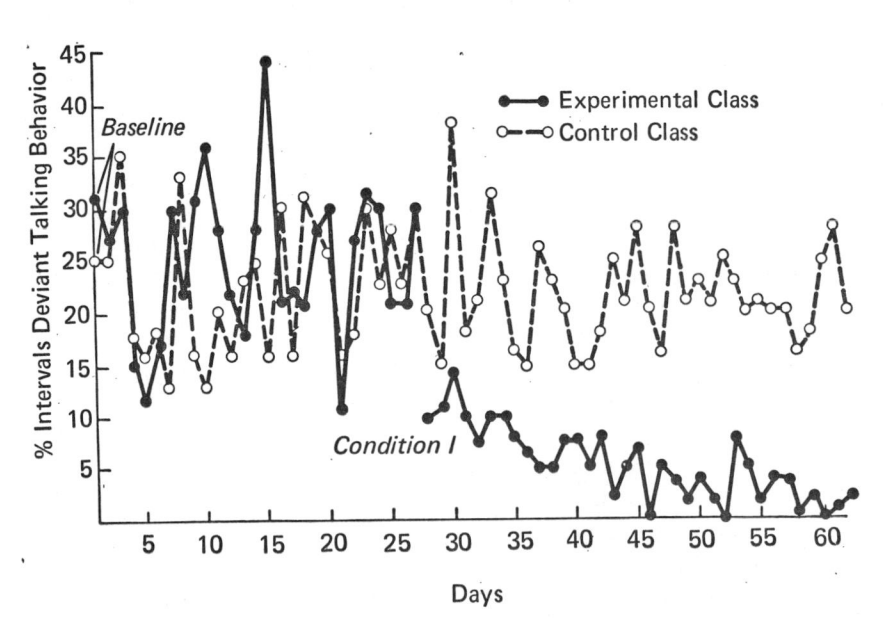

FIGURE 2. Daily percentages of intervals of inappropriate talking behavior in experimental and control classes during Baseline and Experimental Condition I periods.

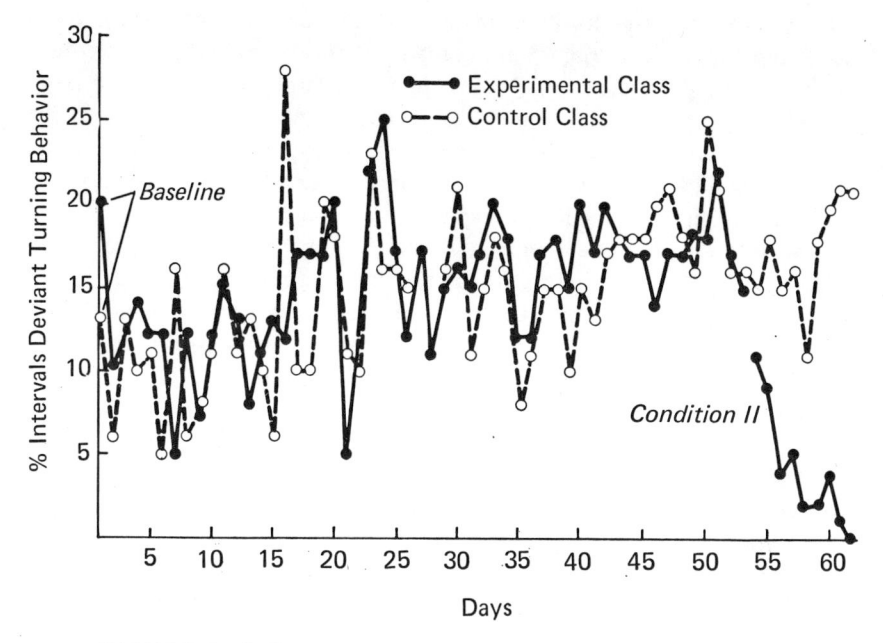

FIGURE 3. Daily percentages of intervals of inappropriate turning behavior in experimental and control classes during Baseline and Experimental Condition II periods.

22.81% in the control class. The two classes were thus approximately equivalent with respect to the amount of inappropriate talking behavior in each before the experimental interventions were made in the experimental class. As can be seen, the introduction of the contingencies in Experimental Condition I on Day 28 immediately reduced the percentage of intervals of inappropriate talking behavior in the experimental class. From this point on, the amount of inappropriate talking behavior in the experimental class continued to decrease and finally stabilized at a level below 5%. Meanwhile, the control class continued to manifest its previous level of inappropriate talking behavior. In the period from Day 28 through Day 62, when the study was concluded, the average daily percentage of inappropriate talking intervals in the control class was 21.51%, compared with an average of 5.34% in the experimental class.

Turning Behavior
The results obtained with the second target behavior, inappropriate turning around, can be seen in Fig. 3, which indicates the daily percentages of intervals of inappropriate turning behavior in both classes during the study. During the Baseline Condition in the experimental class and the equivalent period in the control class (Days 1 through 53), the level of inappropriate

turning behavior was slowly increasing in both classes. The average daily percentage of inappropriate turning intervals during this time was 15.13% in the experimental class and 14.45% in the control class. As with talking behavior, the two classes were roughly equivalent in the amount of inappropriate turning behavior observed before experimental interventions were made. The introduction of Experimental Condition II contingencies on Day 54 again immediately reduced the percentage of inappropriate turning intervals in the experimental class. This behavior continued to decrease during the remaining days of the study. In the control class, the level of inappropriate turning behavior remained essentially the same. In the period from Day 54 through Day 62, the average daily percentage of inappropriate turning intervals in the control class was 17.22% and in the experimental class was 4.11%.

Teacher Behavior
During the Baseline period on talking behavior, the average number of instances of inappropriate talking per class period that received some type of verbal reprimand from the teacher was 25.76% in the experimental class and 22.23% in the control class. The majority of these verbal responses took the form of saying, "Shhh!". On occasion, observers noted that the teacher corrected students directly, using their names. On several occasions she made general threats, stating that she would keep people after school if talking did not subside; however, she was never observed to carry out this kind of threat. During this period there were no observations of the teacher's dispensing any praise for not talking. During Experimental Condition I, the teacher disapproved of an average of 93.33% of inappropriate talking instances per class period in the experimental class. In the control class during this time, she disapproved of an average of 21.38% of inappropriate talking instances per class period. She also praised on an average of 6.07 occasions per experimental class period, contingent on not talking, during this time. With two exceptions, she was not observed directly to praise not talking in the control class.

During the Baseline period on inappropriate turning behavior, the average percentage of inappropriate turning instances per class period that received verbal reprimands from the teacher was 12.84% in the experimental class and 13.09% in the control class. Most of these were simple instructions, like "Turn around!", and she used the student's name in most cases. During Experimental Condition II, the average percentage of inappropriate turning instances per class period that occasioned disapproving responses from the teacher was 95.50% in the experimental class and 18.50% in the control class. In addition, she praised on an average of 5.75 occasions per experimental class period, contingent on not turning. In the control class she was not observed to provide any such praise for not turning.

DISCUSSION

The results indicate quite clearly that the statements of praise and disapproval by the teacher had consistent effects on the two target behaviors observed in the experimental class. Both behaviors decreased. That the statements were, in fact, responsible for the observed modifications in behavior was demonstrated through the multiple baseline procedure in which the target behaviors changed maximally only when the statements were applied. The use of the control class data further substantiates this contention. The observations of teacher behavior in the study provide evidence that the program was being carried out as specified in the two classrooms.

The design of the study does not make it possible to isolate the separate effects of the teacher's statements of praise and disapproval on the students' behaviors. It is possible that one or the other of these was more potent in achieving the observed results. In addition to the possibility that statements of praise or disapproval, in themselves, might have differed in their effectiveness in modifying behavior, the different manner in which these two types of statements were delivered may have resulted in differing effects. The design, it will be remembered, called for disapproving statements to be delivered to individual students, while praise was delivered to the class as a whole. This resulted in a sudden onset of numerous disapproving statements delivered to individual students when Experimental Condition I was put into effect. The observers agreed that the students seemed "stunned" when this essentially radical shift in stimulus conditions took place. The immediate and marked decrease in inappropriate talking behavior at this point may have resulted because of this shift. The phenomenon can be compared to the sudden response rate reductions observed in animals when stimulus conditions are shifted suddenly. The decrease in inappropriate turning behavior observed when Experimental Condition II was put into effect, while immediate, was not of the same magnitude as that observed previously. Perhaps some measure of adaptation to this type of stimulus shift had taken place. Regardless of the possible reasons for the immediate effects observed when the experimental conditions were put into effect, it is also true that the direction of these effects was maintained thereafter in both experimental conditions. The combination of praise and disapproval undoubtedly was responsible for this.

Assuming that praise statements were functioning as positive reinforcers for a majority of the experimental class, they may have operated not only directly to reinforce behaviors incompatible with inappropriate talking and turning but also to generate peer-group pressure to reduce inappropriate behavior because such statements were contingent on the entire class' behavior. Further studies are needed to investigate the effects of peer-group contingencies on individual behavior.

Although it appears that the statements of praise and disapproval by the teacher functioned as positive reinforcers and punishers, respectively, an alternative possibility exists. These statements may have been operating primarily as instructions that the students complied with. It is conceivable that had praise statements, for example, been delivered as instructions independent of the occurrence of inappropriate behavior the same results might have been obtained. Also, it should be noted that results obtained in other studies (Lovaas, Freitag, Kinder, Rubenstein, Schaeffer, and Simmons, 1964; Thomas, Becker, and Armstrong, 1968) indicate that disapproving adult behaviors do not have a unitary effect on children's behavior. What would appear to be punishing types of statements are sometimes found to function as positive reinforcers. Informal observations indicated that this seemed to be the case in this study, at least as far as one student was concerned.

Several comments may be made regarding the practical aspects of the present approach. The study further exemplifies the usefulness of the multiple baseline technique, which makes it unnecessary to reverse variables in order to demonstrate the specific effectiveness of the experimental variables. Many teachers and school administrators will undoubtedly find this approach more acceptable in their schools. The notion of reversing variables to reinstitute what is considered to be maladaptive or inappropriate behavior is extremely repugnant to many educators who are more interested in "getting results" than in experimental verification of the results obtained.

The study differs from most previous operant research in classrooms in that the focus was on recording and modifying target behaviors without specific regard to the individual students involved. Most earlier studies have focused on observing the behavior of one student at a time. With this approach, it takes considerable time to extend observations to an entire class and usually this is not done. While observations of an entire class are not always necessary from a practical point of view (i.e., only a few students are involved in inappropriate behaviors), the present approach does seem feasible when the number of students involved in one or more classes of inappropriate behavior is large. From an experimental point of view, this study was deficient in not providing more exact information as to the number of students actually involved in the target behaviors. Once this facet is determined, however, the essential approach seems quite feasible and practical.

It might be argued that a group-oriented approach will not function in the same way with all members of the group. This is potentially possible, if not probable. However, two practical aspects should be considered. In the first place, such an approach could conceivably remediate the total situation enough to allow the teacher to concentrate on those students who either have not responded or who have become worse. Secondly, perhaps a general reduction in inappropriate behavior is all the teacher desires. In this study, for example, the results obtained were, according to the teacher, more than enough to satisfy her. She did not, in other words, set a criterion of eliminating the target behaviors.

A significant practical aspect of this study was the amount of difficulty encountered by the teacher in recording behavior and delivering contingent praise and disapproval. It might be asked how she found time to teach when she was involved in these activities. Perhaps the best judge of the amount of difficulty involved with these techniques is the teacher herself. She reported that, initially, recording behaviors was difficult. The task did take considerable time and did interrupt her on-going teaching. On the other hand, the large amount of talking and other inappropriate behaviors occurring at the beginning of the study also interrupted her teaching. She felt that as the study went on she became more accustomed to recording and it became easier for her to accomplish. She pointed out that the fact that she usually positioned herself at her desk or rostrum also made recording somewhat easier because the forms were readily available. This was her usual position in the classroom; she did not change to make recording easier. Considerable time was required to deliver contingent praise and disapproval at the beginning of the experimental conditions. This also tended to interrupt teaching tasks as far as the teacher was concerned. However, she felt that this state of affairs did not last long because the target behaviors declined so immediately and rapidly. The overall judgment of the teacher was that the procedures of recording and dispensing contingent consequences did, indeed, interfere with her teaching but that the results obtained more than compensated for this. When the levels of inappropriate behavior had been lowered she felt she could carry out her teaching responsibilities much more efficiently and effectively than before. She felt strongly enough about the practicality and effectiveness of the techniques to present information and data on the study to her fellow teachers and to offer her services as a consultant to those who wanted to try similar approaches in their classrooms.

The senior author held frequent conferences with the teacher after class periods. The aim was to provide her with feedback regarding her performance in class. She was actively praised for appropriate modifications in her classroom behavior and for record-keeping behavior. Likewise, she was criticized for mistakes in her application of program contingencies.

Finally, the data of this experiment are considered significant by reason of the strong implication that teacher praise and disapproval can function to modify the behavior of high-school level students. This potentially extends the implications of earlier research accomplished on the pre-school and elementary levels.

REFERENCES

Baer, D. M., Wolf, M. M., and Risley, T. R. "Some Current Dimensions of Applied Behavior Analysis." *Journal of Applied Behavior Analysis,* 1968, **1,** 91–97.

Becker, W. C., Madsen, C. H., Jr., Arnold, C. R., and Thomas, D. R. "The Contingent Use of Teacher Attention and Praise in Reducing Classroom Behavior Problems." *Journal of Special Education,* 1967, **1,** 287–307.

Bushell, D., Jr., Wrobel, P. A., and Michaelis, M. I. "Applying Group Contingencies to the Classroom Study Behavior of Preschool Children." *Journal of Applied Behavior Analysis,* 1968, **1,** 55–61.

Cohen, H. L., Filipczak, J., and Bis, J. S. *Case I: An Initial Study of Contingencies Applicable to Special Education.* Silver Spring, Md.: Educational Facility Press—Institute for Behavioral Research, 1967.

Hall, R. V. and Broden, M. "Behavior Changes in Brain-Injured Children Through Social Reinforcement." *Journal of Experimental Child Psychology.* 1967, **5,** 463–79.

Hall, R. V., Lund, D., and Jackson, D. "Effects of Teacher Attention on Study Behavior." *Journal of Applied Behavior Analysis,* 1968, **1,** 1–12.

Harris, F. R., Wolf, M. M., and Baer, D. M. "Effects of Adult Social Reinforcement on Child Behavior." *Young Children,* 1964, **20,** 8–17.

Lovaas, O. L., Freitag, G., Kinder, M. I., Rubenstein, D. B., Schaeffer, B., and Simmons, J. B. *Experimental Studies in Childhood Schizophrenia—Establishment of Social Reinforcers.* Paper read at Western Psychological Association, Portland, April 1964.

Madsen, C. H., Becker, W. C., and Thomas, D. R. "Rules, Praise, and Ignoring: Elements of Elementary Classroom Control." *Journal of Applied Behavior Analysis,* 1968, **1,** 139–50.

Patterson, G. R. "An Application of Conditioning Techniques to the Control of a Hyperactive Child." In I. P. Ullman and L. Krasner (eds.), *Case Studies in Behavior Modification.* New York: Holt, Rinehart and Winston, 1966, pp. 37–75.

Rabb, E., and Hewett, F. M. "Developing Appropriate Classroom Behaviors in a Severely Disturbed Group of Institutionalized Kindergarten-Primary Children Utilizing a Behavior Modification Model." *American Journal of Orthopsychiatry,* 1967, **37,** 313–14.

Thomas, D. R., Becker, W. C., and Armstrong, M. "Production and Elimination of Disruptive Classroom Behavior by Systematically Varying Teacher's Behavior." *Journal of Applied Behavior Analysis,* 1968, **1,** 35–45.

Zimmerman, E. H., and Zimmerman, J. "The Alteration of Behavior in a Special Classroom Situation." *Journal of the Experimental Analysis of Behavior,* 1962, **5,** 59–60.

ANALYSIS OF STUDY 9

This study is representative of a growing movement on the part of educational researchers to take their experimentation into the settings in which educational changes must be applied. The theory, as we have pointed out, has been one of the major means for understanding human behavior, especially learning, and the subject of much long term basic research. Yet this experiment was more a test of the applicability of the theory to a particular classroom setting and an educational problem than a test of the validity of the theory itself. The authors begin with references to previous research which substantiates the claim that behavior can be modified in the classroom through the application of operant conditioning techniques. Their experiment was an effort to establish the efficacy of this technique with older learners and with an entire classroom rather than one or two individuals.

Let us look first at the experimental methodology. The basic design, as described by the authors, utilized a control group and pretest and posttest measures—a non-equivalent control group design—although the groups were not equated in any way through random selection. Since the behavior to be altered was social behavior in the classroom, ability variables would have less of an effect and be less important to control than in typical learning experiments.

There are some other factors in the design of this experiment that make a rigorous sampling procedure relatively unnecessary. Each group served as its own control through the multiple baseline technique, i.e., the incidence of target behaviors was established before any experimental manipulation was undertaken. Following the experimental manipulation, observations of the target behaviors would be compared to the baseline, and any change or lack of change would be relative to that baseline. This was the pre- and posttest aspect of the design. The control group was essential to establish that the altered behavior of the teacher was the main factor in the changed classroom behavior, not some unaccounted for variable.

The difference between a laboratory setting and a field setting is quite clear at this point. Had there been full laboratory control, the experimenter would have chosen his two groups randomly from among all juniors and seniors and then varied the treatment. In the field setting there were only intact classes to work with. This difference may mean that the field setting study will have more confounding variables to contend with, but if the experimental effect can be demonstrated in this setting, the utility of the approach is given more credence.

The experiment, then, consisted in measuring the behavior before the experiment, changing conditions for one group and not the other, and measuring the behavior of both groups after the changed conditions to see if there was changed behavior in the experimental group compared both to its earlier behavior and to the behavior of the control group.

Interestingly enough, no statistical test of significance was applied to these results. A simple nonparametric test could have been employed. But the observed differences in behavior before and after the experimental treatment appear to constitute a real, not a chance, difference.

The discussion part of this research should be read carefully, for the *authors pose a number of unanswered questions arising from their research and add some explanatory comments on aspects of the study that many readers may have questioned as they read the report. Chief among these questions is: How does the teacher teach and record observed behavior at the same time, as well as consciously alter her own behavior as teacher in the experimental group?*

Since our concern in this book is with developing an understanding of research as a process, this is not the place to argue the merits of the basic theory of operant conditioning. B. F. Skinner sets forth his own major arguments in his book Beyond Freedom and Dignity (Knopf, 1971) for accepting the environment as the only determinant of our behavior and altering our environment as the way to change behavior. There is plenty of literature that argues against that point of view.

What does seem inescapable is that operant conditioning is at least one easily demonstrable way of changing the behavior of people and of changing behavior that follows from Skinner's theory and research. Our position is that Skinner's theory is not comprehensive enough to account for the full range of human behavior, but it does account for a good deal, and we now know enough about how to apply his theory to begin using it to improve education and to foster greater growth on the part of students.

Experiments such as this one are significant in advancing the process of change in education and in providing solutions to many practical problems of classroom management and improving the learning environment.

INTRODUCTION TO STUDY 10

This experimental study moves into a realm quite different from the previous studies. It deals directly with ideology and the effect of ideology on behavior. In this case the ideology was the belief system of teachers and the behavior was the teacher's instructional behavior. This experiment also moves outside both the laboratory and the simulated classroom. The data were gathered from careful observations of teachers functioning in the classroom setting during a regular instructional period of time.

The study raises a number of interesting questions of the kind that foster expanded thinking about educational problems. If you are a teacher you will find yourself somewhere in this study, and, if you are willing to let it happen, you may discover some good ideas about teaching or at least some things to think about with regard to teaching.

Study 10

Teachers' Belief Systems and Preschool Atmospheres[1]

O. J. HARVEY
B. J. WHITE
M. S. PRATHER
R. D. ALTER
J. K. HOFFMEISTER

Teachers differing in the concreteness-abstractness of their belief or personality systems should also differ in the goals, social milieu, and behavior they seek for and from their students and hence, knowingly or unknowingly in the values and content they communicate, in their styles of communication, and in their reactions to student adherence to or departure from the standards embodied in their beliefs. Because concreteness disposes towards more fixed and categorical belief systems (Harvey, 1966; White & Harvey, 1965), toward an authority orientation rather than a task orientation (Harvey, 1966; Tiemann, 1965), and toward seeking a simple and highly structured environment (Harvey, 1965; Ware & Harvey, in press), more concrete teachers, to a greater extent than more abstract teachers, should impose predetermined

Reprinted by permission from *Journal of Educational Psychology,* 57, 6, December 1966, 373–81. Copyright 1966 by The American Psychological Association.

STUDY 10

goals upon the students, provide structure and detailed means for their attainment, be less tolerant of student deviation from their goals and standards, and, consequently, react more strongly and invariantly to such deviation. A test of some of the more specific aspects of this general hypothesis was the purpose of this study.

METHOD

Head Start teachers differing in concreteness-abstractness according to two different measures were rated on 26 dimensions assumed to reflect educationally desirable and undesirable behavior toward their preschool students. The rating categories were (1) expression of warmth toward the children, (2) perceptiveness of the children's wishes and needs, (3) flexibility in meeting the needs and interest of the children, (4) ability to maintain relaxed relationships with the children, (5) attention to the individual child, (6) task involvement, (7) enjoyment of teaching, (8) enlistment of child participation, (9) encouragement of individual responsibility, (10) encouragement of free expression of feelings, (11) encouragement of creativity, (12) teaching new concepts, (13) ingenuity in improvising teaching and play materials, (14) utilization of physical resources, (15) task effectiveness, (16) diversity of activities simultaneously permitted, (17) smoothness of classroom operation (especially in the transition from one activity to another), 18) consistency of rule enforcement, (19) use of functional explanation of rules, (20) use of nonfunctional explanation of rules, (21) use of unexplained rules, (22) rule orientation, (23) determination of classroom and playground procedure, (24) need for structure in teaching activities and relationships with children, (25) punitiveness, and (26) anxiety induced by the observers' presence.

It was anticipated that the more abstract subjects (Ss) would score higher than the more concrete Ss on dimensions 1–19 and lower than more concrete Ss on dimensions 20–26.

Subject Selection

Teachers were selected for subsequent observation on the basis of their responses to the "This I Believe" (TIB) Test scored according to conceptual systems.

The TIB, developed specifically as a measure of conceptual or belief systems (e.g., Harvey, 1964, 1965, 1966; White & Harvey, 1965), requests S to indicate his beliefs about a number of socially and personally significant concept referents by completing in two or three sentences the phrase, "This I believe about ____," the blank being replaced successively by one of the referents. The referents employed in the present study were comprised of "religion," "friendship," "the American way of life," "sin," "education," "the family," "people on welfare," "punishment," "teaching," and "sex";

the last six substituted for the more standard referents with the aim of insuring their specific relevance to the Ss and to the task of teaching in the Head Start Program.

From the relativism, tautologicalness, novelty, and connotative implications or richness of the completions, together with criteria implied below, respondents may be classified into one of the four principal belief systems posited by Harvey, Hunt, and Schroder (1961) or into some admixture of two or more systems.

More specifically, Ss were classified as representing *predominantly* System 1, the most concrete mode of dimensionalizing and construing the world, if their sentence completions denote such characteristics as high absolutism, high tautologicalness, high frequency of platitudes and normative statements, high ethnocentrism, high religiosity, assertion of the superioty of American morality, and expression of highly positive attitudes toward institutional referents.

The Ss were categorized as representing System 2, the next to the lowest level of abstractness if, in addition to being highly evaluative and absolutistic, they expressed strong *negative* attitudes toward such referents as marriage, religion, and the American way of life, the same referents toward which System 1 representatives manifest highly *positive* attitudes.

Responses to the TIB were scored as representing System 3 functioning, the next to the highest level of abstractness posited by Harvey et al. (1961), if they indicated more relativism and less evaluativeness than Systems 1 and 2 and at the same time expressed strongly positive beliefs about friendship, people, and interpersonal relations.

System 4 functioning, the highest of the four levels of abstractness, was indicated by TIB responses that implied a high degree of novelty *and* appropriateness, independence without negativism, high relativism and contingency of thought, and the general usage of multidimensional rather than unidimensional interpretive categories.

The TIB was administered to the 168 teachers participating in the Head Start training program conducted by the University of Colorado Extension Division during the summer of 1965. From among this number, no instances of System 2, the anti-authority orientation, and only 10 cases of System 4 functioning were found. Ten Ss each from System 1 and 3, selected from a somewhat larger subpopulation of representatives of these systems, were added to the 10 System 4 representatives, for a total of 30 experimental Ss, all women.

An Additional Measure of Concreteness-Abstractness

In addition to the TIB, Ss completed an objective measure of concreteness-abstractness, the Conceptual Systems Test (CST), which was developed through Tryon's cluster and factor analysis (Tryon & Bailey, 1965[2]). Four factors were found which are theoretically consistent with the major characteristics of the four principal conceptual systems or levels of concreteness-abstractness posited by Harvey et al. (1961). These factors, as we have tentatively labeled them, together with some of their representative items, are:

1. *Divine fate control or religious fundamentalism.* This is assessed by such items as "There are some things which God will never permit man to know," "In the final analysis, events in the world will be in line with the master plan of God," and "I believe that to attain my goals it is only necessary for me to live as God would have me live."

2. *Need for certainty or simplicity* is expressed in response to such statements as "I prefer a story that has two themes rather than one that has five or six themes going at once," "People who seem unsure and uncertain about things make me feel uncomfortable," and "The effective person is one who does not hold conflicting beliefs."

3. *Tolerance of complexity and uncertainty* is based on such items as "I have so much trouble finding out what is or is not true that I can't understand how some people can feel so certain that they know the truth," "More often than not, I like some aspects of a person and do not like other aspects of him," and "I find that I cannot help analyzing almost everything I see and hear."

4. *Relativism of truth* is measured by such items as "There can be as many truths as there are individual points of view," "Man is the judge of the truth or untruth of his thoughts and behavior," and "Something is true or untrue depending on one's assumptions and the context."

Of the several ways these factors may be scored, the one utilized for this report was the overall abstractness score, represented by the sum of the item responses on a six-point scale (from "Completely disagree" to "Completely agree") across the four factors.

Subjects

Ten representatives each of System 1, 3, and 4, as selected by the TIB, served as the experimental Ss. The mean score of each system on the CST, the second measure of abstractness, was: System 1, 2.98; System 3, 3.43; and System 4, 4.35. According to t tests, each system differed significantly from each of the others ($p < .05$ for all comparisons).

All Ss had had prior teaching experience, System 1 teachers having taught on the average almost twice as long (10.1 years) as teachers from System 3 (5.8 years) or System 4 (5.4 years). However, only one System 1, two System 3 and three System 4 teachers had taught previously at the preschool level. All Ss participated in a common 1-week training program for Head Start teachers shortly before beginning their teaching of Head Start enrollees.

The geographic locations where the Ss were teaching and were observed ranged from urban housing projects to small towns which served predominantly rural children in their Head Start programs. In an attempt to control for the influence of different administrative structures and physical facilities upon the teachers' classroom behavior, an equal number of teachers of each belief system was selected from a common administration and a common building whenever possible. In the three instances in which representatives of the three belief systems could not be obtained from the same program, a teacher was selected from an alternate program that served children comparable in socioeconomic backgrounds to the children being taught by teachers of the other two belief systems.

The Rating Scale
Teachers were rated on the 26 behavioral dimensions (listed earlier) which had been selected primarily to reflect differences in the extent to which the teacher fostered independence, creativity, diversity of interests, enjoyment, and intrinsic motivation among her students, ends which would be desirable among most educators of today.

Each of the behavioral dimensions was rated on a six-point scale: 3, 2, and 1 for "far," "considerably," and "slightly" above average respectively; and −1, −2, and −3 for "slightly," "considerably," and "far" below average respectively. The "average" category was omitted with the aim (by creating a forced choice condition) of avoiding the common tendency of observers (Os) to assign a wide variety of discriminably different behaviors to this category. Through a training program described below, an attempt was made to establish equivalent "averages" for all Os.

To encourage specificity of ratings, the rating scale provided space for each behavioral dimension to be rated under each of the school activities of free play, directed play, reading and/or story telling, formal instruction, outdoor activity, snack time, and cleanup activity. Owing to variation in their schedules and practices, many teachers were rated in relation to different activities, no teacher being rated for all activities. In addition to each S being rated on the 26 dimensions for as many of the activities as occurred during the observation period, she was also assigned an overall rating on each dimension by each O. An overall rating, instead of being the arithmetic average of the multiple ratings of a dimension under the different activities, represented the overall impression of an O for that dimension based on his interpretation of his specific ratings together with unrated behavior he may have observed or other impressions he may have gathered. In some instances the overall rating of a dimension would closely parallel the arithmetic average of ratings on that dimension and in other instances it would not. All statistical analyses were based on the overall ratings.

Training of Observers and Assessment of Interobserver Reliability
Each O participated in seven training sessions during which seven teachers representing Systems 1, 3, and 4 or admixtures thereof were observed and

independently rated. Each observation session was followed by lengthy group discussion among the *O*s and other staff members aimed at increasing the reliability of the ratings through improving observation techniques and clarifying and standardizing meaning and usage of the rating categories.

Interjudge reliability for the 14 *O*s was assessed at two points, immediately following the last training session and immediately after completion of the experimental observations, 3 weeks later. The mean of the correlations between the ratings of every pair of judges, based both times on observations of a System 3 teacher, was .69 and .68 for the earlier and later time respectively, values which, while lower than the ideal, are as high as could be expected given the number and diversity of *O*s.

Procedure

Each *S* was observed for approximately 2½ hours by two *O*s on two occasions 1 week apart. The administrator of each Head Start program was asked to give the teachers advance notice of the dates they were to be observed; this was done in all but two instances.

The *O*s, in pairs, arrived before class began, introduced themselves, explained (with the aim of allaying the teacher's apprehension and fostering her cooperation) that the purpose of their visit was to gather examples of good teaching procedures which could be utilized as bases for subsequent training programs for Head Start teachers, and requested that they be allowed to observe but to remain as unobtrusive as possible in order to minimize the effects of their presence upon the children. To further *O*s' unobtrusiveness and simultaneously to increase the likelihood of an *S* following her planned program and, in so doing, emitting somewhat typical teaching behavior, each *S* was asked specifically not to converse with the *O*s during the class period.

The observations took place during normal classroom and playground activities on days free of special events in order to render the conditions of observations as comparable as possible for all *S*s. As a further effort toward maximizing the comparability of the judgments, each pair of *O*s was instructed to remain in the same vicinity at all times so that both would witness the same behavior of a teacher.

During the observation period *O*s independently rated *S* on all of the 26 dimensions under each of the activities that occurred during the period. Following the observation period, *O*s independently rated their overall impression of the *S* on each of the behavioral categories. Ratings were subsequently compared and discussed by each pair of *O*s and under the *single* condition where disagreement was found to exist due to different usage of the rating scale, but for no other reason, either *O* was free to make changes in his ratings. The purpose of this rather unorthodox procedure was to insure that *O*s were defining the rating categories in similar ways and in so doing to control for the variance that would otherwise result from difference in scale usage. This procedure was based on findings from two earlier studies (Harvey,

1963; Harvey & Kline, 1965) that postobservation reviews of their ratings by Os effectively counteracted their tendencies to drift away from the original criteria with the passage of time and the accumulation of experience. To avoid biasing the Os who were to observe the S on the second occasion, discussion concerning any S was restricted to the pair of Os who had observed her together.

Any O bias was further controlled and other desired experimental controls achieved through the policies of no O being paired with any other O more than once and no S being observed by the same O more than once. Any S bias resulting from spread of information about the study from one teacher to another was minimized by the procedure of observing on the same day all teachers who were within the same school system.

All Os made their observations and ratings without any knowledge of the system classification of the teacher. Moreover, in order to prevent the Os from establishing particular sets and expectancies from repeated observation of Ss from any one belief system, each O observed a different random order of representatives of the three belief groupings.

RESULTS

Relationships among the Rating Dimensions

The relationships among the rating dimensions were determined by a Tryon cluster analysis (Tryon & Bailey, 1965, 1966) based on the summed overall ratings of each of the 26 dimensions across the 30 teachers and the four judges. Interdimension correlations ranged from .86 to −.90, with a median correlation, without regard to sign, of .53. Fifty-five of the 325 values attained a magnitude of + or − .70 or above and all but one of these were accounted for by the interrelatedness among 15 items which cohered into one of two major clusters.

The first cluster, which may be termed *dictatorialness,* was comprised of 10 rating items. They and their factor loadings were: need for structure (.97), flexibility (−.91), rule orientation (.89), encouragement of free expression of feelings (−.86), determination of procedure (.86), use of unexplained rules (.84), punitiveness (.82), encouragement of creativity (−.78), diversity of simultaneous activities (−.77) and encouragement of individual responsibility (−.71).

The second cluster, which centered around *task orientation,* consisted of five items with factor loadings as indicated: warmth (.89), perceptiveness (.88), task effectiveness (.77), utilization of physical resources (.72), and ingenuity in improvising teaching and play materials (.65).

With the exception of the correlation between anxiety induced by judges' presence and relaxed relationships with the children, none of the correlations among the 11 dimensions not included in one of the two major factors attained the magnitude of + or − .70. Hence, while more than half of the rating items represented different ways of tapping either of two common behavior patterns, some of the items reflected fairly independent teacher behavior.

System Differences
Performance on specific dimensions. According to the hypothesis, System 4 Ss, as classified by the TIB, should score higher than System 1 Ss on dimensions 1–19 and lower than System 1 teachers on dimensions 20–26. A corollary hypothesis was that System 3 teachers would score between Systems 1 and 4 on all 26 dimensions.

The mean and standard deviation of the overall ratings of each system on each dimension are presented in Table 1. All values are based on the ratings of four Os owing to the results of a preliminary analysis of variance which showed that no significant differences existed between the ratings of the teachers at Time 1 and Time 2.

Results in Table 1 show the predicted differences between Systems 1 and 4 on all 26 dimensions. In further accord with the predictions, System 3 Ss scored between Systems 1 and 4 on 23 of the 26 items. Page's (1963) test for ordered hypotheses for multiple treatments, a test for predictions of order and not of magnitude, showed that the number of dimensions on which the predicted ordering of systems was obtained was highly significant ($M = 26$, $N = 3$, $L = 361$, $P < .001$).

While no predictions were made concerning the magnitude of differences between systems on any specific dimension, a test of significance of magnitudes would yield additional relevant information. One-tailed t tests between systems on overall ratings indicated, on the basis of 18 degrees of freedom, that System 1 and 4 teachers differed significantly on 14 dimensions (Table 2). System 4 teachers expressed greater warmth toward the children, showed greater perceptiveness of the children's wishes and needs, were more flexible in meeting the interests and needs of the children, maintained more relaxed relationships with the children, were more encouraging of individual responsibility, gave greater encouragement to free expression of feelings, were more encouraging of creativity, displayed greater ingenuity in improvising teaching and play materials, invoked unexplained rules less frequently, were less rule oriented, were less determining of classroom and playground procedure, manifested less need for structure, were less punitive, and were less anxious about Os' presence.

System 3 teachers differed significantly from System 1 Ss on eight dimensions. The former were more flexible in meeting the needs and interests of the children, were more encouraging of individual responsibility, were more task effective, permitted greater diversity of activities, invoked unexplained rules less frequently, were less rule oriented, manifested less need for structure, and were less punitive.

TABLE 1. Mean and Standard Deviation for Ratings of Each System as Measured by the This I Believe Test

Rating Dimension	System 1 M	System 1 SD	System 3 M	System 3 SD	System 4 M	System 4 SD
1. Warmth	3.65	0.49	3.97	1.07	4.27	1.03
2. Perceptiveness	3.38	0.71	3.90	0.86	4.15	1.02
3. Flexibility	3.30	0.69	3.97	0.85	4.20	0.97
4. Relaxed	4.13	0.68	4.50	0.60	4.72	0.32
5. Attention to individual	3.67	0.60	4.10	0.80	4.00	0.87
6. Involvement	3.90	0.78	4.13	0.84	4.15	0.87
7. Enjoyment	3.67	0.51	4.02	0.53	4.13	0.97
8. Enlistment child participation	4.25	0.35	4.25	0.87	4.32	0.79
9. Encourage individual responsibility	3.63	0.53	4.17	0.67	4.25	0.94
10. Encourage expression of feelings	3.47	0.55	3.92	0.65	4.20	0.92
11. Encourage creativity	3.15	0.49	3.65	0.82	3.82	1.05
12. Teach new concepts	3.95	0.78	4.05	0.59	4.32	1.14
13. Ingenuity	3.30	0.64	3.85	0.88	4.27	0.73
14. Utilization of resources	3.92	0.69	4.15	0.56	4.50	0.80
15. Task effectiveness	3.82	0.44	4.22	0.48	4.35	1.06
16. Diversity of activity	3.52	0.69	4.00	0.50	4.05	1.02
17. Smoothness	3.85	0.77	4.02	0.53	4.15	0.65
18. Consistency	3.95	0.57	4.02	0.55	4.07	0.50
19. Functional explan. rules	3.38	0.66	3.85	0.74	3.77	0.72
20. Nonfunctional explan.	3.02	0.71	2.97	0.61	2.88	0.32
21. Unexplained rules	3.90	0.77	3.30	0.60	3.05	0.84
22. Rule orientation	4.47	0.76	3.70	0.87	3.20	0.91
23. Determination of procedure	4.40	0.94	4.25	0.68	3.63	0.79
24. Need for structure	4.45	1.00	3.67	0.93	3.13	1.05
25. Punitiveness	3.57	0.90	2.90	0.64	2.50	0.78
26. Anxiety	3.27	0.92	2.77	0.82	2.60	0.43

Note.—N = 10 for each system.

System 3 and System 4 Ss differed significantly only on one dimension; the latter were significantly less determining of the classroom and playground procedures.

Dictatorialness and task orientation. The differences on the specific behavioral dimensions may be summarized and highlighted by a between-

TABLE 2. *t* Tests between Ratings of Systems as Measured by the This I Believe Test

Rating dimension	System 1–3	System 1–4	System 3–4
1. Warmth	−.87	−1.73*	−.64
2. Perceptiveness	−1.49	−1.98*	−.59
3. Flexibility	−1.95*	−2.40**	−.55
4. Relaxed	−1.31	−2.52**	−1.04
5. Attention to individual	−1.34	−.97	.27
6. Involvement	−.62	−.68	−.07
7. Enjoyment	−1.49	−1.30	−.29
8. Enlistment child participation	.00	−.27	−.20
9. Encourage individual responsibility	−2.04*	−1.83*	−.21
10. Encourage expression of feelings	−1.68	−2.15**	−.77
11. Encourage creativity	−1.66	−1.85*	−.42
12. Teach new concepts	−.32	−.86	−.68
13. Ingenuity	−1.59	−3.17***	−1.17
14. Utilization of resources	−.80	−1.72	−1.14
15. Task effectiveness	−1.94*	−1.45	−.34
16. Diversity of activity	−1.76*	−1.35	−.14
17. Smoothness	−.59	−.94	−.47
18. Consistency	−.30	−.52	−.21
19. Functional explan. rules	−1.52	−1.29	.23
20. Nonfunctional explan.	.17	.61	.46
21. Unexplained rules	1.94*	2.35**	.77
22. Rule orientation	2.12**	3.40**	1.25
23. Determination procedure	.41	2.00*	1.90*
24. Need for structure	1.80*	2.89***	1.24
25. Punitiveness	1.94*	2.86**	1.25
26. Anxiety	1.29	2.11**	.60

*p = .05 or < .05, 18 *df*, one-tailed.
**p = < .025, 18 *df*, one-tailed.
***p < .005, 18 *df*, one-tailed.

systems comparison on the two major factors extracted from the rating dimensions. With the exception of relaxed relationships with the children and anxiety from Os' presence, all of the specific dimensions on which Systems 1 and 4 differed significantly were contained within either the factor of dictatorialness or task orientation.

The scores on dictatorialness were 3.88, 3.32, and 3.00 for Systems 1, 3, and 4 respectively; and 3.62, 4.02, and 4.31 on task orientation. System 1 teachers were significantly more dictatorial than representatives of either System 3 ($t = 2.17, p < .025$) or System 4 ($t = 2.92, p < .005$) and at the same time significantly less task oriented than teachers from System 3 ($t = 1.73, p < .05$) or System 4 ($t = 2.42, p < .025$). There were no significant differences between Systems 3 and 4 on either factor, although System 3 teachers tended to be somewhat more dictatorial and less task oriented.

Differences betwen Levels of Abstractness Derived from the CST.

The abstractness scores from the CST were divided into three levels of High, Middle, and Low, 10 scores in each group, and t tests were computed between the means of the two extreme groups for each of the 26 teacher behavior dimensions.

Results in Table 3 show that on all but four of the 26 dimensions (enlistment of child participation, teaching new concepts, smoothness of operations, and consistency of rule enforcement) the High-Abstract teachers out-performed the Low-Abstract teachers. In further support of the hypothesis, the Middle-Abstract group was rated more favorably than the Low-Abstract group, but less favorably than the High-Abstract group, on 20 of the 26 dimensions. Page's (1963) test showed the frequency of predicted orderings to be significant ($M = 26, N = 3, L = 341, p < .001$).

While the number of predicted orderings was significant, the magnitude of the difference between the three CST levels, as assessed by t tests, attained significance in only five of the 78 comparisons, a frequency that departs only slightly from chance. Hence none of these t values is reported.

Abstractness scores from the CST correlated .30 ($p < .05$) with both dictatorialness and task orientation, meaning, because of the direction of scoring, that higher abstractness accompanied the tendency to be less dictatorial and more task oriented in the teaching of the Head Start children.

DISCUSSION

The results are consistent in showing that the more abstract teachers differ from the more concrete Ss in their teaching approaches and in the classroom atmospheres they generated for their Head Start students. Two important factors, the selective process inherent in the choice of becoming a Head Start teacher and the 1-week training program in which all teachers participated,

STUDY 10

TABLE 3. Mean and Standard Deviation for Ratings of Low, Middle, and High Abstract Teachers as Measured by the Conceptual Systems Test

Rating dimension	Low M	Low SD	Middle M	Middle SD	High M	High SD
1. Warmth	3.62	0.84	4.10	0.70	4.17	1.13
2. Perceptiveness	3.50	0.81	3.90	0.78	4.02	1.09
3. Flexibility	3.52	0.92	3.90	0.67	4.05	1.08
4. Relaxed	4.28	0.71	4.62	0.50	4.45	0.55
5. Attention to individual	3.78	0.56	3.98	0.88	4.02	0.87
6. Involvement	3.92	0.86	4.05	0.68	4.20	0.93
7. Enjoyment	3.78	0.65	4.00	0.50	4.05	0.94
8. Enlistment child participation	4.38	0.48	4.35	0.83	4.10	0.74
9. Encourage individual responsibility	3.98	0.64	4.00	0.76	4.08	0.94
10. Encourage expression of feelings	3.75	0.69	3.95	0.66	3.90	0.97
11. Encourage creativity	3.20	0.52	3.62	0.76	3.80	1.10
12. Teach new concepts	4.38	0.83	3.92	0.66	4.02	1.05
13. Ingenuity	3.20	0.55	3.80	0.82	4.42	0.68
14. Utilization of resources	3.88	0.72	4.42	0.43	4.28	0.85
15. Task effectiveness	4.02	0.60	4.08	0.59	4.30	0.98
16. Diversity of activity	3.50	0.66	4.05	0.64	4.02	0.95
17. Smoothness	4.15	0.76	3.80	0.63	4.08	0.55
18. Consistency	4.15	0.50	4.10	0.59	3.80	0.45
19. Functional explanation of rules	3.80	0.58	3.60	0.73	3.60	0.87
20. Nonfunctional explanation	3.15	0.76	2.95	0.35	2.78	0.46
21. Unexplained rules	3.70	0.82	3.22	0.80	3.32	0.80
22. Rule orientation	4.22	1.23	3.65	0.79	3.50	0.79
23. Determination procedure	4.40	0.86	4.12	0.92	3.75	0.73
24. Need for structure	4.15	1.19	3.70	0.98	3.40	1.10
25. Punitiveness	3.20	1.12	2.90	0.75	2.88	0.77
26. Anxiety	3.10	0.85	2.80	0.87	2.75	0.63

Note.—*N* = 10 for each group.

should have operated to produce greater similarities in teaching styles and behavior toward children among our *S*s than exist among teachers selected randomly from the different belief systems and/or levels of abstractness. Despite this, the more abstract teachers in this study were clearly superior to the more concrete teachers in the extent to which they produced what are presumed to be educationally desirable atmospheres in their classrooms. Moreover, this superiority existed despite, or possibly because of, the greater teaching experience of the System 1 Ss.

We can only conjecture at this point on the differential effect of the different atmospheres, and hence of teacher differences in concreteness-abstractness, upon the learning and behavior of the children. The answer to this, a truly significant educational question, can come only from study of the children who have been taught by teachers differing in abstractness.

Although both the TIB and CST predicted significantly differential performance in the classroom, the results point clearly to the greater superiority of the TIB. It is possible that this superiority may be reduced or eliminated by a different scoring method of the CST now being tested, one which is based on a profile of factors and categorizing of Ss into profile groupings rather than on any single factor or summation of factors.

ENDNOTES

1. This study was supported by the Head Start Program, Office of Economic Opportunity, under Contract OEO-517 with the University of Colorado Extension Division. This study in whole or part may be used for any purposes of the United States Government. We wish to express our thanks to OEO and Project Head Start for their support, to the many observers for their conscientious effort in collecting the data and to the teachers in and directors of Head Start Programs that permitted us to visit their schools and observe their teaching.

2. R. C. Tryon and D. E. Bailey, "The B. C. Try System of Cluster and Factor Analysis: Multivariate Behavioral Research," in preparation.

REFERENCES

Harvey, O. J. "Cognitive Determinants of Role Playing." Technical Report No. 3, University of Colorado, Contract Nonr 1147(07), 1963.

Harvey, O. J. "Some Cognitive Determinants of Influencibility." *Sociometry*, 1964, **27**, 208–21.

Harvey, O. J. "Some Situational and Cognitive Determinants of Dissonance Resolution." *Journal of Personality and Social Psychology*, 1965, **1**, 349–55.

Harvey, O. J. "System Structure, Flexibility and Creativity." In O. J. Harvey (ed.) *Experience, structure and adaptability*. New York: Springer, 1966.

Harvey, O. J., Hunt, D. E., & Schroder, H. M. *Conceptual systems and personality organization*. New York: Wiley, 1961.

Harvey, O. J., & Kline, J. A. "Some Situational and Cognitive Determinants of Role Playing: A Replication and Extension." Technical Report No. 15, University of Colorado, Contract Nonr 1147(07), 1965.

Page, E. B. "Ordered Hypotheses for Multiple Treatments: A Significance Test for Linear Ranks." *Journal of the American Statistical Association,* 1963, 58, 216–30.

Tiemann, H. A. "Some Social and Personality Determinants of Reaction to Sensory Deprivation." Technical Report No. 14. University of Colorado, Contract Nonr 1147(07), 1965.

Tryon, R. C., & Bailey, D. E. *The B. C. Try User's Manual.* Boulder, Colorado: University of Colorado Graduate School Computing Center, 1965.

Ware, R., & Harvey, O. J. "A Cognitive Determinant of Impression Formation." *Journal of Personality and Social Psychology,* in press.

White, B. J., & Harvey, O. J. "Effects of Personality and Own Stand on Judgment and Production of Statements About a Central Issue." *Journal of Experimental and Social Psychology,* 1965, 1, 334–47.

ANALYSIS OF STUDY 10

The authors of this study have created two constructs based largely on a theory of factors which affect learning and then tested predictions based on the relationship of the two constructs.

At least half of the report is devoted to an extensive and detailed description of the methodology. The first methodological problems were to measure the belief systems and to identify a sample of subjects that would provide for a test of the hypothesis. The design of the study required that the two extremes of the concrete-abstract continuum be clearly represented. (In some respects the design of this study resembles the causal-comparative design of descriptive research. Categorization of research by type is somewhat arbitrary.)

The second methodological problem was much more complex. This involved making observations of teacher behavior. It is worth noting here that it was the teacher's behavior which constituted the measure of the classroom atmosphere Two related problems had to be solved. First, a rating scale for the various dimensions had to be developed which was explicit enough to permit the most objective possible observations to be made. Secondly, observers themselves had to be trained and procedures had to be established which would insure a high degree of reliability in their ratings. How this was done was clearly reported in the study.

Since the possible distortion of data is always a concern in research design, it is worth calling your attention to the manner in which one obvious source of observer bias was controlled. The hypothesis represented a test of the relationship between belief systems and teacher behavior, and the direction of that relationship; therefore the data could be seriously biased if the observers knew the belief system of the teacher they were observing. The researchers were careful to note that not only did the observers not know the system from which the teacher came, they were also assigned to observe teachers from different belief systems, in random order, so as to prevent particular sets and expectancies from developing. There were other safeguards worked out to control observer bias, and you should take note of these as you read through the procedures.

Statistical treatment enabled the researchers to organize their information. By utilizing correlational techniques on the twenty-six rating dimensions and observing how different dimensions tended to cluster, the researchers were able to identify two major clusters of teacher behavior which they labeled dictatorialness and task orientation. Some of the ratings were relatively independent of these two clusters, but they did account for most of the observed dimensions. Later a comparison of the belief systems scores for teachers operating in each of the two major teaching dimensions supported the predicted differences between the two groups.

In addition to this, comparisons between the three belief systems groups were made for every observed teaching dimension. The predicted ordering of scores was supported at a high level of confidence. This finding held up for both belief systems measures.

One new kind of statistic was employed in this study that has not appeared in any of our previous studies. Since the hypothesis predicted that there would be higher scores for the System 4 teachers on dimensions 1–19 as compared to System 1 teachers, and vice-versa for dimensions 20–26, a statistical test of the significance of this ordering was made. If you examine Table 1 again and compare the mean scores of System 1 and System 4 subjects on each of the dimensions, you will see that the predicted difference occurs on twenty-five of the twenty-six dimensions. Page's test for ordered hypotheses for multiple treatments was applied to this observation, and the results indicated a probability of less than one chance in a thousand that such an ordering on these dimensions could have occurred by chance.

We return now to the discussion of the theory. Harvey and his colleagues began with two sets of constructs that were created in the imagination. (This obviously does not mean that other research and other theoretical thinking were not consulted in the process.) The research problem then became one of developing a method for making the kind of observations that would enable them to study the relationship of the two constructs.

The first construct, or model, was that of "belief systems" ranging across a continuum from "concreteness" on one end to "abstractness" on the other. We have in this one example a good illustration of the importance of theory-building. There are a multitude of ways in which we can organize our thinking about human belief systems, but most of them have still fallen along similar dimensions: authoritarian—permissive; open—closed; authoritarian—antiauthoritarian; and so on. These researchers decided to utilize the dimensions of concreteness-abstractness to understand how teachers' belief systems operate. The study did not attempt to validate this theory beyond its usefulness as an organizing construct.

The second of the two major constructs which these researchers created was preschool classroom atmosphere. This was defined operationally as the teacher's classroom behavior. The twenty-five dimensions on which the teachers were rated to establish this atmosphere were also not validated by the study. Some of this behavior was considered desirable teacher behavior and some was considered undesirable. No test was made of either the desirability or undesirability of these dimensions. In other words, these were the presuppositions or givens in this experiment.

Perhaps now it is clear that what was actually tested in this experiment was the relation between the teacher's ideology (belief system) and the teacher's behavior in the classroom.

In developing a basis for their theory the authors cited evidence to support the following idea: "Concreteness disposes towards more fixed and categorical belief systems . . . , toward an authority orientation rather than a task orientation . . . , and toward seeking a simple and highly structured environment. . . ." It was logical, therefore, to hypothesize that

> more concrete teachers, to a greater extent than more abstract teachers, should impose predetermined goals upon the students, provide structure and detailed means for their attainment, be less tolerant of student deviation from their goals and standards, and, consequently, react more strongly and invariantly to such deviation.

The disciplined observations made in the natural classroom setting supported this hypothesis.

What might be the value or importance to educators to have experimental evidence on the relationship of these two constructs? The theory here is clearly dealing with two exceedingly important and relevant variables in education: the value system which the teacher brings to the classroom and the instructional behavior of the teacher. The methodology of the experiment, in turn, provided for a measurement of the teacher's value system by a structured but open-ended device oriented around a rather well-established model of belief systems. The instructional behavior was observed in the natural setting of the classroom; that is, rather than having teachers teach a certain predetermined way, a range of teacher behaviors were specified, and observers simply watched the teachers function and rated their performances on the previously established dimensions.

The theory and the methodology of this experiment bear a close relationship both to the reality of human belief systems and to the reality of teacher behavior in the real classroom setting. It would be expected, therefore, that the results of this study would have considerable significance to educators.

CONCLUDING COMMENTS

One of the indications of the comprehensiveness of this study can be found in the variety of unanswered questions which this study raises.

What effect would the different classroom atmospheres of dictatorialness and task orientation have on the learning and behavior of pupils? (The authors of this study raise this question themselves.)[3]

If the dimensions of teaching behavior included in items 1–19 are more desirable than those included in items 20–26 and if we accept the relationship between those dimensions and the belief systems of teachers, do we implement change by attempting to alter the belief system, by working directly on changing teacher behavior, or by some combination of both efforts? (If this is a "chicken-egg" situation, with belief affecting behavior and vice-versa, the question may simply be one of where it would be most effective to enter the circle. The fact that the teachers with the more concrete belief systems tended to be the more experienced teachers also raises some interesting questions.)

Is there something about the way teachers tend to develop their teaching style over a period of time that also leads them to begin to close down their belief system? If so, how might this be counteracted through in-service training programs?

It is useful to contrast this study with the previous one by McAllister et al. In that study, you recall, the teacher simply agreed to alter her behavior in a prescribed way in order to see if better results (results which the teacher desired and which could logically be considered of benefit to student learning) could be obtained. The Harvey study relates classroom behavior to belief systems, clearly internal phenomena. Both studies substantiate their respective positions.

Would a more abstract teacher be more willing to change her classroom behavior to employ operant conditioning for certain effects than a more concrete teacher would? Would a more concrete teacher who decided to try operant conditioning and was reinforced by positive results become more

---

3. Four of the same five authors followed up this study with a replication that extended the research to this question. Findings supported their hypothesis that "greater abstractness, greater resourcefulness, less dictatorialness, and less punitiveness on the part of the teacher would be associated with more educationally preferable performances of the children."

abstract in her belief system? These are only some of the intriguing questions that we could ask and answering them would not be the task of research alone, at least methodologically speaking, because such questions have ideological dimensions. Choosing what behaviors to eliminate in the classroom and what behaviors to encourage are ideological choices and follow from our belief systems. But once choices are made, operant conditioning becomes one of the most powerful means for implementing and reinforcing our choices.

Means and ends, ends and means—these are inescapable problems for human beings. Research always deals in some sense with both, but research also leaves us with at least as many questions unanswered as when we began and beckons us on to the most all-pervasive conclusion in the field of research—further research is needed!

Index

Analysis of covariance, 114, 141
Analysis of variance, 114, 160–161
Analysis-results section:
  purpose, 25
  use of figures in, 26
  use of tables in, 26
Anthropocentric activity, 3
Applied research, 6–7

Basic research, 6–7
Bias:
  data, 74, 76, 190–191
  experimenter, 130
  sampling, 57, 74
Bibliography-appendix section, 27–28

Causal-comparative research:
  example, 100–106
  purposes, 55–56, 108
Chi-square, 75, 108
Conclusions, 26–27
Consumers of research, 9, 11
Controls, 110–111, 130
Correlational research:
  example, 90–97
  purposes, 53–55
Correlation coefficients:
  effect of range on, 98–99
  interpretation of, 53–54
  multiple, 54–55, 98
  negative, 54
  positive, 54
  purpose, 53
  zero order, 54
Current Index to Journals in Education, 13

Data bias, 74, 76, 190–191
Deductive approach, 3–4
Dependent variables, 110
Descriptive research:
  definition, 51
  examples, 62–74, 77–87, 90–97, 100–106
  interpretation of, 59–60
  problems of, 56–59
  purposes of, 51
  types, 52–56
Designs, 111–116
Discrete data, 108
Dissertation Abstracts, 13
Distributed data, 108

INDEX

Education Index, 13
Empiricism, 2
Equivalency, 112–114
Experimental research:
 controls in, 110–111, 130
 designs, 111–116
 examples, 119–129, 134–140, 143–158, 162–174, 177–190
 invalidity sources, 117–118
 purposes, 109, 116
Experimenter bias, 130
External invalidity, 118

Factor analysis, 55
Factorial designs, 114–116, 159–160
Figures, 26

Generalizations, 3

Historical research:
 contributions to education, 31
 example, 34–48
 methods of, 32–33
 purposes, 30–31
History, 117
Hypotheses:
 characteristics, 19–20
 null form, 18–19
 purposes, 18
 research form, 18–19
 statistical form, 18–19

Ideology (*see* Theory)
Independent variable, 110
Inductive approach, 3–4
Inferences, 3
Information systems, 13–14
Instrumentation, 117
Interaction, 114–116

Internal invalidity, 117–118
Invalidity sources, 117–118

Knowledge in research, 1–2

Limitations of research, 27

Matching, 113–114
Maturation, 117
Models (*see* Theory)
Mortality, 118
Multiple correlation, 54–55, 98

Negative correlation, 54
Non-equivalent control group design:
 basic format, 111–112
 establishing equivalency, 112–114
 format variations, 112

Observations:
 definition, 3
 uses, 15

Population, 56–57
Positive correlation, 54
Prediction, 55, 90, 97
Preliminary sources, 12–14
Problem statement:
 methods of expression, 23–24
 narrowing procedure, 14
 purposes, 12, 15–17
 relation to hypotheses, 20
 sources, 12–14
Psychological Abstracts, 13

Questions (*see* Problem statement)

INDEX

Randomization, 112–114
Random sampling, 57
Rationalism, 3
Regression effect, 113–114, 117
Research:
  definition, 1–2
  methods, 25
  purposes, 25, 194
Research in Education, 13
Research proposal, 20–23
Research report, 23–27
Research review:
  methods, 24–25
  purposes, 22–23
  relation to conclusions, 26
  relation to problem statement, 14
  relation to theory, 18
  uses, 14
Review of Educational Research, 13
Review of Research in Education, 13

Sampling:
  bias, 57, 74
  error, 57
  random sample, 57
Science in research, 4
Second Handbook of Research on Teaching, 12–13
Selection, 117
Selection-maturation interaction, 118
Self-awareness in research, 2, 4
Significance, 8–9
Sociology Abstracts, 13
Statistical significance, 75–76, 116
Summary-conclusions section:
  conclusions, 26–27
  findings, 26–27
  limitations, 27
  purposes, 26
  relation to research review, 26

Survey research:
  example, 62–74
  purposes, 52–53

Tables, 26
Testing, 117
Theory:
  assumptions, 8
  complexity, 5
  comprehensiveness, 5
  data collection in, 88, 107, 131, 159, 191
  hypotheses, 18–19, 74, 97
  interpretation, 59–60, 89, 132–133, 141–142, 161
  origin of, 17–18
  questions, 16, 77, 87–88, 107, 131, 141, 175, 190–191
  research uses of, 4

Unobtrusive measures, 76

Validity, 58–59
Variables:
  definition of, 109–110
  dependent, 110
  independent, 110
  relevant, 110

Zero order correlation, 54